TEXTS AND STUDIES

CONTRIBUTIONS TO

BIBLICAL AND PATRISTIC LITERATURE

EDITED BY

J. ARMITAGE ROBINSON B.D.

FELLOW OF CHRIST'S COLLEGE CAMBRIDGE

VOL. I.

No. 3. THE LORD'S PRAYER IN THE EARLY CHURCH

THE LORD'S PRAYER

IN THE

EARLY CHURCH

BY

FREDERIC HENRY CHASE B.D.

PRINCIPAL OF THE CLERGY TRAINING SCHOOL CAMBRIDGE

Wipf & Stock
PUBLISHERS
Eugene, Oregon

Wipf and Stock Publishers
199 W 8th Ave, Suite 3
Eugene, OR 97401

The Lord's Prayer in the Early Church
By Chase, F.H.
ISBN: 1-59244-849-6
Publication date 9/3/2004
Previously published by Cambridge, 1891

TO

JOHN PEILE LITT. D.

MASTER OF CHRIST'S COLLEGE

WITH

THE RESPECTFUL AFFECTION AND GRATITUDE

OF

A FORMER PUPIL.

PREFACE.

IN the following Essay I have treated the Lord's Prayer simply from the point of view of criticism. Of the sacredness of the Prayer, both because Christ taught it to His disciples and because His disciples have used it 'from the first day until now,' I am deeply conscious. But I believe that no subject however sacred lies outside the rightful province of the critic who regards reverence and the endeavour after accuracy as elementary duties.

Besides those obligations to others which are noted in the Essay from time to time, I gladly avail myself of this opportunity to thank Professor Robertson Smith for answering several questions as to the exact translation of the Arabic version of Tatian's Diatessaron as to which I have no first-hand knowledge; also the Rev. R. H. Kennett, Fellow of Queens' College, for valuable criticism in connexion with my references to the Syriac Versions and for rescuing me from some of the perils which are the proverbial portion of 'a little learning'; he is however in no way responsible for my arguments, conclusions and mistakes. Several other friends have given me the kindest help in the revision of the proof-sheets; to them too my hearty thanks are due.

To one other debt of a wholly different kind I must briefly allude. In the discussion of the petitions for Daily Bread and for Deliverance I have treated of subjects previously handled by Bishop Lightfoot. For many generations to come workers in those fields of Biblical and Patristic literature, which he had made his own, will recognise with reverent gratitude two characteristics of his writings, their suggestiveness and their power of inspiration.

On the one hand they supply both a firm foundation and a plan for future work; on the other hand they quicken and invigorate the worker. It is vain to try to formulate in a brief statement the manifold debt which the younger generation of students owes to the Bishop. But I venture to hope that this Essay may be an illustration however unworthy of the suggestiveness of his work to which I have referred.

I have only to add that this Essay was accepted by the Divinity Professors as an exercise for the degree of B.D., and that I have to thank the Regius Professor for giving me permission to make a few slight additions and alterations before publication.

CHRIST'S COLLEGE, CAMBRIDGE,
July, 1891.

TABLE OF CONTENTS.

INTRODUCTION.

THE CHURCH AND THE SYNAGOGUE.

CHRISTIANITY, absolutely new in its central ideas and aims, employed time-honoured machinery for their furtherance. In itself the most revolutionary force which the world has ever seen, it effected the greatest upheavals of political, social, and religious life by conservative methods. It inherited the powers which were inherent in, or had been won by, Judaism; and it made Judaism a thing of the past.

A special instance of this general characteristic of Christianity is found in the relation of the Church to the Synagogue. To the Synagogue system, speaking from a human point of view, the Church owes it that she outlived the days of her immaturity and weakness. Here was an organization ready to hand, which she could use and gradually mould after her own higher type of life. Here was a network encircling within its meshes the whole Roman Empire, by which the Church could draw Gentile as well as Jew to herself[1]. A purely secular historian would not be far wrong were he to trace both the survival and the spread of the Church, at least during the first half century of her life, to her close alliance with the Synagogue.

Of this system Jerusalem was the centre. Even if extant notices exaggerate[2], we may well conclude that the number of Synagogues in the Holy City was great. In some of these numerous congregations 'the Brethren[3]' after they had learned

[1] Gentiles seem to have frequented the Synagogues (Acts xiii. 44, xiv. 1, xviii. 4).

[2] Edersheim, *The Life and Times of Jesus the Messiah* i. p. 119, gives the references. The Synagogues in Jerusalem are said to have been upwards of 400.

[3] "It is significant that the first title given to the body of believers after the Ascension is 'the brethren' (Acts i. 15 true text)": Bp Westcott *The Epistles of*

to believe in Jesus as the Christ would retain their membership. That 'the Brethren' did not sever themselves from the Synagogues of 'the Dispersion' till forced to do so, is plain from repeated notices in the Acts (xiii. 44, xviii. 4, 26 f., xix. 8).

But, sometimes in consequence of a violent disruption, sometimes because of a sense of growing needs and powers, union would gradually give way to an era of modified imitation. If the number of those who joined the Church as recorded from time to time in the Acts is even approximately correct, we feel that it would be necessary, apart from external influences, to organise some separate system of worship and fellowship. How else could so large a multitude be welded together? In the main outline the course of events at Corinth was probably only the repetition of what had occurred elsewhere[1]. At Corinth St Paul for some considerable time took a prominent part in the worship of the Jewish Synagogue. At length a crisis came which made separation necessary. Henceforth 'the Brethren' met in a private house close to the Synagogue. But the presence of St Paul and of Crispus, the chief ruler of the Synagogue, was, we may suppose, a sufficient guarantee that the worship in the house of Titius Justus would be modelled after the ancient pattern. This natural conjecture finds considerable confirmation when we turn to the picture of Christian worship at Corinth drawn by St Paul in his First Epistle to that Church.

Hence there would arise at Jerusalem in very early times Synagogues of 'the Brethren[2].' The wealthier converts, such as

St John p. 126. See especially Acts xv. 23, where Mr Page's correction of R.V. ('The Apostles and Elders, brethren to the brethren...') is obviously necessary; 1 Cor. v. 11, ix. 5, and the use of the word φιλαδελφία. I have therefore used the term to denote the Christians in the early Apostolic times. But it is important to notice that even this phrase is a witness to the Jewish associations of the early Church. Comp. Matt. v. 47, Acts xxii. 5 (even after his conversion St Paul can say ἐπιστολὰς δεξάμενος πρὸς τοὺς ἀδελφοὺς εἰς Δαμασκὸν ἐπορευόμην), xxviii. 21, Rom. ix. 3.

[1] It would but seldom happen that a whole Synagogue, as apparently at Beroea (Acts xvii. 10 f.), became Christianised.

[2] Since writing this, I have noticed with relief that this was Bp Lightfoot's view (*Philippians* p. 190): "As soon as the expansion of the Church rendered some organization necessary, it would form a 'synagogue' of its own." He too appeals to traces of the Christian use of the word συναγωγή.

Mary the mother of John Mark, would naturally offer their homes as the places of meeting.

The lingering traces of the Christian use of the word *συναγωγή*, to appeal to one line of evidence alone, attest this early stage of the Church's development. We find them, as we should expect, in the writings of those who through old associations or geographical position would be likely to retain the term. St James (ii. 1 ff.) is expressly appealing to those 'who hold the faith of our Lord Jesus Christ,' when he draws the contrasted pictures of the gay dandy and the squalid beggar coming 'into your synagogue.' When, at a somewhat later date, St John (Apoc. ii. 9, iii. 9) inveighs against 'the Synagogue of Satan,' it is surely a mistake to conclude that he wishes to disparage the term *Synagogue* in itself. His phrase 'the throne of Satan' (ii. 13) does not preclude him from speaking of 'the throne of God.' If he condemns 'the deep things of Satan' (ii. 24), another Apostle dwells on the thought of 'the depth' of the divine riches of wisdom and knowledge (Rom. xi. 33, 1 Cor. ii. 10; so Ep. Clem. 11 *τὰ βάθη τῆς θείας γνώσεως*). 'The Synagogue of Satan' is a spurious imitation of a true Synagogue on the part of spurious Jews, 'which say that they are Jews, and they are not, but do lie.' The parody implies the original[1]. Early in the next century the great Syrian martyr writes to Polycarp *πυκνότερον συναγωγαὶ γινέσθωσαν* (Ignatius *Ep. ad Polycarpum* 4). Late in the same century another teacher of Antioch, Theophilus, uses the same term[2]. In Benjamin's prophecy of St Paul in the *Testaments of the Twelve Patriarchs* it is said *ἕως συντελείας τῶν αἰώνων ἔσται ἐν συναγωγαῖς ἐθνῶν*[3]. The so-called Jerusalem Syriac version supplies a proof that at a much later time among Catholic

[1] Cf. Iren. iii. vi. 1 Hi autem sunt Ecclesia. Haec enim est *synagoga Dei*. On the other hand note Tert. *De Spectac.* xxv. (de ecclesia Dei in *diaboli ecclesiam*).

[2] Theophilus *ad Autol.* ii. 14 (*δέδωκεν ὁ θεὸς τῷ κόσμῳ κυμαινομένῳ...τὰς συναγωγάς, λεγομένας δὲ ἐκκλησίας ἁγίας*). But it is to be remembered that Theophilus is addressing a heathen friend and that the word *συναγωγή* was used of the religious assemblies of the Pagans (see Harnack's note on Hermas *Mand.* xi. 9, a note which contains a large collection of passages).

[3] In *Levi* 11, *Ben.* 11 (*διδοὺς τῇ συναγωγῇ τῶν ἐθνῶν*) the reference is rather to O. T. usage (e.g. Ex. xii. 3, 6, 47; Gen. xxviii. 3, xxxv. 11). On the *Testaments* see below p. 87.

Christians in the neighbourhood of Palestine the word Synagogue was still in use[1]. In regard to the Ebionites we have the express statement of Epiphanius (xxx. 18), *συναγωγὴν οὗτοι καλοῦσιν τὴν ἑαυτῶν ἐκκλησίαν καὶ οὐχὶ ἐκκλησίαν*[2].

From the East we turn to the capital of the West. The number of the Jews in Rome is a commonplace of history. But archaeological researches and the study of inscriptions have now added detail and colour to the picture. Unlike the Jews at Alexandria who formed a political corporation, the Jews in Rome were divided into many separate religious communities (*συναγωγαί*), taking their name sometimes from distinguished patrons as 'the Synagogue of the Augustesians,' sometimes from the locality as 'the Synagogue of the Siburesians' (Subura)[3]. Hence a special importance attaches to the use of the word 'Synagogue' by two Christian writers of the second century, who speak to us from Rome. Justin (*Dial.* 287 B) uses the phrase, *τοῖς εἰς αὐτὸν πιστεύουσιν, ὡς οὖσι μιᾷ ψυχῇ καὶ μιᾷ συναγωγῇ καὶ μιᾷ ἐκκλησίᾳ.* Hermas (*Mand.* xi. 9, comp. 13, 14) writes thus, *ὅταν οὖν ἔλθῃ ὁ ἄνθρωπος ὁ ἔχων τὸ πνεῦμα τὸ θεῖον εἰς συναγωγὴν ἀνδρῶν δικαίων...καὶ ἔντευξις γένηται πρὸς τὸν θεὸν τῆς συναγωγῆς τῶν ἀνδρῶν ἐκείνων κ.τ.λ.*

Thus among Catholic Christians in Syria, among Ebionite sectaries widely scattered, in the Roman Church of the second century, we have evidence that the word *συναγωγή* survived to witness to an almost forgotten stage of Christian life and worship.

The Church then in the earliest days of the faith, as far as concerned her discipline and her worship, may be described as an association of Synagogues, gradually multiplying as she gained new territory for her Master.

[1] 'So wird auch im Ev. Hier. *ἐκκλησία* durch כנישתא d. h. *Synagoge* übersetzt. Das Buch finden wir im Gebrauch katholischer Christen Ostpalästinas' (Zahn *Forschungen, Tatian's Diatessaron* p. 335).

[2] Comp. the inscriptions given in Schürer *The Jewish People* Eng. Trans. div. ii. vol. ii. pp. 64, 69. Subsequent references to Schürer, unless it is otherwise stated, are to this volume.

[3] Schürer p. 247 f.; for Jewish cemeteries at or near Rome see p. 240, also div. i. vol. i. p. 32 f. Compare Merivale *Hist. of the Romans* vi. p. 428 f., vii. p. 379 f.

But at this point there comes into light a fact of far-reaching importance. Of the Jews at Jerusalem there were two classes, the Hebrews and the Hellenists (Acts ix. 29 *συνεζήτει πρὸς τοὺς Ἑλληνιστάς*). The former would naturally constitute the larger body. Among the latter would be numbered Jews of the Dispersion, who either were visiting the Mother City at the time of the Festivals (Acts ii. 5 ff.), or, like Saul of Tarsus, had some reason for settling there. Further, the Book of the Acts (vi. 9), confirmed as it is here by independent authority, informs us that the Hellenists had Synagogues of their own at Jerusalem[1]. It is natural that no special mention should be made of 'the Synagogues of the Hebrews' at Jerusalem, for there they were necessarily the prevailing type. At Rome, on the other hand, where Hellenists would vastly preponderate, a notice is preserved of a 'Synagogue of Hebrews' (*συναγωγὴ Αἰβρέων*)[2].

Over and above a general divergence of tone which would separate the two classes of worshippers, a special point of difference would be the use of Greek in the Synagogues of the Hellenists: "R. Levi Bar Chajothah went to Caesarea and heard them קריין שמע אלוניסתין *reciting their 'Shemaa' Hellenistically* [i.e. *in Greek*][3]." It is difficult to suppose that a custom which prevailed among the Hellenists elsewhere would be abjured by those at Jerusalem, where the presence of pilgrims from the Dispersion in all parts of the world would render it most necessary. There is,

[1] Lightfoot (*Horae Hebr.* on Acts vi. 9) quotes the *Hieros. Megilla* (fol. 73. 4) as speaking of the Synagogue of the Alexandrians at Jerusalem. Commentators differ as to the number of synagogues implied in Acts vi. 9. Some of the older commentators (e.g. Calvin, Beza), and later Wieseler, hold that but one Synagogue is meant; Meyer, like Vitringa (p. 253) and Schürer (p. 57), thinks that five are referred to; Wendt and Nösgen hold that the language requires but two, that of the Libertines, Cyrenians and Alexandrians, and that of those of Cilicia and Asia. Mr Page, separating off the Libertines, supposes that three Synagogues are mentioned. Nösgen *in loc.* refers to 'talmudische Angaben über drei hellenistische Synagogen unter den 480 Jerusalems (*Megill.* E. 73, 4 u. ö.).'

[2] *Corp. Inscr. Graec.* 9909 referred to by Schürer, p. 248.

[3] Lightfoot *Horae Hebr.* on Lc. x. 27. On the use of Greek in the worship of the Dispersion see Schürer, p. 283 with reff., Edersheim *Life and Times* i. pp. 30, 446. Schürer (p. 284) writes, 'The Rabbinical authorities in Palestine expressly sanctioned the use of any language whatever in repeating the Shemah, the Shemoneh Esreh and the grace at meals.' Comp. Neubauer in *Studia Biblica* i. p. 50.

however, so far as I know, no direct evidence as to the usage in this matter of the Hellenistic Synagogues at Jerusalem.

But if this twofold division of Synagogues existed at Jerusalem among the Jews, would not a similar division reappear among 'the Brethren'? Would there not spring up Synagogues of the Hellenistic, as well as Synagogues of the Hebrew 'Brethren'? To the latter there would naturally join themselves the 'great company of the priests' who became 'obedient to the faith' (Acts vi. 7), and those 'of the sect of the Pharisees who believed' (xv. 5); to the former, those who were attracted by the teaching of St Stephen, and at a later time the converts of Barnabas and Saul of Tarsus, as well as some of those ancient disciples who were won on the day of Pentecost.

Nor is this picture of the Church at Jerusalem a hypothetical one. Directly the Church began to expand, 'there arose a murmuring of the Hellenists against the Hebrews' (Acts vi. 1). Almsgiving was specially connected with the Synagogue system[1], and to suppose that 'the daily ministration' was a part of that system as it had been transplanted and as it developed among 'the Brethren' would be no violently improbable conjecture. But however that may be, the whole tone of the history makes it clear that this was no private quarrel, but a public dispute which threatened a disruption of the Church. All becomes intelligible at once if in the disputants we recognise two congregations or two groups of congregations, each with a home and an organization of its own. The Apostles dealt boldly with this rising spirit of disunion. They 'called the multitude of the disciples (τὸ πλῆθος τῶν μαθητῶν) unto them,' all, that is, without distinction of party.

It is probably true that the line of cleavage between 'the Brethren' of the Hebrew and 'the Brethren' of the Hellenistic Synagogues does not exactly coincide with that which separated those that were 'of the circumcision' from the more liberal section of the Jewish Christians, but the two lines cannot have been far apart.

[1] Lightfoot *Horae Hebr.* on Matt. vi. 1 f., Vitringa *de Synagoga* pp. 211 f., 809 ff., Schürer p. 66 ('It was in the Synagogues that the collection of alms took place. According to the Mishna the collection was to be made by at least two, the distribution by three persons').

The two principles of classification are closely related. And the view of the Apostolic Church which I am endeavouring to make probable throws much light, as I believe, on the disputes and the tangled negotiations which led up to, and were connected with, the Conference at Jerusalem. It explains individual expressions in the narrative—*πᾶν τὸ πλῆθος* (xv. 12, comp. vi. 2, xxi. 18 *πάντες τε παρεγένοντο οἱ πρεσβύτεροι*), *σὺν ὅλῃ τῇ ἐκκλησίᾳ* (*v.* 22). It accounts, as it seems to me, for the reference to the Mosaic law in the condensed report of St James' speech. The twofold demand of the Pharisaic party (xv. 5) was, 'It is needful to circumcise them, and to charge them to keep the law of Moses.' To this twofold demand St James had a twofold answer. On the one hand, circumcision was not to be insisted on, though the Gentiles should be asked to make certain reasonable concessions. On the other hand, all that was valuable in their requirements as to the Mosaic law was substantially secured already. Moses was not likely to be neglected. 'For Moses from generations of old hath in every city them that preach him, being read in the Synagogues [i.e. in the public worship of *the Jews and the Christians alike*] every sabbath' (xv. 21). Again, if a conclusion can be safely drawn from the names of the envoys (xv. 22), Judas surnamed Barsabbas represented the Hebrews, Silas the Hellenists. Lastly, the fact that the organized influence of men bound together by common worship was enlisted on this side or on that made this crisis in a doctrinal dispute a matter of grave difficulty and danger, as at an earlier time it had embittered a question of administration.

In the same direction we may look for an explanation of the fact that in the first century relations of our Lord were chosen as Bishops of the Church at Jerusalem. The claim to reverence which these men had rose above any title to authority which was based on pre-eminence either among the Hebrews or the Hellenists. Such an appointment was a victory for neither section of the Church[1].

The Hellenistic (Christian) Synagogues, fortified by the work of St Paul and by the alliance first of the Christian Jews of the

[1] Hegesippus (Eus. *H. E.* iv. 22), *Συμεών...ὃν προέθεντο πάντες ἀνεψιὸν ὄντα τοῦ κυρίου δεύτερον.* Compare what the same writer says of the grandsons of Jude (Eus. *H. E.* iii. 20).

Dispersion and then of Gentile converts, gradually won to themselves the supremacy. From the very first theirs, it would seem, had been the greater enlightenment and vigour. And as time went on and the old things of worship and of organization passed away and became new, they were merged in the life of the Catholic Church of the second century, for which they had prepared the way[1].

The main elements in this view of the early Apostolic Church, its adhesion, that is, to the Synagogue system and the existence among the Christian 'Brethren,' as among the Jews, of Hebrew and of Hellenistic Synagogues, may, I venture to think, be taken as historically certain. I pass on to indicate the bearing of these conclusions first on the question of the origin of the Synoptic Gospels, and secondly on the problem of the original form of the Lord's Prayer.

1. In the Synagogues of 'the Brethren' the personal followers of Christ, and especially the Apostles, would bear their witness to His Resurrection and would tell what they remembered of His teaching and His life. This personal testimony would at least form an important part of each λόγος παρακλήσεως (Acts xiii. 15, note especially Hebr. xiii. 22). The lessons from the Law and the Prophets must have had an honoured place in the Christian as in the Jewish Synagogues, and 'the exhortation' would often be based upon some prophetic saying or some ancient type[2]. The analogy of the apostolic speeches and sermons preserved in substance in the Acts bears out these statements.

To these λόγοι παρακλήσεως in the Christian Synagogues we must look for the first beginnings of the Gospels. In them the sayings of the Lord would be brought together for the purposes of immediate edification. The history of His birth, His work, His Passion, His Resurrection, would be linked with the ancient

[1] See note A at the end of the Chapter.

[2] Such surely is the explanation of the opening words of St Paul's speech at Antioch—ὁ θεὸς τοῦ λαοῦ τούτου (xiii. 17). The τούτου must refer to some words in the section of the Prophets (*v.* 15) just read. Compare Luke iv. 18—21. To take τούτου as deictic (Page) or as referring back to ἄνδρες Ἰσραηλῖται (Wendt) gives a very poor sense. The point is important in its bearing on the sources and the credibility of the Acts.

prophecies. And as among the Jews the Synagogues were closely connected with the Schools of the Scribes, so among the early disciples the more public teaching of the assembly would be repeated and brought home in catechetical instruction. Thus in the very first days of the Church different types of an oral Gospel would be in process of formation.

But in two other ways the needs created by this system of Christian Synagogues tended, I cannot doubt, to the growth of the Gospels as we have them now.

In the first place translation would be necessary. In the Synagogues of the Hebrew Disciples the recital of the Lord's words and the story of His life would be in Aramaic. But when transplanted to the Hellenistic Synagogues, the same recital and the same story would have to assume a Greek dress. And the obvious desirability of making the one version a substantial equivalent of the other would tend to generate in both languages fixed types of apostolic tradition. At the same time it is quite possible that through this necessary intercourse with the Hellenists the Hebrew Apostles and teachers may have gained that power over the Greek language which surprises us, for example, in the Epistle of St James.

In the second place, may not the origin of written Gospels be at least in part traceable to the same set of circumstances? When a decree of the Mother Church, and when Apostolic letters, were read in the Christian assemblies, when further the Apostles and the earliest witnesses became scattered and it might therefore seem wise to compensate for their absence by some representation of their teaching, 'many would take in hand to draw up a narrative concerning those things which had been fulfilled.' In this way the story of Christ's life and teaching would pass from the *λόγος παρακλήσεως* to find a place alongside the lessons from the Law and the Prophets, and thus would gradually, even in the lifetime of the Apostles, attain to something of scriptural authority[1]. Here

[1] Comp. Acts xx. 35 (*μνημονεύειν τε τῶν λόγων τοῦ κυρίου Ἰησοῦ*), 1 Thess. iv. 15 (*ἐν λόγῳ Κυρίου*), 1 Cor. vii. 10 (*οὐκ ἐγὼ ἀλλὰ ὁ κύριος*), 1 Cor. ix. 14 (*ὁ κύριος διέταξεν*), 1 Tim. v. 18 (*λέγει γὰρ ἡ γραφὴ Βοῦν ἀλοῶντα οὐ φιμώσεις, καὶ Ἄξιος ὁ ἐργάτης τοῦ μισθοῦ αὐτοῦ*). In Rom. xvi. 25 f. (*κατὰ ἀποκάλυψιν μυστηρίου...σεσιγημένου φανερωθέντος δὲ νῦν διά τε γραφῶν προφητικῶν κατ' ἐπιταγὴν τοῦ αἰωνίου θεοῦ ...εἰς πάντα τὰ ἔθνη γνωρισθέντος*) I cannot but think that the reference is to the

too we get a side light on portions of the Apostolic Epistles. As Clement of Rome incorporates in his letter to the Corinthian Church a prayer which a comparison of his language with that of the ancient liturgies shews to be the substance of a form which as the presiding elder he used in the worship of the Church, so there is much to lead us to think that St James preserves for us in his Epistle portions of his Synagogue addresses. And a most striking characteristic of this Epistle is that it is built up of *λόγια κυριακά*. What is true of this Epistle is true in a less degree of other Apostolic Epistles. Such references, or possible references, in the Epistles to the Lord's words need careful collection and rigorous examination before any real progress can be made towards the solution of the Synoptic question[1].

The adoption of the Synagogue system in the early Church has an intimate connexion with the composition of the written Gospels. But it is not of itself a sufficient explanation. It is but one among many influences. In truth a key of many wards is needed to fit the complicated lock of the Synoptic problem. We shall probably be moving along the lines which will lead to a settlement of the question, so far as a settlement is possible, when we recognise the converging forces of both Aramaic and Greek oral tradition, of Aramaic and Greek written memoranda, and of all these as they would find a place in the Synagogues of 'the Brethren,' in catechetical instruction, and in missionary activity[2].

writings of *Christian* Prophets. For compare (1) Eph. iii. 1—9 (*ὑπὲρ ὑμῶν τῶν ἐθνῶν...κατὰ ἀποκάλυψιν ἐγνωρίσθη μοι τὸ μυστήριον...δύνασθε ἀναγινώσκοντες νοῆσαι τὴν σύνεσίν μου ἐν τῷ μυστηρίῳ τοῦ χριστοῦ, ὃ...νῦν ἀπεκαλύφθη τοῖς ἁγίοις ἀποστόλοις αὐτοῦ καὶ προφήταις ἐν πνεύματι...φωτίσαι [πάντας] τίς ἡ οἰκονομία τοῦ μυστηρίου τοῦ ἀποκεκρυμμένου κ.τ.λ.*); (2) Tit. i. 2 f. (*ἣν ἐπηγγείλατο...ἐφανέρωσεν δὲ...τὸν λόγον αὐτοῦ ἐν κηρύγματι ὃ ἐπιστεύθην ἐγὼ κατ' ἐπιταγὴν τοῦ σωτῆρος ἡμῶν θεοῦ*). Such a reference would be especially in point at the close of the Roman Epistle.

[1] See note B at the end of the Chapter.

[2] Mr A. Wright's singularly fresh and independent though incomplete essay (*The Composition of the Four Gospels*, 1890) emphasises one important factor, viz. catechetical instruction. To what strange results a one-sided theory may lead is seen in the results attained by Resch in his articles *Der Quellenbericht über die ἀνάληψις des Herrn* (Zeitschrift für kirchliche Wissenschaft 1889 pp. 18 ff., 75 ff.). Here is his 'Hebräischer Urtext,'

וַיַּעַל לִפְנֵיהֶם בִּבְשָׂרוֹ הַשָּׁמַיִם אֶל־אֱלֹהָיו וְאֶל־אָבִיהוּ הַשֹּׁלֵחַ אֹתוֹ וַיֵּשֶׁב לִימִינוֹ׃

Such a theory may be safely left to pair with Dr Abbott's telegram theory (*The Common Tradition* p. xi.).

2. From the larger problem of the Synoptic Gospels I turn to another question, closely connected yet not identical with it, viz., the position of the Lord's Prayer in the Apostolic Church and the bearing of this upon its original form.

The two Evangelists who record the Prayer connect it with different occasions in our Lord's ministry. St Matthew represents our Lord as Himself of His own accord teaching this form of prayer to His disciples in the audience of the crowds (Matt. vi. 9, vii. 28 f.). St Luke tells us that the Lord gave it to His disciples privately in answer to the request of one of them, 'Lord, teach us to pray, *even as John also taught his disciples*.' Apart from general questions, there seems in this case to be nothing essentially improbable in the repetition of the same form[1]. Internal evidence confirms the report of the Evangelists. St Luke (v. 33) preserves a notice which has the support of the other Synoptists (Matt. ix. 14, Mc. ii. 18): *οἱ μαθηταὶ Ἰωάνου νηστεύουσιν πυκνὰ καὶ δεήσεις ποιοῦνται.* Here then lay the point of the disciples' request. But the Lord had no esoteric elaborate teaching on this matter. He gave His disciples privately the same simple form which He had already given them in the audience of the crowds[2].

As the occasions described by the two Evangelists differ, so do also the versions of the Prayer which they respectively give. That contained in St Luke's Gospel diverges from that contained in St Matthew's both in regard to the length of the Prayer and in the wording of the clauses which are common to both Gospels.

[1] Our Lord thus would be simply following the usual custom of Jewish teachers. The Prophets, the Pauline Epistles, and the Apocalypse supply many instances of such repetitions.

[2] Mr Page on the other hand (*Critical Notes on the Lord's Prayer*, Expositor, 3rd Series, vol. vii. p. 433 ff.) thinks that 'a single prayer delivered by Jesus to His disciples may be related by two historians in two different shapes and as delivered under different circumstances.' His arguments are, I think, met by the remarks in the text above. At the same time I believe that it would be contrary to analogy to suppose that the longer and the shorter forms belong respectively to the two occasions. Both the Evangelists record how the Lord's Prayer was delivered to the Disciples; both give a form current when they wrote. On the question whether St Luke has inserted in the Prayer phraseology of his own, see below, pp. 42 ff.

When we come to enquire what the original form of the Prayer was, it is needful to remember that the term original is here relative rather than absolute. For in the period which intervened between the occasion when our Lord first taught the Prayer and the time when the Evangelists gave it a place in the Gospels, it had passed through one stage, and had already entered upon the second stage of its history. On the one hand it is unreasonable to suppose that before the day of Pentecost the Apostles did not use it privately among themselves. On the other, when the number of the Disciples began to increase, it passed over into the Synagogue worship of the Church. The first stage eludes our grasp. It is the second only that our investigation can touch.

In connexion with the use of the Lord's Prayer in the Christian Synagogues the following points must be noticed.

(1) Our Lord left three commands which would mould from the first the worship of the Church: *οὕτως...προσεύχεσθε ὑμεῖς* (Matt. vi. 9), *λάβετε, φάγετε...πίετε ἐξ αὐτοῦ πάντες* (Matt. xxvi. 28), *μαθητεύσατε...βαπτίζοντες* (Matt. xxviii. 19). We know that the last two were obeyed. Converts were baptised; the Eucharist was celebrated. The indications that the other injunction was observed from the earliest days are less obvious and direct, but when brought together they are very cogent. For over and above the *a priori* probability, that if the Disciples met for Synagogue worship, they would use the Prayer which their Master had bequeathed to them, there are, as I hope to shew in dealing with the several clauses of the Prayer, many allusions to its petitions in the Apostolic writings, allusions which become quite intelligible if we assume that the Prayer was in constant public use. Again, the hypothesis of this early liturgical use explains various points in the language both of the Prayer as we have it and of certain additions to it which have been preserved. Lastly, this view exactly harmonises with the evidence of the Didaché. In the Didaché the Lord's Prayer holds a prominent position. 'Pray ye not,' it is said (ch. viii.), 'as the hypocrites; but as the Lord commanded in His Gospel, so pray ye.' The Lord's Prayer is then given in the fuller form recorded by St Matthew, with two variations of text and with the addition of a doxology. The

direction is appended 'Thrice a day in this way pray ye.' This last direction links the Lord's Prayer with the Jewish hours of prayer, morning, afternoon, and evening; hours which were observed by religious Jews in private and, at least on certain days, in the public worship of the Synagogue[1]. That the Apostles kept the hours of prayer we know from the Acts (iii. 1, x. 9). Moreover the Didaché (ch. x.) preserves to us a remarkable eucharistic formula which is closely connected with certain clauses of the Lord's Prayer. Such a reference to the Lord's Prayer implies that it had been itself for some time an essential part of the Church's liturgy.

(2) It may, I think, be taken for certain that the Prayer was originally in Aramaic. *A priori* probabilities are very strongly in favour of this view. Further, on this supposition the variations, especially in the tenses used in the two forms found in the Gospels and in probable allusions to the Prayer in other parts of the New Testament, find an easy explanation. The details of this evidence will appear in the discussion of the several clauses. But if the Aramaic form was the original, the existence of Hellenistic congregations among the Disciples at Jerusalem would necessitate from the very first a translation of the Prayer into Greek. Further, the Prayer would have a liturgical history in the Synagogues of 'the Brethren' both Hebrew and Hellenistic. It is clear then that the Prayer holds a position of its own, and in reference to the circumstances of its transmission stands apart from the rest of the matter contained in the Synoptic Gospels. One other point under this head remains. It is this. From the earliest days after Pentecost the faith would be planted in places more or less distant by missionaries and others coming from the

[1] "Thus the regular Synagogue-services would gradually arise; first, on Sabbaths and on feast- or fast-days, then on ordinary days, at the same hours as, and with a sort of internal correspondence to, the worship of the Temple. The services on Mondays and Thursdays were special, these being the ordinary market-days, when the country-people came into the towns....Accordingly, Monday and Thursday were called 'the days of congregation' or 'Synagogue' (*Yom ha-Kenisah*)" (Edersheim *Life and Times* i. p. 432). On the Jewish hours of prayer and their early date comp. Lightfoot *Horae Hebr.* on Acts iii. 1, Vitringa *de Synagoga Vetere* pp. 42 f., 1062 ff., Schürer p. 85. For early Christian custom see Harnack's note on the *Didaché* viii. 3.

Church at Jerusalem. These teachers would bring with them the Lord's Prayer in the form which it had reached at the time of their departure from the Mother Church. Afterwards liturgical changes might be made in the Prayer both in the Mother Church and in the daughter Churches. But this at least is plain, that when at a later time a version of the Gospels was made in the language of a daughter Church, the Lord's Prayer would stand outside the simple work of translation. There would be a current form already sanctioned by long devotional use, a form which the translator could not neglect or forget, though of course he might subject it to a literary revision when he incorporated it in his translation of the Gospels. Thus it is always possible that the criticism of a Version may yield evidence as to the original form of the Lord's Prayer.

(3) The Disciples would only be following Synagogue usage if they adapted a fixed prayer for use on particular occasions, either by alteration, or by addition[1]. This principle of adaptation, as it will appear, I trust, in the succeeding investigation, was applied in three directions.

(i) By means of substituted or added clauses the Prayer was adapted for use at the Laying on of hands and perhaps at Baptism.

(ii) By alterations in the petition for *daily bread* the Prayer was made suitable for morning and evening use.

(iii) By the accretion of varying forms of Doxology the Prayer was fitted especially for Eucharistic use.

A. Note on the Hellenistic Synagogues (see p. 8).

We have speaking evidence not only for the Jewish parentage of Christian liturgical forms, but also in reference to the operation of translation and adaptation, in the sections of the Didaché which deal with worship (see

[1] 'We have evidence that, in the time of our Lord, and even later, there was much personal liberty left; for, not only was much in the services determined by the usage of each place, but the leader of the devotions might preface the regular service by free prayer, or insert such between certain parts of the liturgy' (Edersheim *Life and Times* i. p. 438 with ref. to Zunz *Gottesd. Vortr. d. Jud.* p. 368 f., *Ritus des syn. Gottesd.* p. 2 f.).

Dr Taylor *The Teaching of the Twelve Apostles*, Lecture II.) and in the Epistle of Clement of Rome, especially 58 ff. The intimate acquaintance with the LXX. shewn in this Epistle proves the writer to be a Hellenist; the worship of the Church over which he presides is in Greek, but it is based on Jewish prayers and benedictions (see Bp Lightfoot *Clement*, 1890, i. p. 392 ff.).

The Church at Rome, the very early date of whose foundation is implied by its size and importance when St Paul wrote his Roman Epistle, and which was at first predominantly Jewish, had not as yet wholly passed beyond the stage in which the Christian 'Brethren' formed a Hellenistic Synagogue, or group of Synagogues (on the Jewish Synagogues at Rome see Schürer p. 247; see above p. 4). If the Church at least to some extent still presented this aspect to the Pagan world of Rome, we have perhaps the clue to the partial confusion of Christians and Jews in Tacitus' account of the Neronian persecution (*Ann.* xv. 44). The first batch of those arrested, who gave information which led to the arrest of the 'multitudo ingens,' may well have been Jews (comp. Merivale *History of the Romans* vi. 448 f.). These, if the Christians formed a schismatic Synagogue, would naturally have full knowledge about them, and would be ready enough to implicate them. With this Clement's insistence on jealousy as the cause of the persecution harmonises (c. 6). Further, of this 'great company' Tacitus says, 'haud perinde in crimine incendii quam odio humani generis convicti sunt.' But this is exactly what he says elsewhere (*Hist.* v. 5) of the Jews, 'adversus omnes alios hostile odium' (comp. Juv. xiv. 103 with Prof. Mayor's note). Again, if we turn to Domitian's onslaught, during, or immediately after, which Clement's letter was written, we have a similar notice. How natural does Dion Cassius' account of the emperor's cruelty towards Flavius Clemens, Domitilla and others become (lxvii. 14 *ἐπηνέχθη δὲ ἀμφοῖν ἔγκλημα ἀθεότητος, ὑφ' ἧς καὶ ἄλλοι ἐς τὰ τῶν Ἰουδαίων ἔθη ἐξοκέλλοντες πολλοὶ κατεδικάσθησαν*), if we suppose this charge of adopting Jewish customs to be connected with the Synagogue worship of the Church at Rome[1]? Still further, in the Hellenistic associations of its earliest days (and old associations in the matter of worship are tenacious and wide in their influence), we may see in part the reason why the primitive Church of Rome was mainly Greek, and why its literature remained Greek till the third century. There is indeed an interesting parallel between the relations of Christian Hebrew and Hellenistic Synagogues at Jerusalem and on the other hand the presence of Greek and Latin elements in the Roman Church, the gradual transition of a Greek into a Latin Church, and the survival of liturgical relics of the former, e.g. in the Kyrie eleison[2].

There is a question of considerable interest which seems to me to be

[1] Compare Sueton. *Domit.* 12, Ad quem deferebantur, qui vel inprofessi Judaicam viverent vitam.

[2] Doubtless originally a Greek Jewish liturgical formula based on the LXX. of Is. xxxiii. 2, Ps. cxxii. 3, vi. 3, ix. 14, &c.

suggested by the liturgical element in Clement's Epistle, when it is viewed in connexion with the theory which I have put forward of the Christian Synagogue worship of the Church at Rome and elsewhere. Bp Lightfoot (*Clement* i. p. 394 f.) points out a series of parallels between the letter of Clement and the first two and the last two of the eighteen Jewish benedictions, the *Shemoneh Esreh.* Now it seems clear that the language employed by the Jews at Rome in their worship was commonly Greek, the Rabbinical authorities in Palestine expressly sanctioning 'the use of any language whatever in repeating the Shemah, the Shemoneh Esreh' (see Schürer p. 283 f.). Is Clement's Greek representation of the Hebrew formulas his own or that of the Christian congregation at Rome, or on the other hand is it based on the Greek version of the Hebrew liturgy current in the Jewish (Hellenistic) Synagogues at Rome, itself largely based on the LXX.? Bishop Lightfoot does not hint at the question, but it seems to follow necessarily on the results of his investigation. Possibly a minute examination of the points of resemblance between Clement and the early Liturgies might reveal their common origin in *Greek* Jewish Prayers. Such a comparison, however, would require a critical textual study of the Liturgies. But can anything be gained from a comparison of Clement with the Didaché? The two documents seem to be quite independent of each other. A comparison is difficult, partly because the liturgical fragments in the Didaché, though distinct, are scanty; partly because the liturgical element in the Didaché is mainly eucharistic, that in Clement mainly intercessory. The two documents, if they draw from the same stream, draw from it at different points of its course. The following resemblances, however, are worth noting. (1) Compare Didaché x. 4 *πρὸ πάντων εὐχαριστοῦμέν σοι ὅτι δυνατὸς εἶ σύ* with Clem. 61 *ὁ μόνος δυνατὸς ποιῆσαι ταῦτα...σοὶ ἐξομολογούμεθα.* The use of *δυνατός* in reference to God is to be noted. Does the Didaché give the liturgical phrase which Clement adapts? The word is so used in Lc. i. 49 (*ὁ δυνατός*); Ps. xxiv. 8, Zeph. iii. 17 (=גבור); Ps. lxxxix. 9 (=חסין); comp. Job xxxvi. 5. (2) Compare Did. x. 3 *σύ, δέσποτα παντοκράτορ, ἔκτισας τὰ πάντα ἕνεκα τοῦ ὀνόματός σου, τροφήν τε καὶ ποτὸν ἔδωκας τοῖς ἀνθρώποις* with Clement (a) 60 *σύ, κύριε, τὴν οἰκουμένην ἔκτισας,...ναί, δέσποτα, ἐπίφανον*...61 *σύ, δέσποτα, ἔδωκας...σὺ γάρ, δέσποτα ἐπουράνιε...δίδως τοῖς υἱοῖς τῶν ἀνθρώπων κ.τ.λ.* The phrase *ὁ παντοκράτωρ θεός* occurs in Clem. 2, 32, 62; *ὁ παντεπόπτης δεσπότης* in 55, comp. 64: (b) 59 *τὸ ἀρχεγόνον πάσης κτίσεως ὄνομά σου.* (3) With Did. x. 2 *εὐχαριστοῦμέν σοι...ὑπὲρ τοῦ ἁγίου ὀνόματός σου, οὗ κατεσκήνωσας ἐν ταῖς καρδίαις ἡμῶν* with Clem. 58 *ὑπακούσωμεν οὖν τῷ παναγίῳ καὶ ἐνδόξῳ ὀνόματι αὐτοῦ.. ἵνα κατασκηνώσωμεν πεποιθότες ἐπὶ τὸ ὁσιώτατον τῆς μεγαλωσύνης αὐτοῦ ὄνομα.* Here the impression given is that Clement has in his mind some liturgical phrase which he adapts and amplifies. If so, the phrase given in the Didaché and implied in Clement may be derived from a common source in (*a*) a Jewish formula, (*β*) a Jewish formula Christianised, (*γ*) a purely Christian formula. We are checked in deciding for (*a*) by a comparison of the phrase *διὰ Ἰησοῦ τοῦ παιδός σου* [Did. ix. 2, 3, x. 2, (3)] with *διὰ τοῦ ἠγαπημένου παιδὸς αὐτοῦ Ἰ. Χρ., διὰ Ἰ. Χρ. τοῦ ἠγ. π. σου* (Clem. 59); so *Mart. Polyc.* 14 *Ἰ. Χ. ἀγαπητοῦ σου παιδός.*

(4) Lastly I take the tangled question of the quotation in Clem. 34 *καὶ ἡμεῖς οὖν, ἐν ὁμονοίᾳ ἐπὶ τὸ αὐτὸ συναχθέντες τῇ συνειδήσει, ὡς ἐξ ἑνὸς στόματος βοήσωμεν πρὸς αὐτὸν ἐκτενῶς εἰς τὸ μετόχους ἡμᾶς γενέσθαι τῶν μεγάλων καὶ ἐνδόξων ἐπαγγελιῶν αὐτοῦ. λέγει γάρ Ὀφθαλμὸς οὐκ εἶδεν καὶ οὖς οὐκ ἤκουσεν, καὶ ἐπὶ καρδίαν ἀνθρώπου οὐκ ἀνέβη, ὅσα ἡτοίμασεν τοῖς ὑπομένουσιν αὐτόν.* Comp. 1 Cor. ii. 9. Bp Lightfoot (*Clement* i. p. 390 n.) was not wholly satisfied with the explanation which is content with tracing these words to Is. lxiv. 4, lxv. 16, 17. 'Still the phenomenon in St Clement,' so he wrote, 'suggests that in one form or other it had a place in early liturgical services, for indeed its liturgical appropriateness would suggest its introduction; and, considering its connexion as quoted by Clement here, it is probable that he himself so used it.' May not a solution of the question be found in the supposition that the quotation in St Paul, Clement, and others is from some *Greek* (Jewish) Liturgical formula? The difficulty of St Paul's method of citation is not great, for the *γέγραπται* is justified by the oblique reference to Isaiah, on which indeed the liturgical formula, if it be such, is based. Further, it will be remembered that in one and the same Epistle St Paul introduces alike a passage of Scripture and a Christian Hymn with the formula *λέγει* (Eph. iv. 8, v. 14 : comp. Hebr. i. 7). Again, a reference to Isaiah hardly explains the language of 1 Cor. ii. 9 ; for the *ἅ...* and *ὅσα...* have the appearance of being the rough edges of a direct quotation torn from its context (comp. 1 Tim. iii. 16 *ὃς ἐφανερώθη...*), rough edges which elsewhere (e.g. in Clement) are smoothed down. It remains to state briefly some arguments which appear to support the theory of a *Greek* (Jewish) liturgical origin. (i) The quotation *with variations* occurs very widely (see Resch *Agrapha* pp. 102, 281), often in writings in which there are traces of Jewish traditions and associations, e.g. in Ep. Clement, 'The Ancient Homily' 11 (14), Mart. Polyc. 2, Apostolic Constitutions (vii. 32), Pseudo-Athan. *de Virginitate* (18); to this list Ep. Pseudo-Clem. *de Virginitate* (i. 9) and *Acta Thomae* (36) should perhaps be added. It is not clear what Gnostic sect Hegesippus (see Phot. *Bibl.* 232) refers to as using these words. The heretic Justin seems to have had Jewish affinities, Valentinus to have had considerable knowledge of Jewish opinions; both of these heretics, if we are to believe Hippolytus (*Refut.* v. 24, 26, 27; vi. 24), used these words[1]. (ii) The notion of the *kingdom* is in several references linked with the words; thus Clem. *Protrept.* x. 94 after the word *ἀνέβη* adds *καὶ χαρήσονται ἐπὶ τῇ βασιλείᾳ τοῦ κυρίου αὐτῶν εἰς τοὺς αἰῶνας· ἀμήν.* *Apost. Constit.* vii. 32 after *τοῖς ἀγαπῶσιν αὐτὸν* adds *καὶ χαρήσονται ἐν τῇ βασιλείᾳ τοῦ θεοῦ.* Agathangelus (31, see below pp. 32, 38), gives the closing words of a confessor's prayer thus: *ἐπήγαγες ἂν ἡμῖν καὶ τὴν σὴν βασιλείαν ἣν προητοίμασας εἰς τὴν ἡμετέραν δόξαν πρὸ τοῦ εἶναι τὸν κόσμον, ἣν ὀφθαλμὸς οὐκ εἶδεν, καὶ οὖς οὐκ ἤκουσεν, καὶ ἐπὶ καρδίαν ἀνθρώπου οὐκ ἀνέβη, ἣν*

[1] If Dr Salmon's theory in his art. on *the Cross-references in the 'Philosophumena'* (*Hermathena* v. p. 389) be true, Hippolytus' evidence is probably worthless.

καὶ νῦν δώσεις, δέσποτα, τοῖς ἠγαπηκόσιν τὸ πανάγιόν σου ὄνομα καὶ τὴν παρουσίαν τοῦ σοῦ μονογενοῦς (cf. 2 Tim. iv. 8, 18). Such prayers, as I shall have occasion to notice later on, sometimes have embedded in them ancient liturgical fragments. Probably it is so here. It is worth noticing in passing that both in Clement and in Agathangelus in the previous context the mention of the Divine will and of the hosts of angels is prominent. When we turn to the Didaché (x. 5), we have the prayer *μνήσθητι, κύριε, τῆς ἐκκλησίας σου...καὶ σύναξον*[1] *αὐτὴν ἀπὸ τῶν τεσσάρων ἀνέμων, τὴν ἁγιασθεῖσαν εἰς τὴν σὴν βασιλείαν ἣν ἡτοίμασας αὐτῇ.* Here it will be noticed that the last clause agrees with the first clause of the excerpt from Agathangelus and contains in connexion with 'the kingdom' the key-word *ἡτοίμασας*, which is common to several of these passages[2]. It is possible that the words of the Didaché and of Agathangelus are to be traced to Matt. xxv. 34 *κληρονομήσατε τὴν ἡτοιμασμένην ὑμῖν βασιλείαν.* But it is perhaps more probable that the *wording* in this latter case as well as in the two former passages is to be referred to some liturgical phrase. (iii) Lastly, there are the expressions *τοῖς ἀγαπῶσιν αὐτόν, τοῖς ὑπομένουσιν αὐτόν.* It may well be that both were sanctioned by Hellenistic liturgical usage; that in fact they were alternative phrases. The latter is suggested by Is. lxiv. 3 (*τοῖς ὑπομένουσιν ἔλεον*), also by Ps. lxviii. 7, Lament. iii. 25 (*ἀγαθὸς κύριος τοῖς ὑπομένουσιν αὐτόν*), Zech. vi. 14 (*ὁ δὲ στέφανος ἔσται τοῖς ὑπομένουσι*). The former (*τοῖς ἀγαπῶσιν αὐτόν*) occurs in the N. T. not only in 1 Cor. ii. 9, but also in Jas. i. 12, ii. 5—'the crown of life (the kingdom)' *ὃν* (*ἧς*) *ἐπηγγείλατο τοῖς ἀγαπῶσιν αὐτόν*, compare 2 Tim. iv.

[1] Compare *Did.* ix. 4 *οὕτω συναχθήτω σου ἡ ἐκκλησία ἀπὸ τῶν περάτων τῆς γῆς εἰς τὴν σὴν βασιλείαν*, *Ep. Clem.* 34 (see above) *συναχθέντες*, *Mart. Polyc.* 20 *τῷ δὲ δυναμένῳ πάντας ἡμᾶς εἰσαγαγεῖν [ἐν] τῇ αὐτοῦ χάριτι καὶ δωρεᾷ εἰς τὴν ἐπουράνιον αὐτοῦ βασιλείαν διὰ παιδὸς αὐτοῦ*, 22 *ἵνα κἀμὲ συναγάγῃ ὁ κύριος* 'I. X. *μετὰ τῶν ἐκλεκτῶν αὐτοῦ*, *Clementine Liturgy* (Hammond p. 22) *πάντας ἡμᾶς ἐπισυνάγαγε εἰς τὴν τῶν οὐρανῶν βασιλείαν*, *Lit. of St James* (Hammond p. 26, Swainson p. 218), and (Hammond p. 46 = Syriac p. 76, Swainson p. 301 = Syriac p. 342) *ἐπισυνάγων ἡμᾶς ὑπὸ τοὺς πόδας τῶν ἐκλεκτῶν σου*, *Lit. of St Basil* (Hammond p. 120, Swainson pp. 84, 164) *τοὺς ἐσκορπισμένους ἐπισυνάγαγε.* The source of these prayers is doubtless the tenth of the Eighteen Benedictions, 'Set up a standard to *collect* our captives, and *gather us together from the four corners of the earth.* Blessed art Thou, O Lord, who *gatherest the outcasts* of Thy people Israel.' But the Greek representation thus widely spread must be that current in the Hellenistic Synagogues, founded on such passages in the LXX. as Deut. xxx. 4 *ἐὰν ᾖ ἡ διασπορά σου ἀπ' ἄκρου τοῦ οὐρανοῦ ἕως ἄκρου τοῦ οὐρανοῦ ἐκεῖθεν συνάξει σε ὁ κύριος*, Ps. cvi. 47, cxlvii. 2, Is. xi. 12 *τοὺς διεσπαρμένους Ἰούδα συνάξει ἐκ τῶν τεσσάρων πτερύγων τῆς γῆς*, xlix. 5, lii. 12, Neh. i. 9 *εἰσάξω αὐτοὺς εἰς τὸν τόπον ὃν ἐξελεξάμην κατασκηνῶσαι τὸ ὄνομά μου ἐκεῖ* (note the double coincidence with *Did.* ix. x.), Zech. ii. 6 *ἐκ τῶν τεσσάρων ἀνέμων τοῦ οὐρανοῦ συνάξω ὑμᾶς*, 2 Macc. i. 27, ii. 18. Compare Matt. xxiv. 31, John xi. 52, 2 Thess. ii. 1.

[2] For this connexion compare e.g. 1 Sam. xiii. 13, 1 Chron. xvii. 11, 2 Chron. xii. 1, Is. xxx. 33. The word occurs also (though in a somewhat different connexion) in *Mart. Polyc.* 14, which is clearly a valuable liturgical fragment.

8 (πᾶσιν τοῖς ἠγαπηκόσι τὴν ἐπιφάνειαν αὐτοῦ, comp. Agath. quoted above). The context in all these passages is very similar, and a common liturgical source would explain all the phenomena. This phrase also would be ultimately based on the O. T., Deut. vii. 9 ὁ φυλάσσων...ἔλεος τοῖς ἀγαπῶσιν αὐτόν (לאהביו), Ps. cxlv. 20; comp. Ps. cxix. 165, cxxii. 6. If the original liturgical setting resembled the First of the Eighteen benedictions, 'Blessed art Thou, O Lord our God and the God of Abraham, the God of Isaac, and the God of Jacob...who rememberest the good deeds of the fathers and sendest a redeemer unto their sons' sons,' the phrase might be a reminiscence of Isaiah xli. 8 (אברהם אהבי, LXX. Ἀβραὰμ ὃν ἠγάπησα), 2 Chron. xx. 7.

I am content if this somewhat lengthy discussion makes it in any degree probable that patient investigation may disinter fragments of *Greek* Jewish liturgical forms[1], and if it gives me the opportunity of expressing the belief that the results of such an investigation would throw an unexpected light on many passages of the New Testament, and on the literature and life of the Early Church (compare below p. 147).

B. Note on the Pauline Epistles and the Synoptic Gospels (see p. 10).

Prof. Marshall of Manchester (*Expositor*, July, 1890) points out 'six well established cases in which St Paul directly or indirectly quotes from words of the Lord Jesus which are contained in our present Gospels.' 'In three of the six instances,' he maintains, 'the variation between St Paul and the Evangelist is capable of explanation on the hypothesis that they give a variant translation of a common original, written in the language of Palestine.' The article, which the writer has followed up with others on *the Aramaic Gospel*, is most suggestive.

As the matter is closely connected with the subject of this Essay, I add the following coincidences with the text of our Gospels in the Pauline Epistles[2]:

(1) 1 Thess. i. 6 δεξάμενοι τὸν λόγον ἐν θλίψει πολλῇ μετὰ χαρᾶς πνεύματος ἁγίου. Comp. Lc. viii. 13 μετὰ χαρᾶς δέχονται τὸν λόγον. Matt. xiii. 21 γενομένης δὲ θλίψεως || Mc. iv. 17. Also comp. 1 Thess. ii. 13 with Lc. viii. 11.

(2) 1 Thess. ii. 15 f. τῶν Ἰουδαίων, τῶν καὶ τὸν κύριον ἀποκτεινάντων

[1] Comp. Dr Swainson *The Greek Liturgies* p. xl., 'Dr Westcott, in a note on 1 Jn. ii. 2, has quoted a remarkable passage from Philo *De Monarchia* ii. 6, which suggests that the prayers ὑπὲρ εὐκρασίας ἀέρων, ὄμβρων εἰρηνικῶν κ.τ.λ. (*St Chrys.* p. 111, *St James* pp. 251, 287) may have originated in Jewish usage.' But the prayers in the Alexandrian Synagogues would be in Greek. Hence Dr Swainson's reference becomes a hint which may prove fruitful. A liturgical scholar familiar with Philo might very probably recover large portions of the Greek Jewish Prayers. Compare the discussion below of the doxology at the close of the Lord's Prayer.

[2] Davidson, *Introduction* (Ed. 2, 1882) p. 441, has a somewhat similar table of parallels, which however I have not consulted.

Ἰησοῦν καὶ τοὺς προφήτας καὶ ἡμᾶς ἐκδιωξάντων...εἰς τὸ ἀναπληρῶσαι αὐτῶν τὰς ἁμαρτίας πάντοτε. ἔφθασεν δὲ ἐπ' αὐτοὺς ἡ ὀργὴ εἰς τέλος. Comp. Matt. xxiii. 32 ff. υἱοί ἐστε τῶν φονευσάντων τοὺς προφήτας· καὶ ὑμεῖς πληρώσατε (v. l. πληρώσετε) τὸ μέτρον τῶν πατέρων ὑμῶν...πῶς φύγητε ἀπὸ τῆς κρίσεως τῆς γεέννης;...ἀποστέλλω πρὸς ὑμᾶς προφήτας...ἐξ αὐτῶν ἀποκτενεῖτε...καὶ διώξετε.

(3) 1 Thess. v. 2 οἴδατε ὅτι ἡμέρα κυρίου ὡς κλέπτης ἐν νυκτὶ οὕτως ἔρχεται (Apoc. iii. 3, 2 Pet. iii. 10). Comp. Matt. xxiv. 42 οὐκ οἴδατε ποίᾳ ἡμέρᾳ ὁ κύριος ὑμῶν ἔρχεται...γινώσκετε ὅτι εἰ ᾔδει...ποίᾳ φυλακῇ ὁ κλέπτης ἔρχεται.

(4) 1 Thess. v. 5 πάντες γὰρ ὑμεῖς υἱοὶ φωτός ἐστε καὶ υἱοὶ ἡμέρας (Eph. v. 9 τέκνα φωτός). Comp. Lc. xvi. 8 τοὺς υἱοὺς τοῦ φωτός (Jn. xii. 36).

(5) 1 Thess. v. 14 εἰρηνεύετε ἐν ἑαυτοῖς. Comp. Mc. ix. 50 εἰρηνεύετε ἐν ἀλλήλοις.

(6) 1 Thess. v. 15 ὁρᾶτε μή τις κακὸν ἀντὶ κακοῦ τινὶ ἀποδῷ (Rom. xii. 17, 1 Pet. iii. 9). Comp. Matt. v. 44 ff., Lc. vi. 27 ff.

(7) 2 Thess. i. 5 εἰς τὸ καταξιωθῆναι ὑμᾶς τῆς βασιλείας τοῦ θεοῦ. Comp. Lc. xx. 35 οἱ καταξιωθέντες τοῦ αἰῶνος ἐκείνου τυχεῖν καὶ τῆς ἀναστάσεως τῆς ἐκ νεκρῶν.

(8) 1 Cor. vii. 34 f. μεριμνᾷ...εὐπάρεδρον τῷ κυρίῳ ἀπερισπάστως. Comp. Lc. x. 39 f. παρακαθεσθεῖσα πρὸς τοὺς πόδας τοῦ κυρίου...περιεσπᾶτο... μεριμνᾷς.

(9) 1 Cor. xiii. 2 κἂν ἔχω πᾶσαν τὴν πίστιν ὥστε ὄρη μεθιστάνειν. Comp. Matt. xvii. 20 ἐὰν ἔχητε πίστιν ὡς κόκκον σινάπεως, ἐρεῖτε τῷ ὄρει τούτῳ Μετάβα ἔνθεν ἐκεῖ καὶ μεταβήσεται (xxi. 21, Mc. xi. 23). Note the Syriac Version.

(10) 2 Cor. vi. 10 ὡς λυπούμενοι ἀεὶ δὲ χαίροντες, ὡς πτωχοὶ πολλοὺς δὲ πλουτίζοντες. vii. 6 ὁ παρακαλῶν τοὺς ταπεινοὺς παρεκάλεσεν ἡμᾶς. Comp. Matt. v. 3 ff., Lc. vi. 20 f.

(11) 2 Cor. x. 1 διὰ τῆς πραΰτητος καὶ ἐπιεικίας τοῦ χριστοῦ. Comp. Matt. xi. 29 πραΰς εἰμι καὶ ταπεινὸς τῇ καρδίᾳ Note the Syriac Versions.

(12) 2 Cor. xii. 7 f. ἄγγελος Σατανᾶ...ἵνα ἀποστῇ ἀπ' ἐμοῦ. Comp. Lc. iv. 13 ὁ διάβολος ἀπέστη ἀπ' αὐτοῦ.

(13) Gal. i. 15 f. ὅτε δὲ εὐδόκησεν [ὁ θεὸς]...ἀποκαλύψαι τὸν υἱὸν αὐτοῦ ἐν ἐμοὶ.. εὐθέως οὐ προσανεθέμην σαρκὶ καὶ αἵματι. Comp. Matt. xvi. 17 σὰρξ καὶ αἷμα οὐκ ἀπεκάλυψέν σοι ἀλλ' ὁ πατήρ μου ὁ ἐν τοῖς οὐρανοῖς.

(14) Rom. vi. 11 ὃ δὲ ζῇ, ζῇ τῷ θεῷ. Lc. xx. 38 θεὸς δὲ οὐκ ἔστιν νεκρῶν ἀλλὰ ζώντων· πάντες γὰρ αὐτῷ ζῶσιν.

(15) Rom. viii. 14 ὅσοι γὰρ πνεύματι θεοῦ ἄγονται, οὗτοι υἱοὶ θεοῦ εἰσίν (Gal. v. 18). Comp. Lc. iv. 1 ἤγετο ἐν τῷ πνεύματι. Note the thought of sonship in the context (iii. 22, iv. 3, 9).

(16) Rom. xii. 14 εὐλογεῖτε τοὺς διώκοντας, εὐλογεῖτε καὶ μὴ καταρᾶσθε. Comp. Lc. vi. 28 εὐλογεῖτε τοὺς καταρωμένους ὑμᾶς. Matt. v. 44 προσεύχεσθε ὑπὲρ τῶν διωκόντων ὑμᾶς.

(17) Rom. xiii. 8 ff. ὁ γὰρ ἀγαπῶν τὸν ἕτερον, νόμον πεπλήρωκεν...ἐν τῷ λόγῳ τούτῳ ἀνακεφαλαιοῦται. Comp. Matt. xxii. 37 ff. ἀγαπήσεις κύριον... ἀγαπήσεις τὸν πλησίον σου...ἐν ταύταις ταῖς δυσὶν ἐντολαῖς ὅλος ὁ νόμος κρέμαται καὶ οἱ προφῆται.

(18) There are coincidences of thought, and to some extent of expression, in Mc. vii. 18 ff., and 1 Cor. vi. 13, viii. 13, Rom. xiv. 15 ff.

(19) Phil. ii. 8 *ἐταπείνωσεν ἑαυτὸν...διὸ καὶ ὁ θεὸς αὐτὸν ὑπερύψωσεν.* Comp. Matt. xxiii. 12 *ὅστις ταπεινώσει ἑαυτὸν ὑψωθήσεται* (xviii. 4, Lc. xiv. 11, xviii. 14).

(20) Phil. ii. 15 *φαίνεσθε ὡς φωστῆρες ἐν κόσμῳ.* Comp. Matt. v. 14 *ὑμεῖς ἐστὲ τὸ φῶς τοῦ κόσμου.*

(21) Phil. iv. 6 *μηδὲν μεριμνᾶτε.* Comp. Matt. vi. 25 *μὴ μεριμνᾶτε τῇ ψυχῇ ὑμῶν* (vv. 31, 34).

(22) 1 Tim. i. 13 *ἠλεήθην ὅτι ἀγνοῶν ἐποίησα.* Comp. Lc. xxiii. 34 *ἄφες αὐτοῖς, οὐ γὰρ οἴδασιν τί ποιοῦσιν.*

(23) 2 Tim. iv. 18 *τὴν βασιλείαν αὐτοῦ τὴν ἐπουράνιον.* The phrase is unique in St Paul. Equally with St Matthew's *ἡ βασ. τῶν οὐρανῶν* it would represent the Aramaic phrase.

The following coincidences come under a different category:

(1) 2 Cor. iii. 15 *ἡνίκα ἂν ἀναγινώσκηται Μωυσῆς κάλυμμα ἐπὶ τὴν καρδίαν αὐτῶν κεῖται.* Comp. Lc. xxiv. 32 (Western reading, D and d) *οὐχὶ ἡ καρδία ἦν ἡμῶν κεκαλυμμένη...ὡς διήνοιγεν ἡμῖν τὰς γραφάς;*

(2) Rom. v. 5 *ἡ ἀγάπη τοῦ θεοῦ ἐκκέχυται ἐν ταῖς καρδίαις ἡμῶν διὰ τοῦ πνεύματος ἁγίου.* Tit. iii. 6 *πνεύματος ἁγίου, οὗ ἐξέχεεν ἐφ' ἡμᾶς πλουσίως.*

There is here a reference to the Pentecostal keyword from Joel ii. 28, *ἐκχεῶ ἀπὸ τοῦ πνεύματός μου* (Acts ii. 17), *ἐξέχεεν τοῦτο* (v. 33), *ἡ δωρεὰ τοῦ πνεύματος τοῦ ἁγίου ἐκκέχυται* (Acts x. 45, the account of the 'Gentile Pentecost'). Comp. Ep. Clem. 2, 46, Barn. i. 3, Test. xii. Patriar. *Jud.* 24.

(3) Col. i. 23 *τοῦ εὐαγγελίου...τοῦ κηρυχθέντος ἐν πάσῃ κτίσει τῇ ὑπὸ τὸν οὐρανόν.* Comp. [Mc.] xvi. 15 *πορευθέντες εἰς τὸν κόσμον ἅπαντα κηρύξατε τὸ εὐαγγέλιον πάσῃ τῇ κτίσει.* With this coincidence, compare the following: Hebr. ii. 3 f. *ἥτις* (*σωτηρία*), *ἀρχὴν λαβοῦσα λαλεῖσθαι διὰ τοῦ κυρίου, ὑπὸ τῶν ἀκουσάντων εἰς ἡμᾶς ἐβεβαιώθη, συνεπιμαρτυροῦντος τοῦ θεοῦ σημείοις τε καὶ τέρασιν καὶ ποικίλαις δυνάμεσιν*, and [Mc.] xvi. 19 f. *ὁ μὲν οὖν κύριος* [*Ἰησοῦς*] *μετὰ τὸ λαλῆσαι αὐτοῖς ἀνελήμφθη...ἐκεῖνοι δὲ ἐξελθόντες ἐκήρυξαν πανταχοῦ, τοῦ κυρίου συνεργοῦντος καὶ τὸν λόγον βεβαιοῦντος διὰ τῶν ἐπακολουθούντων σημείων.*

To these coincidences there must be added those which a study of the other Books of the New Testament reveals (see Resch *Agrapha* pp. 248, 252 f.). A rigorous and minute examination of all the coincidences thus brought together, in connexion with the Syriac Versions and especially with what is known of Palestinian Aramaic, would be the next necessary step. Apart from such an investigation no conclusions can be safely drawn. But a study of the evidence thus collected and sifted would, I cannot but believe, bring the Synoptic question sensibly nearer to a solution than it is at present.

I.

πάτερ ἡμῶν ὁ ἐν τοῖς οὐρανοῖς (St Matthew).
πάτερ (St Luke).

There are some independent grounds for thinking that the longer and the shorter forms of this clause were both current in the Apostolic age.

(1) In regard to the longer form. The frequent occurrence in the Synoptists of the phrases *ὁ πατὴρ ὑμῶν ὁ οὐράνιος* (Matt. v. 48, vi. 14, 26, 32, comp. xxiii. 9), *ὁ πατήρ μου ὁ οὐράνιος* (Matt. xv. 13, xviii. 35), *ὁ πατὴρ [ὁ] ἐξ οὐρανοῦ* (Lc. xi. 13), *ὁ πατήρ μου ὁ ἐν τοῖς οὐρανοῖς* (Matt. vii. 21, x. 32, 33, xii. 50 (*ἐν οὐρανοῖς*), xvi. 17, xviii. 10 (*ἐν οὐρανοῖς*), 19 (*ἐν οὐρανοῖς*), *ὁ πατὴρ ὑμῶν ὁ ἐν τοῖς οὐρανοῖς* (Matt. v. 16, 45, vi. 1, vii. 11, Mc. xi. 25) seems to shew that such a form of words was specially endeared to the Disciples, while the fact that the type *ὁ ἐν (τοῖς) οὐρανοῖς* is commoner than the type *ὁ οὐράνιος* is an indication that in St Matthew we have the original Greek form of the first clause of the Prayer[1].

Among the passages referred to above, the following, viz. Matt. vi. 14, xviii. 35, Mc. xi. 25 (*ἀφίετε εἴ τι ἔχετε κατά τινος, ἵνα καὶ ὁ πατὴρ ὑμῶν ὁ ἐν τοῖς οὐρανοῖς ἀφῇ ὑμῖν τὰ παραπτώματα ὑμῶν*), are of special importance, for they refer to the petition for forgiveness as well as to the appeal to the Heavenly Father. The

[1] The two phrases *ὁ οὐράνιος* and *ὁ ἐν τοῖς οὐρανοῖς* equally represent the Hebrew שבשמים and the Syriac ܕܒܫܡܝܐ. The remarks in the text above must to some extent be discounted in view of the fact that both אבינו alone and אבינו שבשמים are found in 'the Jews' Prayer Books' (Dr Taylor *Sayings of the Jewish Fathers* p. 138).

last quoted is the only passage in St Mark in which this name of God, *the Father in Heaven, the Heavenly Father,* is found; and consequently its witness is strongly in favour of the form ὁ ἐν τοῖς οὐρανοῖς being the current Greek form of the first clause of the Lord's Prayer.

The *Didaché* (viii.) is, so far as I know, the only authority which preserves a different wording of this form. In place of ὁ ἐν τοῖς οὐρανοῖς it has ὁ ἐν τῷ οὐρανῷ. The variation is slight. In view of other passages in the Synoptic Gospels[1], it is probable that we have here a trace of divergent translations of an Aramaic original. The fact that ἐν οὐρανῷ occurs later on in the Prayer would seem to make ἐν τῷ οὐρανῷ the more obvious expression in the first clause, and thus to shew that ἐν τοῖς οὐρανοῖς, as being less obvious, has a better claim to be the original Hellenistic translation. But whatever may be the explanation of the variation, its existence indicates that when the *Didaché* was drawn up the Greek form of the Prayer was not absolutely and finally fixed.

(2) In regard to the shorter form[2]. Three passages must be here considered.

καὶ ἔλεγεν 'Αββά *ὁ πατὴρ...ἀλλ' οὐ τί ἐγὼ θέλω ἀλλὰ τί σύ.* St Mark xiv. 36.

ἐξαπέστειλεν ὁ θεὸς τὸ πνεῦμα τοῦ υἱοῦ αὐτοῦ εἰς τὰς καρδίας ἡμῶν, κρᾶζον 'Αββά *ὁ πατήρ.* Gal. iv. 6.

ἐλάβετε πνεῦμα υἱοθεσίας, ἐν ᾧ κράζομεν 'Αββά *ὁ πατήρ.* Rom. viii. 15.

In each of these passages I believe there is a reference to the first clause of the Lord's Prayer.

[1] Comp. (1) Matt. iii. 16 f., Mc. i. 10 f. (plur.) || Lc. iii. 21 f. (sing.), (2) Matt. v. 12 (plur.) || Lc. vi. 23 (sing.), (3) Matt. vii. 11 (plur.) || Lc. xi. 13 (sing.), (4) Matt. xix. 21, Lc. xviii. 22 (plur.) || Mc. x. 21 (sing.). Sometimes there is agreement, e.g. (1) Matt. xiv. 9, Mc. vi. 41, Lc. ix. 16 (sing.); (2) Matt. xxvi. 64, Mc. xiv. 62 (plur.). In the LXX. the plur. is common in the Psalms, rare elsewhere. I do not think that it occurs in the O. T. as equivalent to the late Hebrew שמיא.

[2] In Lc. xi. 2 the Old Latin MSS., *a*, *ff*, *i*, have *Pater sancte qui...;* *mm* (a vulgate text) has *Pater sancte sanctificetur...* Compare John xvii. 11. Such a reading must be traced to a liturgical expansion such as we have in the *Didaché* (x), where we read *πάτερ ἅγιε.* Compare the Christmas preface to the Lord's Prayer in the Gallican Liturgy (Hammond p. 343, see also pp. lxxxii, 290), and the Syrian Baptismal prayer below p. 37.

As to the first of them two points call for notice. (*a*) St Mark, 'the interpreter' of St Peter, records elsewhere Aramaic expressions used by Christ—*ταλειθά κούμ, ὅ ἐστιν μεθερμηνευόμενον* Τὸ *κοράσιον, σοὶ λέγω, ἔγειρε* (v. 41); *κορβάν, ὅ ἐστι Δῶρον* (vii. 11); *λέγει αὐτῷ* 'Εφφαθά, *ὅ ἐστιν Διανοίχθητι* (vii. 34). In these cases St Mark connects the Aramaic word and the Greek equivalent by the phrases, *which is, which is being interpreted.* The absence of such a phrase in xiv. 36 may indeed be accounted for by its incongruity with the solemnity of the context; but it may be better explained by the familiarity of the words 'Αββά *ὁ πατήρ.* (*b*) The Evangelists seem to wish their readers to find in our Lord's words in the Garden of Gethsemane coincidences with the language of the Lord's Prayer [see pp. 61 f., 108 ff.; note especially *γενηθήτω τὸ θέλημά σου* (Matt. xxvi. 42)]. Does not St Mark's use of the words 'Αββά *ὁ πατήρ* harmonise with this undercurrent of thought?

The two Pauline passages confirm this suggestion. In neither of them does the Apostle seem to have the solemn scene in Gethsemane in his thoughts. In both the context breathes a spirit of exaltation. Hence this combination occurring independently in St Mark and in St Paul must be derived from a common source. Now, if the Lord's Prayer were current in the shorter form, what more likely than that the initial word of the Prayer as used by the Hebrew Christians should be coupled with the initial word of a Hellenistic rendering—initial words which, like *Pater noster*, might be used as a name for the Prayer itself? Further, if we substitute in St Paul the two words which recall to *us* the Lord's Prayer—'God sent forth the Spirit of His Son into our hearts, crying, Our Father,' 'Ye received the Spirit of adoption, whereby we cry, Our Father,' the words of the Apostle at once gain, I venture to think, new point and vigour. They are no longer abstract but concrete. In discussing the next clause I shall give another reason for thinking that the Lord's Prayer was at this point in St Paul's mind.

It only remains to point out that in this case the word *Abba* implies the shorter form as given by St Luke, and cannot be the initial word of the longer form; for in a Semitic language the possessive pronoun *Our*, if inserted, becomes part of the noun.

II.

ἁγιασθήτω τὸ ὄνομά σου,
ἐλθάτω ἡ βασιλεία σου.

It will be convenient to consider these two clauses together. In both of them there occurs a remarkable, though but slightly attested, variation of reading. As these variations of reading are cognate, and as the evidence in regard to the latter of the two clauses is clearer, the consideration of this latter will prepare the way for a discussion of the former clause.

In a cursive MS. of the Gospels, of which Mr. Hoskier has published (1890) a full account, the text of which is very remarkable, the opening clauses of the Lord's Prayer in St Luke's Gospel run thus: *πάτερ· ἁγιασθήτω τὸ ὄνομά σου· Ἐλθέτω τὸ πνεῦμά σου τὸ ἅγιον ἐφ' ἡμᾶς καὶ καθαρισάτω ἡμᾶς· γενηθήτω κ.τ.λ.* Mr. Hoskier calls this MS. 'Cod. Ev. 604' (= 700 Gregory)[1].

Of the petition for the coming of the kingdom Gregory of Nyssa *de Oratione Dominica* (ed. Krabinger p. 60) writes thus: *ἢ τάχα καθὼς ἡμῖν ὑπὸ τοῦ Λουκᾶ τὸ αὐτὸ νόημα σαφέστερον ἑρμηνεύεται, ὁ τὴν βασιλείαν ἐλθεῖν ἀξιῶν τὴν τοῦ ἁγίου πνεύματος συμμαχίαν ἐπιβοᾶται. οὕτω γὰρ ἐν ἐκείνῳ τῷ εὐαγγελίῳ φησίν, ἀντὶ τοῦ Ἐλθέτω ἡ βασιλεία σου, Ἐλθέτω, φησί, τὸ ἅγιον πνεῦμά σου ἐφ' ἡμᾶς καὶ καθαρισάτω ἡμᾶς.* A few lines lower down he adds, *ὁ γὰρ Λουκᾶς μὲν πνεῦμα ἅγιον λέγει, Ματθαῖος*

[1] Mr. Hoskier gives a photograph of the page of the MS. containing Lc. xi. 1 f. This important piece of evidence would have escaped my notice but for Dr Hort's kindness.

δὲ βασιλείαν ὠνόμασεν κ.τ.λ. Krabinger's note (p. 141) should be consulted. He mentions a variant, τὸ πνεῦμά σου τὸ ἅγιον, in the former passage, as having some support.

Maximus, a champion of the orthodox party against the Monothelites in the first half of the seventh century, comments thus on the clause (Migne *P. G.* 90 p. 884 f.): ὃ γὰρ ἐνταῦθα Ματθαῖός φησι βασιλείαν, ἀλλαχοῦ τῶν εὐαγγελιστῶν ἕτερος πνεῦμα κέκληκεν ἅγιον, φάσκων Ἐλθέτω σου τὸ πνεῦμα τὸ ἅγιον καὶ καθαρισάτω ἡμᾶς: and lower down, Ἐλθέτω ἡ βασιλεία σου, τουτέστι τὸ πνεῦμα τὸ ἅγιον, ἤδη τῷ τῆς πραότητος λόγῳ τε καὶ τρόπῳ ναοποιηθεῖσι τῷ θεῷ διὰ τοῦ πνεύματος. ἐπὶ τίνα γάρ φησι καταπαύσω, ἀλλ' ἢ ἐπὶ τὸν πρᾶον κ.τ.λ. It thus appears likely that Maximus knew of the words ἐφ' ἡμᾶς, but perhaps by accident did not give them a place in the petition itself.

This evidence, so far as it goes, is clear to the effect that a prayer for the Holy Spirit took the place of the petition for the coming of the kingdom.

A passage, however, from Tertullian (*adv. Marc.* iv. 26), which must next be considered, implies that that writer found at any rate in the text used by Marcion (for otherwise his argument is pointless), probably in the text common to himself and Marcion, a petition for the Holy Spirit in the Lord's Prayer. 'Cui dicam, *Pater*? ei qui me omnino non fecit, a quo originem non traho, an ei qui me faciundo et instruendo generavit? A quo *spiritum sanctum* postulem? A quo mundialis spiritus praestatur, an a quo fiunt etiam angeli spiritus, cujus et in primordio spiritus super aquas ferebatur? Ejus *regnum* optabo venire quem nunquam regem gloriae audivi, an in cujus manu etiam corda sunt regum? Quis dabit mihi *panem quotidianum*?' Thus Tertullian, or possibly Marcion, is at one with Cod. 604, with Gregory and Maximus in witnessing to a petition for the Holy Spirit in the Prayer as given by St Luke; but it is substituted for the petition 'Hallowed be Thy name[1],' and the prayer for the coming of the kingdom is retained. Moreover Tertullian gives no evidence as

[1] Rönsch (*Das Neue Test. Tert.* p. 640) thinks that the words *sanctificetur nomen tuum* may have had a place in the copy from which Tert. quotes, but that he does not notice them because they give him no handle against his opponent. But Tert. was too good a debater not to find a controversial use for whatever lay before him.

to the precise wording of the clause. But another passage in his works (*de Oratione* 4) suggests perplexing questions as to his collocation of the earlier clauses in the Prayer. He quite expressly arranges the clauses thus, 'Sanctificetur nomen tuum, Fiat voluntas tua in coelis et in terra, Veniat regnum tuum[1].' I do not know that there is any other authority for this arrangement of the petitions, and it is hard not to feel that, though Tertullian is here quoting the fuller form of St Matthew's Gospel, this order is connected with the reading which he records in the treatise against Marcion. At first sight this evidence appears to point to little more than a general unsettlement of the earlier petitions. But further examination reveals, I think, an explanation which is at least possible[2]. Tertullian lays some stress on the interpretation (or, to anticipate, a possible relic of an addition to the text) 'ut sanctificetur *in nobis*.' With the clause so interpreted he connects the petition which in his text follows, and on which he gives a similar gloss, 'ut *in nobis* fiat voluntas Dei in terris.' These two clauses then *Sanctificetur*...and *Fiat voluntas*...as explained by Tertullian on the one hand, and on the other the prayer for the Holy Spirit, would come to be regarded as very closely allied. Hence the two former petitions would replace the petition for the Holy Spirit. If this interpretation of the evidence of the *de Oratione* is right, it appears to favour the view that the clause about the Holy Spirit had a place in the MSS. used both by Tertullian and by Marcion,

[1] He expressly says (*a*) Sanctificetur...Secundum hanc formam subjungimus: Fiat...4. (*b*) Veniat quoque regnum tuum ad id pertinet, quo et Fiat voluntas tua, in nobis scilicet...5. (*c*) Post coelestia, id est, post dei nomen, dei voluntatem et dei regnum...6. (*d*) Dei honor in Patre, fidei testimonium in nomine, oblatio obsequii in voluntate, commemoratio spei in regno...9.

The Lord's Prayer as a whole, when the detached clauses are brought together, stands thus in the *de Oratione*: 'Pater qui in coelis es, Sanctificetur nomen tuum, Fiat voluntas tua in coelis et in terra, Veniat regnum tuum, Panem nostrum quotidianum da nobis hodie, Dimitte nobis debita nostra...Ne nos inducas in temptationem. Sed devehe nos a malo.' The omitted clause is implied in the comment, 'remittere nos quoque profitemur debitoribus nostris.' See below p. 58.

[2] The explanation given by Nitzsch, *Studien und Kritiken*, 1830, 4 Heft, p. 846 ff. (quoted by Rönsch *Das Neue Test. Tert.* p. 599), is different. He supposes that the collocation of clauses, to which Tertullian witnesses, arose for the purpose of improving in the way partly of purifying, partly of amplifying, a text of St Luke which Nitzsch represents thus: 'Geheiligt werde dein Name. Zu uns komme dein heil. Geist und reinige uns. Zu uns komme dein Reich.'

while it coincides with the evidence of the *adversus Marcionem* as to the position of the clause.

To sum up; we get evidence in favour of the insertion in the Lord's Prayer of a petition for the Holy Spirit from at least four quarters, from a cursive MS. of the Gospels, from Gregory a Bishop in Cappadocia (from whom perhaps Maximus borrowed his information), from Tertullian of Carthage, from Marcion who seems to have travelled much, and the sources of whose information it is impossible to trace. But the witnesses do not agree as to the position of the petition, substituting it either for 'Thy kingdom come' or for 'Hallowed be Thy name.'

To pass from the form to the occasion of this prayer, we shall be able, I think, to trace it back, through the forms of invocation connected with the Consecration of the Eucharist, the Anointing, and the Imposition of hands, to the passages of the Acts which speak of the Laying on of the Apostles' hands. Indeed the archaic simplicity of this added clause is best seen when it is compared with the passages in the Acts, and when on the other hand it is contrasted with the formulas in use at a later time, which are, as I believe, developments of it.

That such a prayer was in use in connexion with the Laying on of hands is, I think, clear from the following passages, to which others of similar import might be added[1]: Ordo Romanus (Hittorp *de Divinis Cath. Ecclesiae Officiis*, 1568, p. 76) Pontifex veniens ad infantes elevata et imposita manu super capita omnium, dat orationem super eos cum invocatione septiformis gratiae Spiritus Sancti. Then follows a prayer on which the prayer before the imposition of hands in the English 'Order of Confirmation' is based. Augustine *de Trinitate* xv. 26 (Migne *P. L.* 42 p. 1093) Orabant [Apostoli] ut veniret in eos quibus manus imponebant, non ipsi eum dabant. Quem morem in suis praepositis etiam nunc servat ecclesia. Pseudo-Ambrose *de Sacram.* iii. 2 (Migne *P. L.* 16 p. 434) Post fontem superest ut perfectio fiat quando ad invocationem sacerdotis Spiritus Sanctus infunditur. *Constit. Apost.* vii. 44 ἐὰν γὰρ μὴ εἰς ἕκαστον τούτων ἐπίκλησις γένηται ὑπὸ τοῦ εὐσεβοῦς ἱερέως τοιαύτη τις, εἰς ὕδωρ μόνον καταβαίνει...μετὰ

[1] Dr Mason *The Relation of Confirmation to Baptism as taught by the Western Fathers* gives the fullest collection of passages; see especially the Appendix on *Ancient Western Baptismal Prayers.*

τοῦτο ἑστὼς προσευχέσθω τὴν εὐχήν, ἣν ἐδίδαξεν ἡμᾶς ὁ κύριος. Dionysius Alex. (apud Eus. *H. E.* vii. 2) παλαιοῦ γέ τοι κεκρατηκότος ἔθους ἐπὶ τῶν τοιούτων μόνῃ χρῆσθαι τῇ διὰ χειρῶν ἐπιθέσεως εὐχῇ. Cyprian *Ep. ad Jubaianum* Quod nunc quoque apud nos geritur, ut qui in ecclesia baptizantur, praepositis ecclesiae offerantur, et per nostram orationem ac manus impositionem Spiritum Sanctum consequantur et signaculo dominico consummentur. Tert. *de Bapt.* 8 Dehinc manus imponitur per benedictionem advocans et invitans Spiritum Sanctum. It will be noticed that most of these quotations are from Fathers of the Latin Church, where the Apostolic custom of the Laying on of hands maintained its place.

It is remarkable that the Greek offices for Baptism and Anointing do not supply any close parallels[1]. Yet there are the prayers (1) for the sanctification of the water: αὐτὸς οὖν φιλάνθρωπε βασιλεῦ παρέσο καὶ νῦν διὰ τῆς ἐπιφοιτήσεως τοῦ ἁγίου σου πνεύματος καὶ ἁγίασον τὸ ὕδωρ τοῦτο: (2) for the sanctification of the chrism: αὐτὸς εὐλόγησον καὶ τοῦτο τὸ ἔλαιον τῇ δυνάμει καὶ ἐνεργείᾳ καὶ ἐπιφοιτήσει τοῦ ἁγίου σου πνεύματος (Assemani *Codex Liturgicus* ii. pp. 136, 140). In the Latin services there are more obvious resemblances. Thus: Tu, Domine, inmitte in eos Spiritum Sanctum tuum Paracletum; again, Emitte in eos Septiformem Spiritum tuum; and again, Spiritus Sanctus superveniat in vos, et virtus Altissimi sine peccato custodiat vos (Assemani *Cod. Lit.* iii. pp. 2, 3, 5). It is however in the Eucharistic offices that we trace most clearly the expansion of the Apostolic prayer. Thus, compare *Lit. St James* (Hammond p. 38, Swainson p. 260) ἀντικατάπεμψον ἡμῖν τὴν χάριν [add καὶ τὴν δωρεάν, Swainson] τοῦ παναγίου σου πνεύματος. καὶ [ναί, Swainson] ὁ θεὸς ἐπίβλεψον ἐφ' ἡμᾶς κ.τ.λ. *Lit. of Constantinople* (Hammond p. 90, Swainson p. 109) Βασιλεῦ οὐράνιε, παράκλητε, τὸ πνεῦμα τῆς ἀληθείας......ἐλθὲ καὶ σκήνωσον ἐν ἡμῖν, καὶ καθάρισον ἡμᾶς ἀπὸ πάσης κηλῖδος, καὶ σῶσον, ἀγαθέ, τὰς ψυχὰς ἡμῶν. The probable lateness of this Liturgy does not affect the importance of the coincidence with both parts of the petition in Cod. 604.

Similar forms are frequent in the ἐπίκλησις, e.g. *Lit. St James* (Hammond p. 42 f., Swainson p. 276 f.) ἐξαπόστειλον ἐφ' ἡμᾶς καὶ

[1] On a passage from *Acta Thomae* see note A, p. 36; on some Syrian Baptismal Prayers see note B, p. 37.

ἐπὶ τὰ προκείμενα ἅγια δῶρα ταῦτα τὸ πνεῦμά σου τὸ πανάγιον τὸ κύριον καὶ ζωοποιόν......αὐτὸ τὸ πνεῦμά σου τὸ πανάγιον κατάπεμψον, δέσποτα, ἐφ' ἡμᾶς καὶ ἐπὶ τὰ προκείμενα ἅγια δῶρα ταῦτα ἵνα ἐπιφοιτῆσαν τῇ ἁγίᾳ καὶ ἀγαθῇ καὶ ἐνδόξῳ αὐτοῦ παρουσίᾳ ἁγιάσῃ κ.τ.λ. Similar formulas will be found in Hammond pp. 28, 48, 104, 111, 114, 178, 187.

The occurrence of a similar form in the Mozarabic Liturgy (Hammond p. 311, Veni Sancte Spiritus, sanctificator, sanctifica hoc sacrificium de manibus meis tibi praeparatum), and of one very parallel in the Gallican Liturgy (Hammond p. 315), seems to prove the antiquity of this prayer for the Spirit in the Eucharistic office (cf. the 2nd Pfaffian frag. of Irenaeus, Harvey ii. p. 502). Cyril of Jerusalem (Migne *P. G.* 33 p. 1089), closely connecting the *ἐπίκλησις* in the Eucharist with that in the rite of Anointing, shews how easily a prayer originally used in the rite of 'Confirmation' might pass into the Liturgy proper.

The following passages must be compared:

Ep. Clem. 46 *ἢ οὐχὶ ἕνα θεὸν ἔχομεν καὶ ἕνα Χριστὸν καὶ ἓν πνεῦμα τῆς χάριτος τὸ ἐκχυθὲν ἐφ' ἡμᾶς; καὶ μία κλῆσις ἐν Χριστῷ;* See also c. 2.

Barn. 1. *βλέπω ἐν ὑμῖν ἐκκεχυμένον ἀπὸ τοῦ πλουσίου τῆς ἀγάπης κυρίου πνεῦμα ἐφ' ὑμᾶς.* The words *ἐφ' ὑμᾶς* after *ἐν ὑμῖν* imply an allusion to a familiar phrase. They seem to slip in with the word *πνεῦμα.*

Matt. iii. 16 *πνεῦμα θεοῦ...ἐρχόμενον ἐπ' αὐτόν* (comp. Mc. i. 10, Lc. iii. 22, Jn. i. 33; Lc. i. 35, iv. 18).

Acts viii. 15 *προσηύξαντο περὶ αὐτῶν ὅπως λάβωσιν πνεῦμα ἅγιον· οὐδέπω γὰρ ἦν ἐπ' οὐδενὶ αὐτῶν ἐπιπεπτωκός......τότε ἐπετίθεσαν τὰς χεῖρας ἐπ' αὐτοὺς καὶ ἐλάμβανον πνεῦμα ἅγιον.*

Acts x. 44 *ἐπέπεσεν τὸ πνεῦμα τὸ ἅγιον ἐπὶ πάντας τοὺς ἀκούοντας τὸν λόγον.*

Acts xv. 8 f. *θεὸς ἐμαρτύρησεν αὐτοῖς δοὺς τὸ πνεῦμα τὸ ἅγιον καθὼς καὶ ἡμῖν......τῇ πίστει καθαρίσας τὰς καρδίας αὐτῶν.* Here the coincidence with both parts of the formula given by Gregory will be noticed.

Acts xix. 6 *καὶ ἐπιθέντος αὐτοῖς τοῦ Παύλου χεῖρας ἦλθεν τὸ πνεῦμα τὸ ἅγιον ἐπ' αὐτούς.*

1 Thess. iv. 8 *ἐκάλεσεν ἡμᾶς ὁ θεὸς......ἐν ἁγιασμῷ......τὸν*

θεὸν τὸν διδόντα τὸ πνεῦμα αὐτοῦ τὸ ἅγιον εἰς ὑμᾶς (comp. Ezek. xxxvii. 14 δώσω πνεῦμά μου εἰς ὑμᾶς καὶ ζήσεσθε).

Gal. iv. 6 ἐξαπέστειλεν ὁ θεὸς τὸ πνεῦμα τοῦ υἱοῦ αὐτοῦ εἰς τὰς καρδίας ἡμῶν, κρᾶζον Ἀββά ὁ πατήρ.

Rom. viii. 15 ἐλάβετε πνεῦμα υἱοθεσίας, ἐν ᾧ κράζομεν Ἀββά ὁ πατήρ.

The probable connexion of the last two passages with the Lord's Prayer has been already pointed out, see above p. 23 f.

Titus iii. 5 πνεύματος ἁγίου οὗ ἐξέχεεν ἐφ' ἡμᾶς πλουσίως.

1 Peter iv. 14 τὸ τοῦ θεοῦ πνεῦμα ἐφ' ὑμᾶς ἀναπαύεται. Compare Is. xi. 2 ἀναπαύεται ἐπ' αὐτὸν πνεῦμα τοῦ θεοῦ. The change in order by which in the Epistle the words πνεῦμα ἐφ' ὑμᾶς are brought together should be taken into account: comp. Barn. 1, quoted above p. 30.

Compare also 1 Cor. iii. 16, 2 Cor. i. 22, Rom. viii. 9 ff., Eph. i. 13, 2 Tim. i. 14.

We pass to the other clause, *Hallowed be Thy name.* In St Luke xi. 2 Codex Bezae reads ἁγιασθήτω ὄνομά σου ἐφ' ἡμᾶς. The corresponding Latin Version has, 'super nos.' There is no other evidence that I know of to be derived from any MSS.

The petition thus read is a conflation of two types of phrases found in the Prophets. On the one hand we compare Is. xxix. 23 δι' ἐμὲ ἁγιάσουσι τὸ ὄνομά μου, Ezek. xxxvi. 23 ἁγιάσω τὸ ὄνομά μου τὸ μέγα: on the other Is. iv. 1 (cf. Jer. xiv. 9) τὸ ὄνομα τὸ σὸν κεκλήσθω ἐφ' ἡμᾶς (יִקָּרֵא...עָלֵינוּ), lxiii. 16, 19 σὺ γὰρ εἶ πατὴρ ἡμῶν...σὺ κύριε πατὴρ ἡμῶν ῥῦσαι ἡμᾶς, ἀπ' ἀρχῆς τὸ ὄνομά σου ἐφ' ἡμᾶς ἐστί... ἐγενόμεθα ὡς τὸ ἀπ' ἀρχῆς, ὅτε οὐκ ἦρξας ἡμῶν οὐδὲ ἐκλήθη τὸ ὄνομά σου ἐφ' ἡμᾶς. In the latter passage the coincidence with three leading thoughts of the Lord's Prayer—Our Father, Thy name, deliver us—is remarkable. The language of the Old Testament passed into the Synagogue Prayers and into the Christian Liturgies. Thus in the Morning Service of a modern Jewish Prayer Book, we find the words,

אָבִינוּ מַלְכֵּנוּ חָנֵּנוּ וַעֲנֵנוּ כִּי שִׁמְךָ הַגָּדוֹל נִקְרָא עָלֵינוּ :

and the following remarkable coincidence with the Lord's Prayer,

קַדֵּשׁ אֶת־שִׁמְךָ עַל מַקְדִּישֵׁי שְׁמֶךָ וְקַדֵּשׁ אֶת־שִׁמְךָ בְּעוֹלָמֶךָ...

מְקַדֵּשׁ אֶת־שִׁמְךָ בָּרַבִּים׃

In the last passage the occurrence of the two prepositions ב and על in parallel clauses should be noticed for a reason which will appear later on[1]. Similar phrases are found in the Christian Liturgies. Compare the 'Clementine' Liturgy (Hammond p. 22) *τὸ ὄνομα τοῦ χριστοῦ σου ἐπικέκληται ἐφ' ἡμᾶς*. A similar phrase has a marked connexion with other clauses of the Lord's Prayer in the Embolismus of the *Liturgy of St James* (Hammond p. 48, Swainson p. 307), *διὰ τὸ ὄνομά σου τὸ ἅγιον, τὸ ἐπικληθὲν ἐπὶ τὴν ἡμετέραν ταπείνωσιν.*

Some passages in early Christian literature bear on this form of the petition.

There is such a passage in Agathangelus' history of the Conversion of Armenia[2]. Agathangelus, the secretary of Tiridates king of Armenia, relates at length the story how his master was at first the persecutor and then the patron of Gregory the apostle of Armenia in the first quarter of the fourth century. Incidentally the book records the history of a body of religious women who fled from Rome to rescue one of their number Rhipsima from the foul designs of Diocletian. They fly to Armenia and there build a nunnery. The fame however of the beauty of Rhipsima reaches Tiridates and he sends for her to the palace. In the prayer which Agathangelus puts into her mouth at this point of the history (c. 73 ed. Lagarde) there occur the following words: *ὁ διδάξας καὶ παιδεύσας καὶ δοὺς τοὺς λόγους σου ἐν τῷ στόματι ἡμῶν, ἵνα ἐν τούτοις δυνηθῶμεν σωθῆναι ἀπὸ τῆς παγίδος τοῦ ἐχθροῦ, καὶ εἰπὼν ὅτι* Τὸ *ὄνομά μου ἐπικέκληται ἐφ' ὑμᾶς, καὶ ὑμεῖς ἐστὲ ναὸς τῆς θεότητός μου, καὶ πάλιν ὅτι* Τὸ *ὄνομά μου ἁγιάσεται* [sic] *ἐν ταῖς καρδίαις*

[1] These extracts are taken from the *Authorised Daily Prayer Book...Published under the sanction of Chief Rabbi Dr Nathan Marcus Adler*, 1890, pp. 60, 9; comp. pp. 37, 45, 59, 61, 75. I cannot think that these clauses are modern. But I have not traced the words in the different groups of the Jewish Prayer Books. The intricacy of the subject may be seen from Dr Schiller-Szinessy's article *Mahzor* in the *Encyclopaedia Britannica*.

[2] See detached note C on p. 38.

ὑμῶν· καὶ ἔδωκας λόγον ἐν τῷ στόματι ἡμῶν αἰτήσασθαι καὶ λέγειν Ἁγιασθήτω τὸ ὄνομά σου, νῦν τοῦτο αἰτούμεθα παρὰ σοῦ. ἰδοὺ συνήχθη πλῆθος κακῶν, μιᾶναι τὸ πανάγιον ὄνομά σου ἐφ' ἡμᾶς καὶ τὸν ναὸν τοῦ ὀνόματός σου. εἰ γὰρ καὶ ἡμεῖς ἀσθενεῖς καὶ ταπειναὶ ὑπάρχομεν, πλὴν αὐτὸς φύλαξον τὰς ψυχὰς ἡμῶν ἀπὸ τῆς ἀκαθάρτου ἀτιμίας, φιλάνθρωπε σῶτερ, ὁ ἐάσας ἐπελθεῖν ἡμῖν τὸν πειρασμὸν τοῦτον· δὸς ἡμῖν νίκην τῇ σῇ δυνάμει. σὴ γάρ ἐστιν ἡ νίκη καὶ νικήσει τὸ σὸν ὄνομα.

There are, it will be seen, in this story two grounds for suspicion. First, though Diocletian was in Rome more than once in the early years of the fourth century, yet the representation of him suggested by Agathangelus has every appearance of being apocryphal. Secondly, a nunnery in Rome, well established by the beginning of the fourth century, is a plain anachronism. But the importance of the passage for our purpose is independent of the question of date. In martyrologies the prayers of the saints are always worth careful inspection from the point of view of criticism, for there is always the probability that they may contain relics of ancient formulas. In this case it is clear that the prayer is based on liturgical forms[1]. It is to the setting of the petition of the Lord's Prayer that I would call attention.

In the *Didaché* we have a very early witness carrying back the evidence to the confines of the Apostolic age. The form of thanksgiving which is to be said after the reception of the Eucharist (x. 1 f.) is the resultant of two converging forces, the Prayers of the Synagogue and the Lord's Prayer. The petitions for daily bread and for deliverance from evil (or the evil one) are paraphrased in the later part. The form begins thus, *εὐχαριστοῦμέν σοι, πάτερ ἅγιε*[2], *ὑπὲρ τοῦ ἁγίου ὀνόματός σου, οὗ κατεσκήνωσας ἐν ταῖς καρδίαις ἡμῶν, καὶ ὑπὲρ τῆς γνώσεως καὶ*

[1] The liturgical character of the prayer becomes clear when we compare e.g. (1) the *Embolismus* of the Liturgy of St James (Hammond p. 48), ὁ εἰδὼς τὴν ἀσθένειαν ἡμῶν...ῥῦσαι ἡμᾶς ἀπὸ τοῦ πονηροῦ...πάσης ἐπηρείας καὶ μεθοδείας αὐτοῦ διὰ τὸ ὄνομά σου τὸ ἅγιον, τὸ ἐπικληθὲν ἐπὶ τὴν ἡμετέραν ταπείνωσιν, (2) the prayer for the Emperor in the Lit. of St Mark (Hammond p. 172), δὸς αὐτῷ, ὁ θεός, νίκας, εἰρηνικὰ φρονεῖν πρὸς ἡμᾶς, καὶ πρὸς τὸ ὄνομά σου τὸ ἅγιον. The word φιλάνθρωπε is very common in the Liturgies.

[2] The reading *Pater sancte* in some old Latin MSS. should be compared: see p. 23.

πίστεως καὶ ἀθανασίας, ἧς ἐγνωρίσας ἡμῖν διὰ Ἰησοῦ τοῦ παιδός σου· σοὶ ἡ δόξα εἰς τοὺς αἰῶνας.

The latter part of this thanksgiving is substantially a repetition of a formula used in an earlier passage (ix. 3), and should be compared with the second and fourth of the Jewish 'Eighteen Benedictions.' We may disregard it, for at most it vaguely corresponds with the clauses about the Divine Kingdom and Will. But the earlier portion clearly refers to a petition immediately succeeding the opening words of the Prayer. At first sight the word ὀνόματος is a stumbling block. Our first impression is that it must have taken the place of an original πνεύματος. To this latter word, side by side with κατεσκήνωσας ἐν ταῖς καρδίας ἡμῶν, many parallels at once suggest themselves, e.g. Hermas *Mand.* iii. 1, v. 1, 2, x. 2, *Sim.* v. 6. 5, passages which in their turn are based on James iv. 5. But against this correction either of the text of the *Didaché* or of the Didachist's report of his original there are at least three objections. (*a*) The correction is too obvious. Neither the Didachist himself nor the copyists would be under any temptation to change an easy word into a hard one. (*b*) The actual phrase is found in the LXX., ἐν Σηλώ, οὗ κατεσκήνωσα (שִׁכַּנְתִּי) τὸ ὄνομά μου ἐκεῖ ἔμπροσθεν (Jer. vii. 12), τὸν τόπον ὃν ἐξελεξάμην κατασκηνῶσαι (לְשַׁכֵּן) τὸ ὄνομά μου ἐκεῖ (Neh. i. 9). In Deut. xii. 11, xiv. 23, xvi. 6, 11, xvi. 2 the translators represent לְשַׁכֵּן שְׁמוֹ שָׁם by ἐπικληθῆναι τὸ ὄνομα αὐτοῦ ἐκεῖ. In all these places the reference is to the Sanctuary (see Dr Taylor *The Teaching of the Twelve Apostles* p. 73 f.). Compare also Ezek. xliii. 7 ἐν οἷς κατασκηνώσῃ τὸ ὄνομά μου ἐν μέσῳ οἴκου Ἰσραὴλ τὸν αἰῶνα (אֲשֶׁר אֶשְׁכָּן־שָׁם), Ps. lxxiv. 8 ἐβεβήλωσαν τὸ σκήνωμα τοῦ ὀνόματός σου (מִשְׁכַּן־שְׁמֶךָ). (*c*) The phrase as it stands in the *Didaché* has remarkable points of contact with the passage in Agathangelus—τὸ ὄνομά μου ἐπικέκληται ἐφ' ὑμᾶς καὶ ὑμεῖς ἐστὲ ναὸς τῆς θεότητός μου......μιᾶναι τὸ πανάγιον ὄνομά σου ἐφ' ἡμᾶς καὶ τὸν ναὸν τοῦ ὀνόματός σου. Compare Barn. 16 οἰκοδομηθήσεται δὲ ἐπὶ τῷ ὀνόματι κυρίου. προσέχετε, ἵνα ὁ ναὸς τοῦ κυρίου ἐνδόξως οἰκοδομηθῇ. πῶς; μάθετε. λαβόντες τὴν ἄφεσιν *τῶν ἁμαρτιῶν καὶ ἐλπίσαντες ἐπὶ τὸ ὄνομα ἐγενόμεθα καινοί, πάλιν ἐξ ἀρχῆς κτιζόμενοι. διὸ ἐν τῷ κατοικητηρίῳ ἡμῶν ἀληθῶς ὁ θεὸς κατοικεῖ ἐν ὑμῖν.* In the last passage the reference is clearly to Baptism (comp. Hermas *Vis.* iii. 3. 5)[1].

Of the *ἐφ' ἡμᾶς* of Cod. D a faint trace[2], I think, survives in the gloss 'in nobis,' *ἐν ἡμῖν* (compare ב, על, p. 32). Thus,

Tertullian *de Oratione* iii. Cum dicimus: Sanctificetur nomen tuum, id petimus, ut sanctificetur *in nobis*, qui in illo sumus, simul et in ceteris, quos adhuc gratia dei expectat, ut et huic praecepto pareamus, orando pro omnibus, etiam pro inimicis nostris. Ideoque suspensa enuntiatione non dicentes, Sanctificetur *in nobis*, in omnibus dicimus.

Cyprian *de Orat. Dominica.* Sanctificetur nomen tuum. Non quod optemus Deo ut sanctificetur orationibus nostris, sed quod petamus ab eo ut nomen ejus sanctificetur *in nobis.*

Cyril *Catech. Mystag.* v. *εὐχόμεθα ἐν ἡμῖν ἁγιασθῆναι τὸ ὄνομα τοῦ θεοῦ· οὐχ ὅτι ἐκ τοῦ μὴ εἶναι ἅγιον ἐπὶ τὸ εἶναι ἔρχεται· ἀλλ' ὅτι ἐν ἡμῖν ἅγιον γίνεται, ἁγιαζομένοις καὶ ἄξια τοῦ ἁγιασμοῦ ποιοῦσιν.*

Such is the evidence as to this clause, so far as I have been able to collect it. Dr Hort (*Notes on Select Readings* p. 60) appears to accept Dr Sanday's suggestion that the *ἐφ' ἡμᾶς* of Cod. D in the petition about the Divine Name 'may be a trace of *ἐλθέτω τὸ ἅγιον πνεῦμά σου ἐφ' ἡμᾶς κ.τ.λ.*' The fresh evidence however here discussed tends, I think, to shew that the two clauses are separate, though very cognate, developments of petitions in the Lord's Prayer.

The analogy of the petition for the Holy Spirit discussed above and a study of the passages in the New Testament which speak of the Divine Name in reference to Baptism suggest that this *ἐφ' ἡμᾶς* is connected with an adaptation of the Lord's Prayer for use at Baptism. The following passages should be compared:

Acts xxii. 16 *βάπτισαι καὶ ἀπόλουσαι τὰς ἁμαρτίας σου ἐπικαλεσάμενος τὸ ὄνομα αὐτοῦ.*

[1] The language in several passages in Hermas should be compared, e.g. *εἰς τὴν βασιλείαν τοῦ θεοῦ οὐδεὶς εἰσελεύσεται, εἰ μὴ λάβοι τὸ ὄνομα τοῦ υἱοῦ αὐτοῦ* (*Sim.* ix. 12. 4, 8).

[2] It is curious that the English version of the Lord's Prayer in the *Bishops' Book* (1537) has *Thy kingdom come unto us.*

Jas. ii. 7 *οὐκ αὐτοὶ βλασφημοῦσιν τὸ καλὸν ὄνομα τὸ ἐπικληθὲν ἐφ' ἡμᾶς;* Compare the imagery of the Apocalypse (iii. 12 f., xxii. 4), also Ep. Clem. 64.

2 Thess. i. 12 *ὅπως ἐνδοξασθῇ τὸ ὄνομα τοῦ κυρίου ἡμῶν Ἰησοῦ ἐν ὑμῖν καὶ ὑμεῖς ἐν αὐτῷ.* The addition of *ἐν ὑμῖν* is striking when this passage is compared with Is. lxvi. 5 *ἵνα τὸ ὄνομα κυρίου δοξασθῇ.*

The idea of the Baptismal formula (*εἰς τὸ ὄνομα...*) lies at the root of these expressions. The Divine Name is invoked upon the man who is baptized, and he is brought into union with the Name. So he becomes a 'sanctuary' in which the Divine Name dwells, a *σκεῦος ἐκλογῆς...τοῦ βαστάσαι τὸ ὄνομα* (Acts ix. 15)[1].

A. Note on *Acta Thomae*, c. 27 (Ed. Bonnet; see above p. 29).

I have to thank the Editor of this series for pointing out to me the following passage in the *Acta Thomae* c. 27: *λαβὼν δὲ ὁ ἀπόστολος ἔλαιον καὶ καταχέας ἐπὶ τῆς κεφαλῆς αὐτῶν καὶ ἀλείψας καὶ χρίσας αὐτοὺς ἤρξατο λέγειν Ἐλθὲ τὸ ἅγιον ὄνομα τοῦ χριστοῦ τὸ ὑπὲρ πᾶν ὄνομα· ἐλθὲ ἡ δύναμις τοῦ ὑψίστου καὶ ἡ εὐσπλαγχνία ἡ τελεία· ἐλθὲ τὸ χάρισμα τὸ ὕψιστον· ἐλθὲ ἡ μήτηρ ἡ εὔσπλαγχνος...ἐλθὲ τὸ ἅγιον πνεῦμα καὶ καθάρισον τοὺς νεφροὺς αὐτῶν καὶ τὴν καρδίαν, καὶ ἐπισφράγισον αὐτοὺς εἰς ὄνομα πατρὸς καὶ υἱοῦ καὶ ἁγίου πνεύματος.* We have here a Gnostic formula based on the Prayers of the Church (see below n. 1). The following points are to be noticed: (*a*) the prayer *ἐλθὲ τὸ ἅγιον πνεῦμα κ.τ.λ.* is here clearly seen to be connected with the Chrism; (*b*) the prayer *ἐλθὲ τὸ ἅγιον ὄνομα κ.τ.λ.* confirms the suggestion that the *ἐφ' ἡμᾶς* of Cod. D is an addition to the Lord's Prayer closely parallel to the prayer for the Holy Spirit; (*c*) the prayer *ἐλθὲ ἡ δύναμις τοῦ ὑψίστου* (Lc. i. 35) illustrates the Latin form quoted above on p. 29.

The following passages of these Acts, clearly derived from formulas of the Church, are worth notice as illustrating the petitions under discussion: (*a*) *Baptismal prayers: ἐλθέτω σου ἡ εἰρήνη καὶ σκηνωσάτω ἐν αὐτοῖς, ὅπως καθαρισθῶσιν ἀπὸ τῶν προτέρων αὐτῶν πράξεων* (p. 35; comp. *ἐπιθεὶς αὐτοῖς τὴν χεῖρα εἶπεν Ἔσται ἐφ' ὑμᾶς ἡ εἰρήνη τοῦ κυρίου*, p. 48), *ἐλθὲ καὶ σκήνωσον ἐν τοῖς ὕδασι τούτοις, ἵνα τὸ χάρισμα τοῦ ἁγίου πνεύματος τελείως ἐν αὐτοῖς τελειωθῇ* (p. 37), *ἵνα...καὶ δέξομαι κἀγὼ σφραγῖδα καὶ γένωμαι ναὸς ἅγιος* (p. 56), *ἐλθέτω ἡ δύναμίς σου· ἱδρυνθήτω ἐπὶ τὴν δούλην σου Μυγδονίαν ἡ ἐλευθερία αὕτη*

[1] Compare the prominence of 'the Name' in the strange Gnostic Baptismal rite, in many points clearly a parody of the Church's service, which Irenaeus (i. 14. 2) describes, and especially the words, *εἰρήνη πᾶσιν, ἐφ' οὓς τὸ ὄνομα τοῦτο ἐπαναπαύεται.* Compare note A on this page.

(p. 68), *ἁγίασον αὐτοὺς ἐν τῷ σῷ ὀνόματι...ποίησον αὐτοὺς ναοὺς τοῦ ἁγίου σου πνεύματος* (p. 81), *ἐλθέτω, Ἰησοῦ, ἡ νικητικὴ αὐτοῦ δύναμις, ἐνιδρύων τοῦτο τὸ ἔλαιον...ἐλθέτω δὴ καὶ ἡ δωρεὰ δι' ἧς τοῖς ἐχθροῖς αὐτοῦ ἐμφυσήσας εἰς τὰ ὀπίσω ὑποχωρῆσαι ἐποίησας...καὶ ἐπιδημῆσαι τῷ ἐλαίῳ καταξίωσον τούτῳ εἰς ὃ καὶ τὸ σὸν ἅγιον ἐπιφημίζεται ὄνομα* (p. 82). The use of *ναός* in this connexion (comp. pp. 56, 89 *σὺ εἶ ὁ μηνύσας με σὸν ὄνομα...ἵνα ὁ ναὸς σοῦ ἄξιος ἐν μολυσμῷ μὴ εὑρεθῇ*) is to be compared with the words of Agathangelus quoted above, p. 32. (*b*) *A Eucharistic prayer:* Ἰησοῦ Χριστέ... *ἰδοὺ κατατολμῶμεν τῆς εὐχαριστίας καὶ ἐπικλήσεως τοῦ ἁγίου σου ὀνόματος... ἐλθὲ τὰ σπλάγχνα τὰ τέλεια...ἐλθὲ ἡ τὰ ἀπόκρυφα ἐκφαίνουσα καὶ τὰ ἀπόρρητα φανερὰ καθιστῶσα, ἡ ἱερὰ περιστερὰ ἡ τοὺς διδύμους νεοσσοὺς γεννῶσα, ἐλθὲ ἡ ἀπόκρυφος μήτηρ...ἐλθὲ καὶ κοινώνησόν ἡμῖν ἐν ταύτῃ τῇ εὐχαριστίᾳ ἣν ποιοῦμεν ἐπὶ τῷ ὀνόματί σου κ.τ.λ.* The Gnostic character of this passage is clear, as is also the fact that it is a parody of the Church's Eucharistic *ἐπίκλησις*.

B. Note on some Syrian Baptismal Prayers (see p. 29).

I append some prayers from the Latin translation of a Syriac Book of Baptismal Offices: 'D. Severi Alexandrini quondam Patriarchae de ritibus baptismi...liber...Guidone Fabricio Boderiano Exscriptore et Interprete, Antverpiae...1572' (see Resch *Agrapha* pp. 361 ff.). The date of the Book in its present form must be late; for in what is substantially the 'Constantinopolitan' Creed the words *et a Filio procedit* occur. In the title there is probably a confusion with Severus Patriarch of Antioch early in the sixth century (Resch p. 372). The prayers to which I wish to call attention are these:

(1) p. 63. 'Velis igitur Domine super eos immittere tuum illum Spiritum Sanctum; et inhabita et scrutare omnium eorum membra; ac praepurga et sanctifica eos, O Trinitas, ita ut adaequentur sanctae unctioni...'

(2) p. 65. 'Pater Sancte, qui per manus Apostolorum sanctorum dedisti Spiritum Sanctum tuum illis qui baptizabantur: Nunc autem cum etiam in umbra manuum mearum familiarem te exhibeas, mitte Spiritum Sanctum super eos qui baptizandi sunt, et cum repleti fuerint illo, afferant tibi fructum trigesimum...'

(3) p. 13. 'O qui super unicum Filium tuum Deum verbum, dum in terra baptismi ordinationem faceret, Sanctum illum Spiritum tuum misisti in specie columbae, qui Jordanides undas sanctificavit; nunc etiam, Domine mi, velis ut Spiritus ille Sanctus tuus hosce servos tuos qui baptizantur operiat, eosque perfice ac domos Christi tui eos constitue, expurgans eos sancto lavacro tuo.'

(4) p. 92. 'Immitte super eos illius spiritus tui vivificantis gratiam, et eos imple ipsius sanctitate.'

In referring to the Latin forms (see above p. 30) I omitted to notice that through these we may trace back to the apparently apostolic formula ἐλθέτω τὸ ἅγιον πνεῦμά, κ.τ.λ., the great Pentecostal hymns of the Western Church: *Veni, superne Spiritus; Veni, Creator Spiritus* (Newman *Hymni Ecclesiae* pp. 91, 94). From the same source are probably derived the words of the Collect (familiar to us in its English dress): Purifica per infusionem Sancti Spiritus cogitationes cordis nostri.

C. Note on Agathangelus (see above p. 32).

For the reference to Agathangelus I am indebted to Resch *Agrapha* pp. 443, 450. It is edited by Lagarde 'aus dem fünfunddreissigsten Bande der Abhandlungen der königlichen Gesellschaft der Wissenschaften zu Göttingen,' 1887. I gather into a note some points of interest. (1) Lagarde bases his opinion (*a*) that the Greek is a translation, on the barbarous character of the language; (*b*) that it is a translation from an Armenian original, on an investigation of the quotations from the New Testament (pp. 134, 129 ff.). Some passages of the New Testament are taken, Lagarde allows, from the original Greek. This he says would be natural; the translator would know the Greek of passages occurring frequently in the worship of the Church at Byzantium (p. 134). The following points however are worthy of note, (*a*) the translator knew the Greek of 2 Peter; for he speaks (c. 32) of the Prophets οἳ καὶ ἐγένοντο φωστῆρες ἐν τῷ αὐχμηρῷ τόπῳ (2 Pet. i. 19); (*b*) a paronomasia occurs (c. 75) which could not be a translation, εἰ δὲ μάλιστα, Ῥιψίμη, κατὰ τὸ ὄνομά σου ἀληθῶς ἐξερρίφης κ.τ.λ.: the words of course may be an interpolation of the translator; (*c*) the translator was apparently acquainted with the Martyrdom of Polycarp in Greek, for, besides the passage given by Resch p. 281, compare c. 75 καὶ ἐγένετο σφοδροτάτη βροντὴ ὥστε ἐκφοβεῖσθαι τὸν ὄχλον. καὶ ἤκουσαν φωνῆς λεγούσης πρὸς αὐτὰς Ἀνδρίζεσθε καὶ θαρσεῖτε with *Mart. Polyc.* IX. (2) As to the clauses of the Prayer other than that about the hallowing of the Divine Name: (*a*) to the words quoted above (p. 32) ἀπὸ τῆς παγίδος τοῦ ἐχθροῦ, add c. 62 ἵνα νικήσωμεν τὰς δολίας καὶ δεινὰς τοῦ ἐχθροῦ παγίδας, καὶ τὸ ὄνομά σου, δέσποτα, δοξασθῇ κ.τ.λ., c. 87 ὁ δὲ πονηρὸς ἅμα τῷ συνεργῷ αὐτοῦ, ὡς πάντοτε, καὶ νῦν ἐντραπήσεται: (*b*) note the gloss (quoted p. 33) ὁ ἐάσας ἐπελθεῖν κ.τ.λ.; comp. p. 68. (3) There is an account of Gregory's consecration as Bishop by Leontius at Caesarea (c. 139) τὸ δὲ ἅγιον εὐαγγέλιον κατὰ τῆς κεφαλῆς αὐτοῦ κουφίσαντες ἐπέθηκαν τὰς χεῖρας κ.τ.λ. (4) In the account of the baptism of the king, &c., there is a reminiscence of the fire kindled in the Jordan at our Lord's baptism: φῶς σφοδρότατον φανὲν καθ' ὁμοίωμα στύλου φωτοειδοῦς ἔστη ἐπὶ τῶν ὑδάτων τοῦ ποταμοῦ, ἔνθα ἐβαπτίζοντο. (5) In Rhipsima's prayer quoted above (p. 32 f.), with ναὸς τῆς θεότητός μου......τὸν ναὸν τοῦ ὀνόματός σου, compare the Syrian Baptismal rite of Severus (see above p. 37) 'domos Christi tui eos constitue.' I cannot help thinking that Agathangelus would well repay more careful examination by some competent liturgical scholar.

III.

γενηθήτω τὸ θέλημά σου,
ὡς ἐν οὐρανῷ καὶ ἐπὶ γῆς (St Matthew).

Three points here demand notice. (1) There are clear reminiscences of the petition in the N. T.: Matt. xxvi. 42 *γενηθήτω τὸ θέλημά σου* (comp. *v.* 39, Mc. xiv. 36), Lc. xxii. 42 *πλὴν μὴ τὸ θέλημά μου ἀλλὰ τὸ σὸν γινέσθω* (the reading *γενέσθω* has very slight attestation), Acts xxi. 14 *τοῦ κυρίου τὸ θέλημα γινέσθω* (where there is some slight authority for *γενέσθω*); comp. *Mart. Polyc.* vii. *τὸ θέλημα τοῦ θεοῦ γενέσθω* (Eus. *H. E.* iv. 15 *γινέσθω*). Comp. Matt. vii. 21, xii. 50, xviii. 14, Mc. iii. 35. The variation in these passages (*γενηθήτω, γενέσθω, γινέσθω*) is easily accounted for if we assume an Aramaic original[1], which would be indeterminate in regard to tense. The Vulgate Syriac has ܢܗܘܐ in Matt. vi. 10, xxvi. 42, Lc. xxii. 42, Acts xxi. 14[2].

(2) The Old Syriac has ܘܢܗܘܘܢ ܨܒܝ̈ܢܝܟ (and-let-there-be thy-wills)[3]. The plural *τὰ θελήματα* is used of the divine will in Ps. xv. 3, cii. 7, cx. 2, Is. xliv. 28 (quoted in Acts xiii. 22). In the N. T. in Mc. iii. 35 *ὃς ἂν ποιήσῃ τὸ θέλημα τοῦ θεοῦ* (Matt. xii. 50 *τοῦ πατρός μου τοῦ ἐν οὐρανοῖς*), *οὗτος ἀδελφός κ.τ.λ.* Cod. B, supported by a quotation given by Epiphanius (*Haer.*

[1] The Syriac Versions may be taken to represent *approximately* the original Aramaic form of our Lord's sayings. 'Although Josephus says that the Jews could understand the Syrians, the Jewish Aramaic was nevertheless a distinct dialect in some respects, as may be seen from the words λαμά (Matt. xxvii. 46, in Syriac *lemana*), Βοανεργές (Mc. iii. 17, in Syriac *bene ra'ma*)': Neubauer in *Studia Biblica* i. p. 53. In the case of the Lord's Prayer, which in the earliest Syriac Version is the result not so much of later translation as of continuous tradition reaching back to the earliest Apostolic times, probably the form given in this Version is practically identical with the Aramaic original.

[2] We may compare the phrase which forms a very common beginning of Jewish prayers, e.g. *The Authorised Prayer Book* p. 69

יהי רצון מלפני אבינו שבשמים

But the Hebrew N. T. of Delitzsch and that of Salkinson-Ginsburg both have יֵעָשֶׂה. In this connexion a passive voice of עשה seems less natural than the Qal; the latter occurs e.g. in the Rabbinic saying (*Pirqe Aboth* v. 30)

הוה אז...לעשות רצון אביך שבשמים:

[3] In Lc. xxii. 42 it has the singular.

xxx. 14) from an Ebionite Gospel, has *τὰ θελήματα*. Again, in Matt. vii. 21 *ὁ ποιῶν τὸ θέλημα τοῦ πατρός μου τοῦ ἐν τοῖς οὐρανοῖς* Cod. ℵ has *τὰ θελήματα*. In Eph. ii. 3, the only other passage of the N. T. where the plural occurs, it seems to point to the manifoldness of unsatisfied lust (comp. Is. lviii. 3, 13, Jer. xxiii. 26). There appears to be no other authority for this reading in the Lord's Prayer[1].

(3) Bengel in his note on the petition quotes the following words from the *Catechismus Romanus* put forth by the Council of Trent[2]: 'Pastoris erunt partes monere fidelem populum verba illa *Sicut in coelo et in terra* ad singulas referri posse singularum (*trium*) primarum postulationum, ut, Sanctificetur nomen tuum, sicut in coelo et in terra. *Item* Adveniat regnum tuum, sicut in coelo et in terra. *Similiter* Fiat voluntas tua, sicut in coelo et in terra.' For this interpretation, which is thus enjoined upon her teachers by the Church of Rome, there is much to be said.

For in the first place this interpretation harmonises both with the twofold division of the petitions of the Prayer and with the invocation with which it opens: God is *our* Father, the Father of His sons on earth; He is *in Heaven*. It is natural that this thought should exercise a continuous influence on the petitions which immediately follow, rather than that it should at once fall into the background to reappear at a later point of the Prayer. In the second place, if this connexion of the petitions in the Prayer as given by St Matthew was recognised in early times, we have an explanation why the additions made for the purpose of adaptation, i.e. the prayer for the Holy Spirit and the *ἐφ' ἡμᾶς* of Codex Bezae, attach themselves to the Prayer as given by St Luke, where the words *ὡς ἐν οὐρανῷ καὶ ἐπὶ γῆς* do not occur.

Further confirmation is derived from a consideration of the several clauses. (*a*) Little need be said of the petition to which the words *as in heaven so on earth* are immediately joined. We should however compare Ps. cxxxiv. 6 (*πάντα ὅσα ἠθέλησεν ἐποίησεν ὁ κύριος ἐν τῷ οὐρανῷ καὶ ἐν τῇ γῇ*) and 1 Macc. iii. 60

[1] The reading of the Old Syriac (plural verb and noun) is reproduced, as Prof. Bensly has kindly pointed out to me, in the Syriac *Acts of Judas Thomas* (ed. Wright, vol. i. p. [illegible]; vol. ii. p. 279, Eng. Tr.).

[2] Pars IV. c. x. qu. iii.

(*ὡς δ' ἂν ᾖ θέλημα ἐν οὐρανῷ οὕτω ποιήσει*). (*b*) No less naturally do the words connect themselves with the petition *Thy kingdom come*[1]. Compare 1 Chron. xxix. 11 *σὺ πάντων τῶν ἐν τῷ οὐρανῷ καὶ ἐπὶ τῆς γῆς δεσπόζεις*. The thought conveyed by this connexion is indeed implied in all the very numerous passages which speak of the coming of the *kingdom of Heaven* or *of God*, e.g. Dan. ii. 44, vii. 14, Matt. iii. 2, xvi. 28, Lc. xi. 20, xvii. 20, xxi. 31, Apoc. xi. 15. It harmonises with what is at least a probable reading of the Angelic song which prefaces the history of our Lord's life in St Luke's Gospel (ii. 14) *δόξα ἐν ὑψίστοις θεῷ καὶ ἐπὶ γῆς*[2], and with the words of our Lord which close St Matthew's Gospel (xxviii. 18) *ἐδόθη μοι πᾶσα ἐξουσία ἐν οὐρανῷ καὶ ἐπὶ [τῆς] γῆς*. If it be objected that this arrangement of the clauses introduces the idea of the *coming of the kingdom of God in Heaven*, it is sufficient to reply that such an objection overlooks a common idiom: the *coming* of the kingdom on earth answers to its *existence* in heaven. Further, we may compare Col. i. 20 (*ἀποκαταλλάξαι τὰ πάντα εἰς αὐτὸν...εἴτε τὰ ἐπὶ τῆς γῆς εἴτε τὰ ἐν τοῖς οὐρανοῖς*), Eph. i. 10, iii. 15. (*c*) The sequence *Hallowed be Thy name, as in heaven, so on earth* presents no difficulty and commends itself by its intrinsic fitness. Compare Ps. viii. 2 *Κύριε ὁ κύριος ἡμῶν, ὡς θαυμαστὸν τὸ ὄνομά σου ἐν πάσῃ τῇ γῇ· ὅτι ἐπήρθη ἡ μεγαλοπρεπία σου ὑπεράνω τῶν οὐρανῶν*. In the *Authorised Daily Prayer Book* I find (p. 45, comp. p. 37) the prayer:

נְקַדֵּשׁ אֶת־שִׁמְךָ בָּעוֹלָם כְּשֵׁם שֶׁמַּקְדִּישִׁים אוֹתוֹ בִּשְׁמֵי מָרוֹם׃

This formula, part of the קדושה, is probably of ancient origin[3].

[1] Compare Cyprian *de Oratione Dominica*, Bene autem regnum Dei petimus, id est, regnum caeleste, quia est et terrestre regnum.

[2] Dr Hort *Introduction*, *Notes on Select Readings* p. 56.

[3] When *ἐν τοῖς οὐρανοῖς* of the first clause of the Prayer is compared with *ἐν οὐρανῷ*, we notice a double contrast. (1) In the second case the article is wanting. Its absence emphasises character—heaven as compared with earth (comp. 2 Cor. xii. 2). (2) The plural is used in the first, the singular in the later clause. In the N. T. the plural (*οὐρανοί*) expresses the idea of majesty through the notion of vastness, e.g. Phil. iii. 20, Hebr. vii. 26, viii. 1, xii. 23, 25. Note especially Eph. iv. 10 (*πάντων τῶν οὐρανῶν*), Hebr. iv. 14, vii. 26. The singular is commonly used when heaven as one place is contrasted with earth, e.g. Matt. xi. 25, xxviii. 18, 1 Cor. viii. 5, Jas. v. 12; yet see Matt. xvi. 19, Eph. i. 10, iii. 15.

IV.

τὸν ἄρτον ἡμῶν τὸν ἐπιούσιον
δὸς ἡμῖν σήμερον (St Matthew).

τὸν ἄρτον ἡμῶν τὸν ἐπιούσιον
δίδου ἡμῖν τὸ καθ' ἡμέραν (St Luke).

There are two points here in which the two Gospels differ, (1) *δὸς*, *δίδου*, (2) *σήμερον*, *τὸ καθ' ἡμέραν*. Both of these variations demand a brief notice before we enter upon (3) the discussion of the main problem suggested by this clause.

(1) The Old and the Vulgate Syriac versions have in both Gospels ܗܒ. This word, like the Hebrew תֵּן (תְּנָה), is indeterminate in regard to tense. If the Prayer then was originally in Aramaic, the original for 'give' could be represented in Greek equally well by the aorist and by the present imperative. *δός* would naturally be used in the Greek form in which *σήμερον* had a place, *δίδου* as naturally in the form in which *τὸ καθ' ἡμέραν* occurred[1].

(2) But what of the variations *σήμερον*, *τὸ καθ' ἡμέραν*? Mr T. E. Page (*Expositor*, Third Series, vol. vii. p. 436), arguing from the use in both Gospels of the solecism *ἐπιούσιος* that 'the tradition—whether written or oral—which the writers employed was, as regards these particular words, expressed in Greek,' goes on to say, 'the phrase *τὸ καθ' ἡμέραν* occurs only three times in the

[1] Compare the following variations: (1) Matt. v. 42 (*δός*) || Lc. vi. 30 (*δίδου*), (2) Matt. xiv. 19 (*ἔδωκεν*) || Mc. vi. 41, Lc. ix. 16 (*ἐδίδου*), Jn. vi. 11 (*διέδωκεν*), (3) Matt. xxiv. 45 (*δοῦναι*), Lc. xii. 42 (*διδόναι*), (4) Matt. xxvii. 34 (*ἔδωκαν*), Mc. xv. 23 (*ἐδίδουν*).

New Testament, namely here and Luke xix. 47, Acts xvii. 11[1]; so that it is certainly Luke's own (*ächt Lukanisch,* Weiss), and therefore the *σήμερον* of Matthew is much more likely to be original.' There are strong reasons for thinking that the Prayer existed originally in an Aramaic form, and I hope presently to dispose of the argument which Mr Page founds on the use of *ἐπιούσιος*. Further, assuming that *of-the-day* was the original word in this clause, there is much probability in the assumption that *day-by-day* was a primitive variation (see below p. 45). Even in this case however Mr Page's question only takes a new form. Does not the fact, he might ask, that the phrase *τὸ καθ' ἡμέραν* is peculiar to St Luke among the writers of the New Testament go far to shew that St Luke, instead of simply incorporating in his Gospel a form of the Lord's Prayer current among the Hellenistic Disciples, interweaves into that current form phrases of his own? An answer to this important question is supplied by the fact that *τὸ καθ' ἡμέραν*, in itself a classical phrase (e.g. Aristoph. *Eq.* 1126), may also be regarded as a shortened form of a somewhat clumsy phrase of the LXX.; a phrase which, occurring in the account of the giving of the Manna, would very naturally be used by the Hellenists in their translation of the Lord's Prayer, but which at the same time in its full form was unfit for liturgical use[2]. The presence then of this phrase in St Luke becomes to

[1] In the latter passage, it should be noticed, there is considerable authority (including ℵADE$_2$ 13 61) for the omission of *τό*. For *καθ' ἡμέραν* see Matt. xxvi. 55, Mc. xiv. 49, Lc. ix. 23, xxii. 53, Acts ii. 46 (*καθ' ἡμέραν τε προσκαρτεροῦντες ὁμοθυμαδὸν ἐν τῷ ἱερῷ, κλῶντές τε κατ' οἶκον ἄρτον, μετελάμβανον τροφῆς κ.τ.λ.*), ii. 47, iii. 2, (xvii. 17), xix. 9, 1 Cor. xv. 31, 2 Cor. xi. 28, Hebr. vii. 27, x. 11.

[2] Ex. xvi. 5 *ὃ ἐὰν συναγάγωσι τὸ καθ' ἡμέραν εἰς ἡμέραν* = אֲשֶׁר יִלְקְטוּ יוֹם יוֹם. Comp. ver. 4 *τὸ τῆς ἡμέρας εἰς ἡμέραν* (1 Chron. xvi. 37) = דְּבַר־יוֹם בְּיוֹמוֹ. This last Hebrew phrase occurs in Ex. v. 13 (LXX. *τὰ ἔργα τὰ καθήκοντα καθ' ἡμέραν*), v. 19 (*τὸ καθῆκον τῇ ἡμέρᾳ*), Lev. xxiii. 37, 1 Kings viii. 59, 2 Kings xxv. 30 (*λόγον ἡμέρας ἐν τῇ ἡμέρᾳ αὐτοῦ*), Ezra iii. 4, Jer. lii. 34 (LXX. *ἐξ ἡμέρας εἰς ἡμέραν*), Dan. i. 5 (Theodot. *τὸ τῆς ἡμέρας καθ' ἡμέραν*); comp. 1 Chron. xvi. 37, 2 Chron. viii. 13, 14, ix. 24. 'The occurrence of several allusions (Ps. lxxviii. 24; cv. 40; Nehem. ix. 15; Sap. Sol. xvi. 20; &c.) to the corn, or bread, of heaven makes it sufficiently probable *a priori* that the Lord's Prayer also should have some reference to the giving of the manna' (Dr Taylor *Sayings* p. 139). Compare John vi. 32, 1 Cor. x. 3. In the *Authorised Daily P. B.* (p. 92), the 'section of the manna' (פרשת המן), i.e. Ex. xvi. 4—36, has a place in the Morning Service by the side of Gen. xxii. 1—19.

some extent an indication that he preserved a form of the Lord's Prayer which was in actual use in the worship of the Disciples.

(3) From these easier questions I turn at once to the difficult problem which the clause suggests, viz., the meaning and the origin of the word ἐπιούσιος.

If we could put ourselves in the position of one reading this clause for the first time, after our first sense of bewilderment at the appearance of a stranger unknown heretofore in Greek, we should be impressed with the fact that this stranger has a unique function in the Prayer. There is no other epithet in the Prayer, for the phrase ὁ ἐν τοῖς οὐρανοῖς can hardly be said to fall under this category. The language of each clause is characterised by the brevity of severe simplicity. Further, this unique function does not seem to justify itself as necessary or useful. If ἐπιούσιος is to be connected, as it seems certain it must be, with ἡ ἐπιοῦσα[1], and to be taken to mean *of the coming day*, the word is exposed to the charge of introducing tautology into the Prayer as well as of being alien to its simplicity of language. This becomes clear at once if the translation is given in a literal and bald form 'Give us to-day (day-by-day) our bread of the coming day.' This poverty of meaning has been used as a powerful argument in favour of what I venture to consider an impossible mystical interpretation of the word. 'Is it conceivable,' Mr McClellan asks (*New Testament* p. 645), 'that in this inimitably concise and sublime prayer there could have been perpetrated so

[1] Bp Lightfoot's conclusion as to the meaning of ἐπιούσιος (*On a Fresh Revision, Appendix*), it will be seen, I absolutely accept, though it is only fair to add that I venture to interpret some of the evidence on which he bases it in a different way. I am indebted to that *Appendix* for a large part of the material I have used in the investigation which follows. On the other hand Mr McClellan (*New Testament* p. 632 ff.) argues fervently for the meaning *future*. His conclusion may be stated in his own words (p. 646), 'As the food *given for nourishing a life which shall be perfected and enduring in the future world*, it is ἐπιούσιος, מחר, *crastinus*, that is, οἰκεῖος τοῦ ἐπιόντος or μέλλοντος αἰῶνος, "*proper to the world to come.*"' The italics are his. The statement of this view is, it seems to me, its best refutation. If so many layers of meaning,—future, i.e. pertaining to the future world, i.e. spiritual food in the present in preparation for the future,—could be wrapped up in one single word, human language could not bear the strain.

diffuse and mean a tautology as this, "*Our bread which is daily give us daily?*"' I admit the cogency of the reasoning so vigorously expressed, but I think it points to a conclusion different from that which the writer maintains.

I hazard then the conjecture, as a working hypothesis, that the original form of the clause might be represented thus in Syriac:

ܠܚܡܢ ܕܝܘܡܐ ܗܒ ܠܢ

to-us give of-the-day our-bread

This Syriac form is based on the Old Syriac Version which reproduces, we can hardly doubt, the original Aramaic (see above p. 39 n.). Looking at Luke xi. 3 in the same version we may further suppose that there were from the first two variations. *The-bread* (ܠܚܡܐ) was current as well as *our-bread; of-every-day* (ܕܟܠܝܘܡ) as well as *of-the-day*[1].

We have already seen how the two clauses *Hallowed be thy name, Thy kingdom come* were in all probability adapted for liturgical use. These adaptations, being only needed for special occasions, have left but slight traces behind. The word ἐπιούσιος is, I believe, a similar adaptation, but, being in daily use among the Greek-speaking Christians of the earliest days, it has won for itself a permanent place in the Prayer.

There seems to be evidence that considerable latitude was allowed as to the insertion in the Synagogue prayers of petitions suitable to the season or the day[2]. At least equal freedom would be claimed in the assemblies of 'the Brethren.' Thus it is no

[1] Compare the prayer (Berakoth 60 b) 'And give me over this day and every day (היום ובכל יום) to grace &c.' (Dr Taylor *Sayings* &c. p. 142). Comp. Acts vi. 1 ἐν τῇ διακονίᾳ τῇ καθημερινῇ (Syr. ܕܟܠܝܘܡ, Hieron. cotidiano: comp. the Old Syr. of Lc. xi. 3 and the Old Latin of the Lord's Prayer). The διακονία of the Father in Heaven must be reflected in the διακονία of the Church on earth. We may perhaps suppose that St Luke's record of the custom of the Church is shaped by a remembrance of the Prayer. As to the custom itself, it may well have been connected with the Synagogue system of 'the Brethren' (see p. 6), and, if so, with the petition of the chief Prayer. Comp. Chrys. (viii. p. 257) τοῦ ἄρτου τοῦ ἐπιουσίου, τουτέστι, τοῦ καθημερινοῦ. Cf. Judith xii. 15 τὴν καθημερινὴν δίαιταν.

[2] See above p. 14. For the prayers used in the morning and the evening recitation of the Shema see Vitringa *de Synagoga Vetere* p. 1054; for the original form of these see Zunz *Die Gottesd. Vorträge* p. 369.

violently improbable hypothesis if we suppose that when the Lord's Prayer was used in the morning or in the evening Prayers[1] of the Hebrew 'Brethren' and of the Hellenistic 'Brethren,' at first at Jerusalem and later in Northern Syria, it became customary to adapt the one clause which speaks of time to the particular hour of prayer.

Among the Hebrew and Syrian Christians the phrase as it stood, *Our-bread of-the-day*, would be appropriate for the morning Prayer. Of this form, as one very familiar to them, Ephrem reminds his readers (see below p. 49 f.). When however the Prayer was used in the evening, a slight adaptation would be necessary; and such an adaptation we actually find in the word *Mahar* (Syr. ܡܚܪ), which Jerome quotes from 'the Gospel according to the Hebrews' (see below p. 52)[2].

The case of the Hellenistic 'Brethren' was different. Here there was need of translation. And the requirements both of translation and of adaptation were satisfied when, *ἡ ἐπιοῦσα* being adopted in place of ܝܘܡܐ, the word *ἐπιούσιος* was coined to represent ܕܝܘܡܐ. This rendering would have a double advantage. It would be appropriate when the Prayer was used in the morning—*our bread for the coming day*: it would be equally appropriate in the evening[3]. Thus the petition would assume this form—*τὸν ἄρτον ἡμῶν τὸν ἐπιούσιον δὸς ἡμῖν*. It is at least possible that the

[1] Comp. *Didaché* viii. 3 (*τρὶς τῆς ἡμέρας οὕτω προσεύχεσθε*). The writer throughout is giving rules for public, not private, devotion.

[2] A trace of this adaptation of the petition for evening use seems to survive in the Memphitic Version (Matt.) *Our bread of to-morrow give it to us to-day*. On which Version two remarks: (*a*) I take this as an example of a version preserving a clause of the Lord's Prayer as it was brought by the earliest converts and missionaries of the Apostolic age (see p. 13 f.): (*β*) The clause as it stands is the product of a literary revision, the strength of devotional conservatism maintaining *of to-morrow* when *to-day* had been added to represent *σήμερον*.

[3] Mr Wratislaw in an article in *The Churchman* (July 1888) shews conclusively that *ἡ ἐπιοῦσα* is used of the day already begun. But it should be noticed that *ἡ ἐπιοῦσα* could always be substituted for *ἡ αὔριον*, though the converse does not hold: comp. Acts vii. 26, xvi. 11, xx. 15 (on which see Mr Wratislaw's remarks), xxi. 18. Hence I am not sure that Mr Wratislaw does not carry his point too far when he claims Prov. xxvii. 1 (*μὴ καυχῶ τὰ εἰς αὔριον, οὐ γὰρ γινώσκεις τί τέξεται ἡ ἐπιοῦσα*) as an illustration in his favour. It seems to me that the last passage gives some confirmation to my theory in regard to the Lord's Prayer. For *ἡ ἐπιοῦσα*, not found elsewhere in the LXX., here translates יום.

apparent analogy of *περιούσιος*, occurring in a group of passages (Ex. xix. 5, Deut. vii. 6, xiv. 2, xxvi. 18) which we know to have occupied an important place in Apostolic teaching (Tit. ii. 14, 1 Pet. ii. 9; comp. Acts xx. 28, Eph. i. 14), may have suggested or facilitated this representation of the original Aramaic word.

Liturgical forms soon get the sanction of usage. The instincts of devotion are singularly tenacious of a familiar word, even when (perhaps even in proportion as) its meaning and origin have become obscure. And thus before the time when the first and third Gospels in their present form were composed, the epithet *ἐπιούσιος* had firmly attached itself to the substantive.

No doubt, in our ignorance of the relations between the Hebrew and the Hellenistic 'Brethren,' much must remain ambiguous. The living witness of the Apostles as well as the morning Prayers of the Hebrews would be sufficient to prevent the original phrase (ܕܝܘܡܐ) and the alternative (ܕܟܠܝܘܡ) becoming forgotten. When the Lord's Prayer assumes a literary shape in the Gospels according to St Matthew and St Luke, the well-known liturgical formula is preserved, but side by side with it there appears in the one Gospel the original *of-the-day* in the natural adverbial form *to-day*, in the other the very early, if not original, alternative *day-by-day*. In this petition then, owing to the influence of devotional conservatism combined with reverence for any remembered word of Christ, there meets us a double rendering of the original word, a phenomenon to which most chapters of the LXX. will supply a parallel.

So far I have endeavoured to reconstruct the history of this clause as it stands in our present Gospels. The results may be taken as confirming to some extent the working hypothesis (p. 45) from which we started. But is there any independent support of the conjecture that the original form of the clause was *Our-bread of-the-day give to-us*? I venture to think that there is some evidence worth consideration.

(1) There is a passage in the Epistle of St James (ii. 15 ff.), which, I believe, bears on this problem:

ἐὰν ἀδελφὸς ἢ ἀδελφὴ γυμνοὶ ὑπάρχωσι καὶ λειπόμενοι τῆς ἐφημέρου τροφῆς, εἴπῃ δέ τις αὐτοῖς ἐξ ὑμῶν Ὑπάγετε ἐν εἰρήνῃ, θερμαίνεσθε καὶ χορτάζεσθε, μὴ δῶτε δὲ αὐτοῖς τὰ ἐπιτήδεια τοῦ σώματος, τί ὄφελος;

The Epistle of St James is a mosaic of *λόγια κυριακά*, among which those 'oracles' which have a place in the Synoptists' record of the Sermon on the Mount are especially numerous. Sometimes these references to Christ's teaching are obvious; sometimes they lie beneath the surface; sometimes they have become so assimilated to the context in which they are embedded that they fail to attract attention[1]. It must be sufficient to refer to the Introduction to any of the Commentaries on the Epistle for a list of the more patent of these coincidences. But no tabulated statistics can give any idea of the living connexion which, even with our fragmentary knowledge of the Lord's discourses, we feel to exist between the letter of the Disciple and the words of his Master.

In the passage from St James quoted above it is very probable that he has in his mind the words of Christ recorded in Matt. xxv. 35—45. But it appears to me still more likely that in the phrase *ἡ ἐφήμερος τροφή* we have a reminiscence of the petition for 'the bread of the day'; and further that in the succeeding words *τὰ ἐπιτήδεια τοῦ σώματος* we have a very early comment on the scope of the petition[2].

Such a conjecture is incapable of proof. The phrase *ἡ ἐφήμερος τροφή* is not in itself a remarkable one[3], neither indeed is the phrase which I suppose it to recall, 'the bread of the day.' The probability allowed to the suggestion will vary in proportion

[1] Compare e.g. James i. 21 (*ἐν πραΰτητι δέξασθε τὸν ἔμφυτον λόγον*) with Mc. iv. 15 (*τὸν λόγον τὸν ἐσπαρμένον εἰς αὐτούς*), Lc. viii. 13 (*μετὰ χαρᾶς δέχονται τὸν λόγον*). See also Barn. ix. 9.

[2] Based perhaps on Matt. vi. 32 (*οἶδεν γὰρ ὁ πατὴρ ἡμῶν ὁ οὐράνιος ὅτι χρῄζετε τούτων ἁπάντων*). Compare the probable reference in *Didaché* x. (*τροφήν τε καὶ ποτὸν ἔδωκας ἀνθρώποις...ἡμῖν δὲ ἐχαρίσω πνευματικὴν τροφὴν καὶ ποτόν*).

[3] Wetstein quotes Aristid. T. ii. p. 398 *αὐτὸς προσαιτῶν, καὶ τῆς ἐφημέρου τροφῆς ἀπορῶν, καὶ βλέπων εἰς β̄ καὶ γ̄ ὀβολούς*: Dion. Hal. *Ant.* viii. 41 *ἀπῆλθεν ἐκ τῆς οἰκίας...ἄδουλος ἄπορος, οὐδὲ τὴν ἐφήμερον ὁ δύστηνος ἐκ τῶν ἑαυτοῦ χρημάτων τροφὴν ἐπαγόμενος*. To these Field (*Otium Norvicense*, Pars Tertia) adds Chrys. ix. p. 677 B *ἀλλ' ὁ μὲν δεσπότης σου καὶ ἥλιον αὐτῷ ἀνατέλλει, σὺ δὲ καὶ τῆς ἐφημέρου τροφῆς ἀνάξιον αὐτὸν κρίνεις*, which however may be a reminiscence of St James. We may compare also Eur. *El.* 429 *τῆς ἐφ' ἡμέραν βορᾶς*, Herod. i. 32 *οὐ γάρ τοι ὁ μέγα πλούσιος μᾶλλον τοῦ ἐπ' ἡμέραν ἔχοντος ὀλβιώτερός ἐστι*.

as the general indebtedness of the Apostle to the Lord's teaching is admitted. It becomes very strong if we recognise that the words of Christ form the woof and web of the language of the Epistle.

That the phrase *ἡ ἐφήμερος τροφή* comes very close to the wording of the Prayer is clear from the Latin versions and from Chrysostom's comments on the petition.

The Old Latin 'panis quotidianus,' retained by Jerome in his version of St Luke, finds a close parallel in the earliest extant Latin version of St James (ii. 15) 'victus quotidianus[1]', a rendering which Jerome preserves. Again, Chrysostom in dealing with the clause as it stands in St Matthew says, *τί ἐστι, τὸν ἄρτον τὸν ἐπιούσιον; τὸν ἐφήμερον...δεῖται γὰρ* [*ἡ φύσις*] *τροφῆς τῆς ἀναγκαίας*. In another place (iv. 530) he uses similar language, *τὸν ἄρτον ἡμῶν τὸν ἐπιούσιον δὸς ἡμῖν σήμερον, ἀντὶ τοῦ, τὴν τῆς ἡμέρας τροφήν*, a phrase in which he stumbles into a curiously literal representation of the original Aramaic.

It is however when we take into consideration the Syriac versions that the importance of the passage in St James is fully seen. In the Syriac Vulgate *τῆς ἐφημέρου τροφῆς* is represented by the words ܡܣܝܒܪܬܐ ܕܝܘܡܐ (the-food of-the-day)[2]. Thus St James gives the natural Greek translation of the Aramaic *of-the-day*, and his whole phrase, excepting the substitution of 'food' for 'bread,' is the very form which we assumed just now as the original of the petition, 'the-(*or* our-)bread of-the-day.'

(2) "I had also hoped," wrote Bp Lightfoot (*On a Fresh Revision* p. 217), "that I might find this petition quoted in the works of one of the earlier Syriac writers, Aphraates or Ephrem, but my search has not been attended with success. An indirect reference in Ephrem (*Op.* vi. p. 642) omits the word in question. 'The

[1] Cod. Corbeiensis has 'sive frater sive soror nudi sint et desit eis victus quotidianus.' Jerome's version is 'Si autem frater aut soror nudi sint et indigeant victu quotidiano.' The writings of neither Tertullian nor Cyprian supply evidence as to the text of St James (Bp. Westcott *Canon*, ed. 5, pp. 258, 373, Rönsch *Das N. T. Tertullian's* p. 572).

[2] The references given in Liddell and Scott are sufficient to shew that Mr McClellan is mistaken in supposing that in later Greek *ἐφήμερος* always means 'lasting but a day.' Such was doubtless the classical sense of the word, a use which lasted on side by side with the meaning 'daily' (see Suicer *Thes.* sub voce). The words *ἐφημερία* and *ἐφημερίς* both illustrate the meaning *daily*.

bread of the day (ܠܚܡܐ ܕܝܘܡܐ) shall suffice thee, as thou hast learnt in the Prayer'. At the same time Ephrem agrees with the Curetonian against the Peshito in ܕܝܘܡܐ, so that it seems *probable* that he used the Curetonian Version." The fact that Ephrem 'omits the word in question,' constitutes, I believe, the importance of the reference.

For in the first place Ephrem refers to some popular version of the Lord's Prayer, a part of catechetical instruction ('as thou hast learned in the Prayer').

And in the second place this popular version cannot have been the Old Syriac. For had it been, his citation would have at once recalled to his hearers (for the reference occurs in a sermon on Fasting) the whole clause as it stood in the Old Syriac (and-our-bread *continual* of-the-day give to-us), and the word *continual* would have refuted the lesson which he wished to draw.

We learn then from an examination of Ephrem's evidence that there was some popular version of the Lord's Prayer still in use among the Syrian Christians of the Fourth Century, and that in this traditional version, on which the Old Syriac itself was based, the form of the petition under discussion was '*the-bread of-the-day.*'

The conclusion to which a cross-examination of Ephrem leads us is confirmed by the clear testimony of another witness. The Arabic version of Tatian's Diatessaron published by Ciasca in 1888 gives what is to all appearance the whole of the matter contained in Tatian's work. But the Syriac text on which the Arabic version is based seems to have been brought into conformity with the Vulgate Syriac text[1]. All the more emphatic therefore is its support of an earlier Syriac text, whenever such support is given. The literal translation of the Arabic version of the petition for 'daily bread' (§ IX.) is 'Give us the bread of our day' (i.e. the day in which we now are). The epithet 'continual' which has a place in the Old Syriac, and the epithet 'of-our-necessity' which is given in the Vulgate Syriac, are alike absent. Thus the pre-Curetonian form has the support of an unwilling witness. We are not only confirmed as to the main conclusion which we drew from Ephrem's evidence, but we are able to identify the popular version

[1] Hemphill p. xxix, Rendel Harris p. 5.

of the Lord's Prayer to which he refers in his Sermon with the form contained in Tatian's Diatessaron[1].

Thus St James, Tatian, and Ephrem, who probably repeats after a long interval the witness of Tatian, combine to attest the shorter form of the clause, 'Give us the bread of the day.'

(3) Does the Old Syriac version itself throw any light on the matter?

In Matt. vi. 11 this version has:

ܘܠܚܡܢ ܐܡܝܢܐ ܕܝܘܡܐ ܗܒ ܠܢ

to-us give of-the-day continual and-our-bread

In Luke xi. 3

ܘܗܒ ܠܢ ܠܚܡܐ ܐܡܝܢܐ ܕܟܠܝܘܡ

of-every-day continual the-bread to-us and-give

Now about the Syriac word *continual* two remarks may be made. In the first place it is difficult to see that it represents any probable meaning of the Greek ἐπιούσιος. In the second place Cureton in his note (referred to by Bp Lightfoot p. 215) remarks that the word *continual* is in fact derived from Numb. iv. 7, where the Hebrew ולחם התמיד עליו יהיה is translated in the Syriac version by the words ܘܠܚܡܐ ܐܡܝܢܐܝܬ ܥܠܘܗܝ ܢܗܘܐ (and-the-bread continually let-it-be thereupon). The Old Syriac then of this clause of the Lord's Prayer appears to be a literary revision of the popular version current since the Gospel was brought to Syria from the Church at Jerusalem in the earliest days of the faith, a revision which represented the seemingly unintelligible ἐπιούσιος, which had meantime come into the Prayer, by a classical phrase about bread in the Old Testament slightly changed, much as Delitzsch in his Hebrew translation of the N. T. uses for the same purpose another classical phrase of the O. T. (לֶחֶם חֻקֵּנוּ) derived from Prov. xxx. 8 (לֶחֶם חֻקִּי).

This conclusion receives some additional confirmation from the fact that in the revision of the Old Syriac (the Vulgate or Peshito Syriac) the epithet ܕܣܘܢܩܢܢ (of-our-necessity) is substituted for

[1] That the Diatessaron was the form of the Gospels used in public worship is clear from the *Doctrine of Addai* c. xxxv, Thdt. *de Fab. Haer.* i. 20.

ܐܡܝܢܐ (continual), as though the latter were not sanctioned by immemorial usage[1].

The position of these Syrian Christians in the third century was in fact very parallel to our own. A Christian preacher in England to-day would say 'Pray God to forgive us our trespasses, as we forgive them that trespass against us, as thou hast learned in the Prayer,' regardless of the fact that the Authorised Version has 'Forgive us our debts, as we forgive our debtors', and that the Revised Version has 'Forgive us our debts, as we also have forgiven our debtors.' Literary revisions are powerless against ancient formulas.

(4) Lastly, there is the notice of the clause in the *Gospel according to the Hebrews* preserved by Jerome (on Matt. vi. 11): 'In evangelio, quod appellatur secundum Hebraeos, pro supersubstantiali pane reperi Mahar, quod dicitur crastinum, ut sit sensus: Panem nostrum crastinum, id est futurum, da nobis hodie.'

Here, it will be noticed, Jerome does not profess to give us the precise words of the whole clause which he found in the Hebrew Gospel. He is content to quote the single word *Mahar*, and then adds his own conclusion as to the general meaning (*ut sit sensus*).

[1] Of this alteration Bp Lightfoot says (p. 215), 'This is only one of the many instances where the Peshito betrays the influences of the fourth century whether in the text or in the interpretation.' This explanation may be the right one. But on the one hand the word *of-our-necessity* does not represent what is essential in the later interpretation of ἐπιούσιος referred to, viz. its connexion with οὐσία. On the other hand the notion of *necessary* would seem to have a place in the earliest expositions of the clause; for such an exposition I believe Jas. ii. 16 (τὰ ἐπιτήδεια τοῦ σώματος) to be. It is worth noting that the Syriac Version in St James ii. 16 (ܣܘܢܩܢܗ ܕܦܓܪܐ) answers to this revised translation of ἐπιούσιος. Jas. ii. 16 might itself be based on Mat. vi. 32, if the gloss were not so natural (comp. Ex. xvi. 22 τὰ δέοντα=לחם, Prov. xxx. 8 τὰ δέοντα καὶ τὰ αὐτάρκη=לחם חקי). So Tert. *de Oratione* vi. (Panem enim peti mandat, quod solum fidelibus *necessarium* est; cetera enim nationes requirunt), and the familiar words 'All things that be *needful* both for our souls and bodies.' In the Peshito then may we not have the substitution of a familiar gloss for the unsatisfactory word of the Old Syriac, a substitution which would be in harmony, as the Old Syriac rendering was at variance, with the form of the clause in common use as preserved to us by Ephrem (see above p. 49 f.)? We have the somewhat similar case of a well-known gloss derived from a phrase of the N. T. gaining a place in the text in the African Latin Version of Matt. vi. 13 (e.g. Cod. Bobiensis, ne passus fueris induci nos in temptationem). Here Tertullian preserves the gloss which has become part of the text in Cyprian's time. See p. 64 f.

It seems impossible that the two words *to-morrow* and *to-day* could have stood side by side in the clause[1], and Jerome disguises the contradiction lurking in his fusion of quotation and comment by the gloss which he slips in (*crastinum, id est futurum*).

The evidence taken together is no doubt scanty; it must be so from the nature of the case. But when we cross-question such witnesses as we have, their testimony appears to me to be consistently and unanimously in favour of the theory that the original form of the clause in the Lord's Prayer ran thus: 'Give us our (*or* the) bread of the day.'

In reviewing the evidence we must remember that in such a reconstruction of the history of a phrase as I have attempted, there must necessarily be many hypotheses whose only support is mutual agreement and inherent likelihood. Further, the general result does not depend on the minute accuracy of each step of the reconstruction. To pretend to recall stages of change and revision which were bound up with the manifold life of the Church of the First Days, liturgical custom among Christian Hebrews and Christian Hellenists, the influence of oral tradition and written memoranda both in Aramaic and Greek, catechetical instruction, the teaching of Missionaries and other converts leaving the Mother Church at different times, the influence of usage and of translation in the Churches which they founded, would be a palpable absurdity. An approximation to such a work is all we can hope for.

The general result is this:

(1) This petition of the Prayer refers to bodily needs[2].

(2) The epithet is temporal, not qualitative.

(3) The epithet is not part of the original form of the petition, and is due to liturgical use.

(4) All the phenomena may be reasonably explained if we assume, an assumption for which there is some independent evidence, that the clause originally was 'Give us our (*or* the) bread of the day.'

[1] On the Memphitic Version see note on p. 46.

[2] In *Didaché* x. 2, where we practically have the earliest exposition of the Lord's Prayer, the reference to actual food comes first: *σύ, δέσποτα παντοκράτορ, ἔκτισας τὰ πάντα ἕνεκα τοῦ ὀνόματός σου, τροφήν τε καὶ ποτὸν ἔδωκας τοῖς ἀνθρώποις εἰς ἀπόλαυσιν, ἵνα σοι εὐχαριστήσωσιν, ἡμῖν δὲ ἐχαρίσω πνευματικὴν τροφὴν καὶ ποτὸν καὶ ζωὴν αἰώνιον διὰ τοῦ παιδός σου.*

V.

καὶ ἄφες ἡμῖν τὰ ὀφειλήματα ἡμῶν,
ὡς καὶ ἡμεῖς ἀφήκαμεν τοῖς ὀφειλέταις ἡμῶν (St Matthew).

καὶ ἄφες ἡμῖν τὰς ἁμαρτίας ἡμῶν,
καὶ γὰρ αὐτοὶ ἀφίομεν παντὶ ὀφείλοντι ἡμῖν (St Luke).

Four problems are suggested by the variations in the two forms of this petition.

(1) Which is the more original, the *τὰ ὀφειλήματα* of St Matthew, or the *τὰς ἁμαρτίας* of St Luke? In the discussion of this question I again assume that the Old Syriac may be taken as representing approximately the original Aramaic.

(*a*) Do the Syriac and the Greek words meaning 'forgive' throw any light on the question?

The Syriac ܫܒܘܩ, the word in the Old and in the Vulgate Syriac, is not decisive. The late Hebrew word שבק (= to leave or desert, Dan. iv. 12, 20, 23; comp. Matt. xxvii. 46) is used (see Gesenius *Thesaurus*) in the Targums as an equivalent to סלח and נשא (= to forgive), words, which are not, I think, applied to the remission of a debt. The Syriac word is used both of the remission of a debt (Matt. xviii. 32, Lc. vii. 42) and of the forgiveness of sins (Rom. xi. 27, 2 Cor. ii. 10).

The case of the Greek *ἀφιέναι* is somewhat different. This word indeed is used in the LXX. to represent שמט (to remit a debt, Deut. xv. 1, 2), but it is also the common equivalent of the words meaning to 'forgive sins,' i.e. נשא (e.g. Gen. l. 17, Ex. xxxii. 32, Ps. xxv. 18), סלח (e.g. Lev. iv. 20, v. 10). In this latter sense the imperative *ἄφες* is very common in prayers (Gen. l. 17 *ἄφες αὐτοῖς τὴν ἀδικίαν καὶ τὴν ἁμαρτίαν αὐτῶν*, Ex. xxxii. 32 *εἰ μὲν ἀφεῖς αὐτοῖς τὴν ἁμαρτίαν αὐτῶν ἄφες*, Numb. xiv. 19 *ἄφες τὴν ἁμαρτίαν τῷ λαῷ τούτῳ*, Ps. xxiv. 18 *καὶ ἄφες πάσας τὰς ἁμαρτίας μου*). Compare Ecclus. xxviii. 2

ἄφες ἀδίκημα τῷ πλησίον σου, καὶ τότε δεηθέντος σου αἱ ἁμαρτίαι σου λυθήσονται. Hence a Hellenist, familiar with the LXX., would be under the temptation to strain a point in translation that he might secure the familiar sequence *ἄφες τὰς ἁμαρτίας.*

(*b*) But is there any ambiguity in the original word meaning 'debt' to minimise the unfaithfulness of such a translation?

The word both in the Old and in the Vulgate Syriac is ܚܘܒܝܢ. The verb ܚܘܒ (= חוב, 'In Targg. persaepe pro hebr. אשם, חטא,' Ges. *Thes.*), properly meaning 'impar, haud capax, fuit' (see Payne Smith *Thes. Syr.*), is frequently used in connexion with sin (e.g. Lev. iv. 22, 27), and defeat (e.g. 2 Kings xiv. 12 Hex., 1 Cor. vi. 7). It occurs also in the derived sense 'debuit,' e.g. in Deut. xxiv. 10, Rom. xiii. 8. Further, the causative signifies 'reum fecit,' 'condemnavit,' without any idea of debt, e.g. in Deut. xxv. 1, 1 Kings viii. 32, Matt. xii. 41, Lc. vi. 37. Moreover the substantive used in the Lord's Prayer, though occurring in the phrase ܡܪܐ ܚܘܒܐ (lord of-the-debt, i.e. creditor; Ex. xxii. 25, 1 Sam. xxii. 2, Lc. vii. 41), yet in the plural means simply 'sins' (Dan. ix. 20 'my sins...the sins of my people'). The precise word used in the Lord's Prayer (ܚܘܒܝܢ), though in Col. ii. 14 the context gives it the sense of 'our-debts,' is yet used without any thought of debt in Ex. xxxiv. 9. Hence, although in the Lord's Prayer the words 'our debtors' fix the meaning, the word itself might be translated in Greek by *τὰς ἁμαρτίας ἡμῶν.*

It is easy therefore to account for this Greek phrase *τὰς ἁμαρτίας* intruding itself as the equivalent of the original Aramaic word here meaning 'debts'; and thus I am led by quite another road to Mr Page's conclusion (*Expositor*, 3rd Series, vol. vii. p. 437) that 'we seem to have...in Matthew a more accurate reproduction of the original.'

(2) The Didaché has *τὴν ὀφειλὴν ἡμῶν* in place of *τὰ ὀφειλήματα ἡμῶν.* A sufficient explanation of the variation in the Didaché might perhaps be found in Matt. xviii. 32 *πᾶσαν τὴν ὀφειλὴν ἐκείνην ἀφῆκά σοι.* But the variation may, I think, be better explained as reflecting a slightly different reading of the original Aramaic. The difference between ܚܘܒܢ (our-debt) and ܚܘ̈ܒܝܢ (our-debts) is very small.

(3) The phrase in St Luke *παντὶ ὀφείλοντι ἡμῖν*, as compared with that in St Matthew *τοῖς ὀφειλέταις ἡμῶν*, has the appearance of a paraphrastic rendering. We can hardly doubt that the terse ܠܚܝ̈ܒܝܢ (our-debtors) is more likely to be the original than ܠܟܠ ܕܚܝܒ ܠܢ (to-every-one who-is-indebted to-us).

(4) There remains still the more perplexing variation, *ὡς καὶ ἡμεῖς ἀφήκαμεν* (St Matthew), *καὶ γὰρ αὐτοὶ ἀφίομεν* (St Luke).

In St Matthew the Old Syriac has,

ܐܝܟܢܐ ܕܐܦ ܐܢܚܢ ܢܫܒܘܩ.

will- (*or* may-) remit we also as (*or* in-order-that)

In St Luke,

ܘܐܦ ܚܢܢ ܢܫܒܘܩ.

will-remit we and-also

The Old Syriac, it will be noticed, has the 'future' in both Gospels; in both Gospels the Vulgate Syriac substitutes the 'perfect.' There is therefore strong reason to believe that the 'future' is the original form. This supposition is supported by the *ἀφίομεν* of St Luke and the *ἀφίεμεν* of the Didaché. But if this be so, is not the original connexion between the two parts of the petition the simple form preserved by the Old Syriac of Lc. xi. 4, 'remit to us *and we also will* remit'[1]? The whole petition becomes thus a prayer and a promise, a prayer for forgiveness, and a promise that the suppliant *will* forgive. This interpretation has very strong support in the parable of the unmerciful servant (Matt. xviii. 23 ff.). Here the divine forgiveness precedes, and is represented as the model of, human forgiveness (comp. Col. iii. 13, Eph. iv. 32). The servant is forgiven, but lacks the grace to forgive. The remission of the debt which he owed becomes invalid, when he refuses remission to another.

It is remarkable that this view of the petition in the Lord's Prayer is supported by what I believe is the earliest reference to the words in Christian literature. In his letter to the Philippians (c. 6) Polycarp writes, *εἰ οὖν δεόμεθα τοῦ κυρίου ἵνα ἡμῖν ἀφῇ, ὀφείλομεν καὶ ἡμεῖς ἀφιέναι.* That Polycarp is here referring to the Lord's Prayer is put beyond dispute by the fact that he refers

[1] See the additional note on p. 57.

in the following chapter to the next clause of the Lord's Prayer, and by the mode in which this reference is introduced: *δεήσεσιν αἰτούμενοι τὸν παντεπόπτην θεὸν μὴ εἰσενεγκεῖν ἡμᾶς εἰς πειρασμόν.* The evidence derived from Tertullian, the earliest witness to the Latin text of the New Testament, is at one with that of Polycarp. It is given in the additional note at the end of this section (p. 58).

One point more in this connexion remains. Matt. vi. 14, 15 and Mc. xi. 25 seem somewhat out of place where they stand, the former passage singling out for emphasis one petition of the Lord's Prayer at the close of the section of the Sermon on the Mount which deals with prayer, the latter following the lesson of faith drawn from the withered fig-tree. Is it rash to suggest that they are re-settings of the words in which the Lord sums up the lesson of the parable, *οὕτως καὶ ὁ πατήρ μου ὁ οὐράνιος ποιήσει ὑμῖν ἐὰν μὴ ἀφῆτε ἕκαστος τῷ ἀδελφῷ*[1] *αὐτοῦ ἀπὸ τῶν καρδιῶν ὑμῶν?* In that case the *ἐὰν γὰρ ἀφῆτε...ἀφήσει καὶ ὑμῖν ὁ πατὴρ ὑμῶν* of St Matthew (vi. 14, cf. Lc. vi. 37) and the *ἀφίετε... ἵνα καὶ ὁ πατὴρ ὑμῶν...ἀφῇ ὑμῖν* of St Mark (xi. 25) will refer, in accordance with the teaching of the parable, to the continuance and consummation of the divine forgiveness; though the language has perhaps been slightly altered in accordance with the Hellenistic translation of the Lord's Prayer, *ὡς καὶ ἡμεῖς ἀφήκαμεν* (comp. Ep. Clem. 13, Ep. Polyc. 2).

In this part of the petition St Luke seems to me to preserve a form nearer to the original as far as the verb (*ἀφίομεν*) is concerned. Neither Gospel very exactly reproduces what appears to be the original connexion of the clauses.

NOTE ON SYRIAC VERSIONS OF THIS CLAUSE (see p. 56).

I am inclined to think that the Old Syriac of St Luke represents the traditional form[2]. (i) It is not here a *translation* of the Greek, as it omits the all important *γάρ*. Contrast the Peshito ܐܦ ܚܢܢ ܫܒܩܢ. (ii) Though

[1] In Westcott and Hort's text should not *τῷ ἀδελφῷ* be printed in uncials? See Deut. xv. 2, 3 (*τὸν ἀλλότριον ἀπαιτήσεις ὅσα ἐὰν ᾖ σοι παρ' αὐτῷ, τῷ δὲ ἀδελφῷ σου* (Cod. B *τοῦ ἀδελφοῦ*) *ἄφεσιν ποιήσεις τοῦ χρέους σου*). The old command is (1) widened, for the Lord's whole teaching gave a new meaning to *brotherhood* (Lc. x. 27 ff.); (2) deepened, by the addition of *ἀπὸ τῶν καρδιῶν ὑμῶν.*

[2] No argument can be founded on the fact that the Arabic of Ciasca's Tatian has the perfect, 'as we have forgiven,' for it seems certain that this text has been largely modernised. See Harris *The Diatessaron of Tatian* p. 5.

Ephrem (iii. p. 641) has what is substantially the Vulgate Syriac, Aphraates twice quotes the petition as it is in the Old Syriac of St Matthew, except that the connecting word between the clauses is (ܕܐܦ) ܘܐܦ. The passages are worth quoting in full. (*a*) *Homilies of Aphraates* ed. Wright p. ܠܒ, Hom. 2, § 14. 'Again when the Lord taught His disciples the Prayer, He said to them, Thus shall ye pray, Forgive us our debts and also we will forgive (ܘܐܦ ܚܢܢ ܫܒܩܝܢܢ) our debtors. And again He said, If thou bring thy gift to the altar...... (Matt. v. 23, 24), lest when any one prayeth, Forgive us our debts and also we will forgive our debtors, he be caught out of his own mouth, and it be said to him by Him who receiveth (or, him who beareth up, i.e. Gabriel) his prayer, Thou dost not forgive (ܐܢܬ ܠܐ ܫܒܩ ܐܢܬ) him who is indebted to thee, how shall they forgive (ܫܒܩܝܢ ܠܟ) thee? And so thy prayer shall remain on the earth.' (*b*) p. ܥܐ, Hom. 4, § 7. 'Forgive us our debts that also we may forgive (ܕܐܦ ܚܢܢ ܫܒܩܝܢܢ[1]: but there is another reading ܘܐܦ ܐܢܚܢܢ='and also we') our debtors......Thou prayest that it should be forgiven thee, and thou professest that thou dost (or wilt) forgive (ܕܫܒܩ ܐܢܬ). Think first within thy mind whether thou forgivest; then profess that thou dost (or wilt) forgive. For do not lie to God and say I do (or will) forgive (ܕܫܒܩ ܐܢܐ), when thou dost not forgive (ܫܒܩ ܐܢܬ). [Matt. v. 23f. is then quoted]......If He finds in thy prayer, Forgive me and I do (or will) forgive (ܘܫܒܩ ܐܢܐ), then shall it be said to him that prayeth by him that beareth up the prayer (i.e. Gabriel), First forgive thy debtor, then will I also bear up thy prayer before thy creditor (i.e. God): do thou forgive a hundred pence according to thy poverty and thy creditor will forgive thee a thousand talents according to His greatness.' In these passages Aphraates seems to treat ܫܒܩܝܢܢ as a present, using the participle to represent it; but the thought of the present seems to merge into that of the future in several clauses. But however Aphraates interprets the words himself, his evidence as to the current form of the clause is clear, for in the second passage the context seems to require ܘܐܦ, and not ܕܐܦ. It should be added in reference to Aphraates' use of the participle in his paraphrases that the Jerusalem Syriac has the plural participle ܫܒܩܝܢ in the second clause of the petition.

The Old Syriac and Aphraates' comments on it find a curious parallel in Tertullian's reference to the Latin Version of the clause. Tertullian does not quote, so far as I know, the second clause of the petition for forgiveness.

[1] This is the reading in the form of the Lord's Prayer found in the Syriac *Acts of Judas Thomas* (ed. Wright, vol. i. p. ܫܩܛ; vol. ii. p. 279 Eng. Tr.). The whole clause is remarkable, 'Forgive us *our debts and our sins, that we too* may forgive our debtors.' I have to thank Prof. Bensly for pointing out to me this reference.

Neither in *de Oratione* vii. nor in *adv. Marcionem* iv. 26 does he give us the exact words. In the former passage however he gives the following gloss: 'Quod idem servus a domino liberatus non perinde parcit debitori suo ac propterea ......tortori delegatur......eo competit, quod *remittere nos quoque profitemur debitoribus nostris.* Jam et alibi ex hac specie orationis, Remittite, inquit, et remittetur vobis.' Again, in the tract *de Pudicitia* ii. he writes, 'Dimittis autem, ut dimittatur tibi a deo. Delicta mundantur quae quis in fratrem, non deum admiserit. *Debitoribus denique dimissuros nos in oratione profitemur.*' This latter passage (*dimissuros*) certainly appears to suggest that in some Old Latin copies the reading in the Prayer was *dimittemus.* I do not know that there is any MS. authority for such a reading. Cyprian's text and comment (*de Oratione Dom.*) seem clearly in favour of the common reading and interpretation: 'Scientes impetrari non posse quod pro peccatis petimus, nisi et ipsi circa debitores nostros paria fecerimus.'

As these sheets are passing through the press, I notice that Prof. Marshall in his article on *the Aramaic Gospel* in the current number of the *Expositor* (April, 1891) discusses this petition of the Prayer. His remarks confirm what I have said on the variation *ὀφειλήματα* and *ἁμαρτίας.* It seems to me however that his method of accounting for the variation *ὡς καὶ ἡμεῖς* (Matt.) and *καὶ γὰρ αὐτοί* (Lc.) is open to criticism. He writes thus: 'The [Aramaic] word for "as," "sicut" is כְּמָא. The equivalent of "for" in this connexion is בְּמָא, "in eo," "quatenus," "seeing that." The difference in Aramaic is therefore merely that of two letters very much alike and easily confounded.' But in the first place this suggestion, ingenious as it is, neglects the evidence of the Syriac Versions as a guide to the original Aramaic (see above p. 39 n.). And in the second place *γάρ* does not seem to me so obvious an equivalent of במא, the meaning of which Buxtorf (*Lex. Chald.*) gives as *in quantum, quatenus, in eo, de eo,* as to lead one to think that it would expel the word *ὡς* (=כמא) already familiar; in fact *ὡς* would be nearer to במא than *γάρ* would be. If such a confusion of Aramaic words alike in sound is to be postulated to account for the variation, it would be simpler to suppose that the Aramaic words were אֵיךְ (הֵיךְ) and כִּי. I think however that the Old Syriac of Lc. xi. 4 preserves the original connexion of the two parts of this petition. In the version given by St Matthew this petition is modelled after the type of the petitions in the earlier part of the Prayer (p. 40 f.) as preserved in his Gospel—human forgiveness must correspond to (*ὡς*) divine forgiveness, just as the earthly doing of the Will, the coming of the Kingdom, and the hallowing the Name should correspond to (*ὡς*) the heavenly. St Luke gives a version of the clause (current perhaps in the Apostolic Churches of Macedonia and Greece) which aims at a more idiomatic Greek rendering. Here however, as so often, we want a knowledge of the text of the Diatessaron.

VI.

ΚΑῚ ΜῊ ΕἸΣΕΝΈΓΚῌΣ ἩΜᾶΣ ΕἸΣ ΠΕΙΡΑΣΜΌΝ.

THE last word of the clause suggests a question of interest with which it will be convenient to deal at once. The Syriac versions have a word which, as it is obvious to remark, according to its vocalization may be either singular (ܢܶܣܝܽܘܢܳܐ, temptation) or plural (ܢܶܣܝܽܘܢܶ̈ܐ, temptations). There is the same ambiguity in regard to St Luke xxii. 28 (ܢܶܣܝܽܘܢܰ̈ܝ, my temptations, or ܢܶܣܝܽܘܢܝ, my temptation).

It is therefore at least possible that the original form of the petition was 'Bring us not into *temptations*,' and such a form would be in harmony with the circumstances of our Lord's temptation (*πάντα πειρασμόν* Lc. iv. 13), and with the phrase *ποικίλοι πειρασμοί* which is common to St James (i. 2) and St Peter (1 Pet. i. 6)[1]. The Old Syriac, it may be added, reads in St Luke xxii. 40 'Pray that ye enter not *among* temptations' (see below p. 62 n.), where the preposition shews that the noun is plural. Further, in this form the petition would perhaps present less difficulty when viewed from a theological and religious standpoint. The evidence however does not seem to warrant more than the suggestion of the possibility that this may have been the earliest form.

The words *μὴ εἰσενέγκῃς* invite discussion in more directions than one.

[1] In 2 Pet. ii. 9 (*οἶδεν Κύριος εὐσεβεῖς ἐκ πειρασμοῦ ῥύεσθαι*), which is very possibly a reminiscence of the Lord's Prayer, there is considerable authority for the plural *πειρασμῶν*.

I. The Syriac versions, as probably representing the original Aramaic, are of special interest here. The Old Syriac in St Luke has

ܠܢܣܝܘܢܐ	ܬܥܠܢ	ܘܠܐ
into-temptation(s?)	make-us-to-enter	and-do-not

The Vulgate Syriac in both Gospels adopts these words[1]. The Old Syriac of St Matthew has ܬܝܬܝܢ (make-us-to-come). The fact that the Vulgate Syriac has in both Gospels the phrase *make-us-to-enter* tends to shew that this was the current traditional form. Other reasons also, which will appear immediately, point to the conclusion that this word 'make-us-to-enter' is the original.

In discussing the interpretation of the words ἀπὸ τοῦ πονηροῦ I shall have to point out the close connexion between the Lord's Prayer and the sayings of the Lord on the night of the betrayal (see below p. 108 f.). Fresh links come into view when we turn to the Syriac versions.

The Old Syriac rendering of St Luke xxii. 40, 46 is happily preserved in the Curetonian fragments.

v. 40 προσεύχεσθε μὴ εἰσελθεῖν εἰς πειρασμόν.

ܢܣܝܘܢܐ	ܠܓܘ	ܬܥܠܘܢ	ܕܠܐ	ܨܠܘ
temptations	among	ye-enter	that-not	pray-ye

v. 46 προσεύχεσθε ἵνα μὴ εἰσέλθητε εἰς πειρασμόν.

ܠܢܣܝܘܢܐ	ܬܥܠܘܢ	ܕܠܐ	ܨܠܘ
into-temptation(s?)	ye-enter	that-not	pray-ye

The Syriac Vulgate has in both places the words which the Old Syriac has in *v.* 46.

In St Matthew xxvi. 41 (προσεύχεσθε ἵνα μὴ εἰσέλθητε εἰς πειρασμόν) and in St Mark xiv. 38 (προσεύχεσθε ἵνα μὴ ἔλθητε εἰς πειρασμόν), verses which are wanting in what remains to us of the Old Syriac, the Syriac Vulgate has the same words as it has in the two passages just cited from St Luke.

A comparison of these passages in the Syriac versions suggests the following conclusions: (1) The same verb which is used in the *Peal* in St Matthew xxvi. 41, St Mark xiv. 38, St Luke xxii. 40,

[1] The ܬܥܠܝܢ in the Vg. Syr. of St Luke is only a difference of form. The Arabic of Ciasca's Tatian has 'make us not to enter.'

46 is used in the *Aphel* in the Lord's Prayer as the clause is given by both versions in St Luke, and by the Vulgate in St Matthew. The close relation therefore between the Lord's Prayer and the history of the evening of the betrayal, which a study of the Greek Gospels suggests, is strongly confirmed. (2) So far as a single case can be urged, the revelation of a harmony, so natural and so simple, between the Lord's words spoken at different times, supports the theory that our Lord spoke in Aramaic and that His sayings were current in that language. (3) The gloss (for such, however ancient, I suppose it to be) in the Old Syriac in St Luke xxii. 40 '*among* temptations' seems to point to the plural interpretation of ܢܣܝܘܢܐ being the common one[1]. (4) Lastly and chiefly we seem to have a clear indication that the verb in the petition originally was, ܬܥܠܢ (make-us-to-enter). This indication is confirmed in two directions. (*a*) In St James i. 2 (ὅταν πειρασμοῖς περιπέσητε ποικίλοις) the Vulgate Syriac has ܬܥܠܘܢ ܠܢܣܝܘܢܐ (ye-enter into-temptations). Here there is no attempt to represent the somewhat remarkable word περιπέσητε: a word which, it may be noted in passing, seems to suggest that St James had some such phrase in his mind as that which is represented by the Old Syriac of St Luke xxii. 40 ('enter *among* temptations'). Of the other passages in the New Testament where the word occurs, one (Acts xxvii. 41) is somewhat different from our present passage; in the other, viz. St Luke x. 30 (καὶ λῃσταῖς περιέπεσεν), the two great Syriac versions endeavour to give an adequate rendering of the word, the Old Syriac having 'he fell into the hands of robbers,' the Vulgate 'there fell upon him robbers.' In St James however it seems as if the Syriac translator could not help reproducing the familiar juxtaposition, 'enter,' 'temptation[2].' (*b*) The word εἰσφέρειν is the natural Greek equivalent of such an Aramaic word as ܐܥܠ. Except in five

[1] The plural appears regularly to follow the preposition ܒܝܬ (=among): see Matt. xiii. 7, xxviii. 15, Mc. ii. 3, 23, Lc. i. 25, vi. 1, viii. 43, xvi. 15, John x. 39, xi. 54, xxi. 23, Acts ii. 9, vii. 2.

[2] We might have expected a similar turn in the Syriac translation of 1 Tim. vi. 9 (ἐμπίπτουσιν εἰς πειρασμὸν καὶ παγίδα). But here the literal rendering is accounted for by the metaphor which follows and by the need of conformity with the translation of the cognate phrases εἰς κρίμα ἐμπ. τοῦ διαβόλου (iii. 6), εἰς ὀνειδισμὸν

passages out of the eighty in which it is found in the LXX., εἰσφέρειν is the translation of הביא, a Hebrew word which very frequently is represented in the Syriac by the Aphel form ܐܥܠ.

If this account of the original phrase is true, and if we may look to the Syriac word rather than to the Greek as a guide to the true meaning of the petition, light is thrown on the difficulties which have often been found in this prayer. There is a certain elasticity about the so-called causative voices. They sometimes approach a permissive sense. So it may be here. Certainly the notion of deliberate guidance has no necessary place in the Syriac word. The fact that this idea of guidance is not prominent in εἰσφέρειν, especially when it is contrasted with the other equivalents of הביא in the LXX. viz., ἄγειν, εἰσάγειν, and more rarely προσάγειν, may have been the reason why the Hellenistic 'Brethren' chose this word to stand in the Lord's Prayer rather than the other possible renderings of the Aramaic.

II. The last subject touched on makes it an easy transition to pass from the Syriac versions to two glosses which found their way into certain forms of the Old Latin version.

(1) In two passages Augustine deals with an interesting form of this clause found in some Old Latin authorities.

In the first, *de Sermone Domini* (Migne *P. L.* 34 p. 1282), he writes thus:

'*Et ne nos inferas in temptationem.* Nonnulli codices habent *inducas*, quod tantumdem valere arbitror; nam ex uno Graeco quod dictum est εἰσενέγκῃς utrumque translatum est. Multi autem precando ita dicunt, *ne nos patiaris induci in temptationem*, exponentes videlicet quomodo dictum sit *inducas*.' Sabatier, referring to this passage, notes that Augustine himself is consistent in the use of 'inferas' in this clause.

Again, in *de Dono Perseverantiae* vi. (Migne *P. L.* 45 p. 1000) Augustine writes as follows:

'Unde sic orant nonnulli et legitur in codicibus plurimis et hoc sic posuit beatissimus Cyprianus: *ne patiaris nos induci in temp-*

ἐμπ. καὶ παγίδα τοῦ διαβόλου (iii. 7). The word הביא appears in Jewish prayers in connexion with temptation. 'The Jews' Morning Prayer (cf. Berakoth 60 b) has the petition, ואל תביאנו...לידי נסיון' (Dr Taylor *Sayings* p. 141 f.).

tationem. In Evangelio tamen Graeco nusquam inveni nisi *ne nos inferas in temptationem.*'

In these two passages Augustine makes three assertions, which we may consider in the following order, giving to the first of them a somewhat larger scope.

(*a*) The words *ne nos patiaris induci in temptationem* are found in some Latin writings, and first occur in Cyprian.

The writer commonly called Arnobius Junior (Migne *P. L.* 53), the inferior limit of whose date is the Eutychian controversy, in the dialogue called *de Deo Trino et Uno* (Lib. ii. ch. xxx.) assumes this as the true reading. 'Qui autem orat et dicit, *ne nos induci patiaris in temptationem,* non utique id orat ut homo sit...neque id orat ut habeat liberum arbitrium,...neque orat peccatorum remissionem...sed orat plane ut faciat mandatum. Orat ut non peccet, hoc est, ne quid faciat mali.'

The same form of the clause is given in a Sermon (lxxxiv.) printed in the Appendix to Augustine's Sermons. The passage is quoted below p. 67 f.

The passage in Cyprian (*de Oratione Dom.*) is clear, and is as follows:

'Illud quoque necessarie monet Dominus ut in oratione dicamus *Et ne patiaris nos induci in temptationem.* Qua in parte ostenditur nihil contra nos adversarium posse, nisi Deus ante *permiserit,* ut omnis timor noster et devotio atque observatio ad Deum convertatur, quando in temptationibus nostris nihil malo *liceat,* nisi *potestas inde tribuatur.*'

I have italicised the words in which Cyprian dwells on the peculiar form of the clause as he accepts it.

It should further be noticed that Hartel, whose text is followed above, records two variations of reading in Cyprian's quotation from the Lord's Prayer: (i) Cod. Veronensis substitutes *passus fueris* for *patiaris,* (ii) Cod. Sangallensis and Cod. Veronensis have *induci nos.*

(*b*) The reading has found its way into several MSS. (1) 'The close affinity of Cod. Bobiensis (k) with Cyprian,' so writes Bp Wordsworth (*Old-Latin Biblical Texts,* No. i. p. lxvii), is 'the first and surest clue that we have to guide us through the maze' of the questions connected with the early history of the Old Latin

Version. This MS. reads *ne passus fueris induci nos in temptationē.* (2) Cod. Colbertinus (*c*), which gives (see below p. 158) a 'mixed' Latin text, has *ne passus nos fueris induci in temptationem.* Sabatier gives *ne patiaris nos induci* as the reading of (3) Cod. Sangermanensis (g^2), and of (4) *gat.*, a MS. of the Hieronymian text of the Gospels at St Gatien's, Tours. To these must be added two MSS. referred to in the critical note on Matt. vi. 13 in Bp. Wordsworth and Mr White's edition of the Vulgate text of St Matthew, viz. (5) 'Cod. *Dublinensis* olim *Armachanus* (Book of *Armagh*),' (6) "Cod. Evang. *Rushworthianus* vel 'Gospels of *Mac Regol.*'" Both of these MSS. read *ne patiaris nos induci.*

The evidence derived from the MSS., taken with that of the Latin writers quoted above, shews (i) that the gloss took more than one form; (ii) that it appears in the text at almost the earliest date at which we have evidence in regard to the African Version, and that it was widely known, though not commonly adopted into the text of the Gospel.

(*c*) 'Sic orant nonnulli,' 'multi precando ita dicunt,' such is Augustine's account of the form of the petition which we are considering. It was common in devotional use; hence it gained currency.

Three passages of Tertullian are instructive in this connexion. I will quote them in the probable order of date.

De Oratione viii. '*ne nos inducas in temptationem,* id est, ne nos patiaris induci ab eo utique qui temptat.'

De Fuga ii. '*Erue nos a maligno,* id est, ne nos induxeris in temptationem permittendo nos maligno. Tunc enim eruimur diaboli manibus, cum illi non tradimur in temptationem.'

Adv. Marcionem iv. 26 'Quis non sinet nos deduci in temptationem? Quem poterit temptator non timere, an qui a primordio temptatorem angelum praedamnavit?'

The thought of the divine permission in the matter of temptation is the turning point of Tertullian's interpretation of the last two clauses of the Prayer, as later on (see p. 134 f.) will appear more clearly. In these passages we see the words in which that thought found expression in the very act, as it were, of securing a place for themselves in the text. In the passage from *de Fuga* the thought is clearly expressed; in the earlier passage from *de*

Oratione the form which in Cyprian is part of the prayer itself is given as the proper expansion of the petition; in the treatise against Marcion, the thought of permission must needs be included in a hasty reference to the clause. Thus the gloss is already laying aside its guise and boldly assuming a higher place.

There is no need to suppose that Tertullian is the author of this *scholium*. He is probably only repeating a devotional adaptation, already current, of a hard saying. That this adaptation is due to liturgical usage will appear presently, when the discussion of the other kindred gloss on this petition has cleared the way for an investigation into their common origin. For the present it is sufficient to notice that the gloss now under consideration is ultimately to be traced back to the words of St Paul in 1 Cor. x. 12, 13, which seemed to offer an authoritative explanation of this petition. The Pauline passage is not quoted by Tertullian. Cyprian however (*Testimonia* iii. 91) represents it thus, 'Temptatio vos non occupabit nisi humana. Fidelis autem Deus, qui non patietur vos temptari super quod potestis, sed faciet cum temptatione etiam evadendi facultatem, ut possitis tolerare[1].'

(2) The passage of St Paul however was pressed into the service by Latin writers in another way. It had helped them to soften down the difficult *ne nos inducas*. It also suggested a limitation of *temptatio*. This gloss appears to be later than the former; it hung about the actual text, but has not, so far as I know, been found in any MS.

I quote in full, as they are instructive in many ways, the passages referred to by Sabatier.

Hilary *in Ps.* cxviii. (Migne *P. L.* 9 p. 510) 'Scientes quidem frequenter nos ab eo ob temptationes derelinqui, ut per eas fides nostra probabilis fiat. Verumtamen secundum Prophetam ne nos penitus derelinquat deprecandus est: ait enim, Non me derelinquas usquequaque nimis. Quod et in dominicae orationis

[1] I quote Hartel's text. He notices that (1) Cod. A (=Cod. biblioth. Sessorianae, saec. vii.) has *quod ferre potestis*; (2) Cod. W (=Cod. Würzeburgensis) has *proventum facultatis* in place of *evad. facult.* The Vulgate (*Cod. Amiatinus*) has 'Temptatio vos non adprehendat nisi humana. Fidelis autem Deus est, qui non patietur vos temptari super id quod potestis, sed faciet cum temptatione etiam proventum, ut possitis sustinere.'

ordine continetur, cum dicitur *Non derelinquas nos*[1] *in temptatione quam ferre non possimus.* Scit Apostolus derelinqui nos ad temptandum; sed novit et mensuram infirmitatis nostrae Deum nosse, dicens *Fidelis est Deus, qui non permittat nos temptari super quam possumus.* Job Deus temptationi permittens a iure diaboli potestatem animae eius excerpsit.'

Chromatius Bp of Aquileia, a contemporary and supporter of Chrysostom, a friend of Ambrose, Jerome, and Rufinus (Migne *P. L.* 20 p. 362) 'Dehinc ait *Et ne nos inducas in temptationem, sed libera nos a malo*....Non ergo ne in toto tentemur oramus, sed ne supra quam virtus fidei patitur temptationi tradamur; quod ipsum in alio libro Evangelii [he is here commenting on the Sermon on the Mount in St Matthew] ostensum est: sic enim scriptum est *Et ne nos inferas in temptationem, quam sufferre non possumus.* Apostolus quoque, ut id ipsum ostenderet, ita testatus est, dicendo *Fidelis autem Deus, qui non patitur temptari super id quod potestis, sed faciet cum temptatione etiam transgressum, ut possitis tolerare.* Et ideo non illam temptationem a nobis auferri, quae esse potest utilis, deprecamur, sed illam, quae ad fidei nostrae eversionem modum infirmitatis excedit. Et idcirco congrue et necessario in fine orationis etiam *liberari* nos postulamus *a malo*, qui fidem nostram diversis temptationibus quotidie expugnare non desinit, a qua nos non immerito quotidiana oratione deprecamur, ne immissionibus ipsius impediti praecepta divina minime possimus implere.' The masculine interpretation of *a malo* is to be noticed.

Jerome *in Ezek.* xlviii. 16 (Migne *P. L.* 25 p. 484) 'Cumque recesserimus ab aquilone, vento frigidissimo, transimus ad meridiem, et post ortum in nobis lumen scientiae, occasum fortitudinum formidamus, nequaquam praeterita sed futura considerantes, nec habentes certam virtutis possessionem sed quotidie in oratione dicentes, *Ne inducas nos in temptationem quam ferre non possumus.*'

Augustine *De Serm. Dom.* ii. 9 'Aliud est induci in temptationem, aliud temptari...Inducimur enim si tales acciderint *quas ferre non possumus.*' This passage is not noticed in Sabatier.

Pseudo-Augustine *Serm.* lxxxiv. (Migne *P. L.* 39 p. 1909) '*Et ne patiaris nos induci in temptationem quam ferre non possumus,*

[1] Here is another Scriptural gloss making its way into the text. Comp. Ps. cxviii. 8 (non me derelinquas usquequaque), xxvi. 9, xxxvii. 22, lxx. 9.

Vide quid dicat *quam ferre non possumus:* non dicit, *non inducas nos in temptationem;* sed quasi athleta talem vult temptationem quam ferre possit humana conditio, et unusquisque ut *a malo*, hoc est, ab inimico et a peccato, *liberetur.* Potens est autem Dominus qui abstulit peccatum vestrum, et delicta vestra donavit, tueri et custodire vos adversum diaboli adversantis insidias, ut non vobis obrepat inimicus, qui culpam generare consuevit[1].' The masculine interpretation of *a malo* again should be noticed.

Hitherto we have confined our attention to Latin writers in reference to both these glosses. It is in Latin writers that they both attach themselves to the text of the Prayer, though it is only the first of them which has gained a place in extant Latin copies of the N.T. But it is important to remark that the first gloss is found in a fragment of Dionysius of Alexandria (Migne *P. G.* 10 p. 1601, see below p. 140) *καὶ δὴ καὶ μὴ εἰσενέγκῃς ἡμᾶς εἰς πειρασμόν· τουτέστι, μὴ ἐάσῃς ἡμᾶς ἐμπεσεῖν εἰς πειρασμόν*, where 1 Tim. vi. 9 is combined with 1 Cor. x. 13. Further, a similar phrase embedded in a prayer has been already quoted (p. 33) from Agathangelus, *ὁ ἐάσας ἐπελθεῖν ἡμῖν τὸν πειρασμὸν τοῦτον.* I have pointed out that there appears to be a large liturgical element in Agathangelus, and this fact at once suggests that we have only partially followed up the clue given in Augustine's words (p. 63), 'sic orant nonnulli,' 'multi precando ita dicunt.' Compare Jerome (above p. 67) 'quotidie in oratione dicentes.' The true origin of these allied glosses appears at once when we turn to the following passages from the Liturgies[2].

Liturgy of Alexandria (Swainson p. 6) *μὴ εἰσενέγκῃς ἡμᾶς εἰς πειρασμόν, ὃν ὑπενεγκεῖν οὐ δυνάμεθα.* The *Embolismus* of the same Liturgy (Swainson p. 62 f., Hammond p. 189) *ναὶ κύριε, κύριε, μὴ εἰσενέγκῃς...πονηροῦ. οἶδεν γὰρ ἡ πολλή σου εὐσπλαγχνία, ὅτι οὐ δυνάμεθα ὑπενεγκεῖν διὰ τὴν πολλὴν ἡμῶν*

[1] This whole passage is also found in Pseudo-Ambrose *de Sacramentis* v. 4. 29.

[2] Dr Hort has already suggested this explanation. After speaking of the doxology, he adds (*Notes on Select Readings* p. 9), 'Another apparently liturgical interpolation occurs in several Latin Fathers, the addition of *quam ferre (sufferre) non possumus* to *temptationem*: it is not known to exist in any Latin MS. of the Gospel itself.' He does not notice the first gloss.

ἀσθένειαν· ἀλλὰ ποίησον σὺν τῷ πειρασμῷ καὶ τὴν ἔκβασιν, τοῦ δύνασθαι ἡμᾶς ὑπενεγκεῖν.

Liturgy of St James (Swainson p. 225 f.) *ῥῦσαι ἡμᾶς...μὴ ἀποστήσῃς ἀφ' ἡμῶν τὴν σὴν βοήθειαν, μηδὲ βαρυτέρας τῆς ἡμετέρας δυνάμεως παιδείας ἐπαγάγῃς ἡμῖν.* The *Embolismus* of the same Liturgy (Swainson p. 306 f., Hammond p. 48) *μὴ εἰσενέγκῃς ἡμᾶς εἰς πειρασμόν, κύριε, κύριε τῶν δυνάμεων, ὃν ὑπενεγκεῖν οὐ δυνάμεθα, ὁ εἰδὼς τὴν ἀσθένειαν ἡμῶν, ἀλλὰ ῥῦσαι κ.τ.λ.*

The Syriac Liturgy of St James (Swainson p. 343, Hammond p. 78) has, 'Domine, Deus noster, ne inducas nos in temptationem, quam virtute destituti sustinere non possimus, [sed fac etiam cum tentatione proventum, ut possimus sustinere,] et libera....

The *Embolismus* of the Coptic Liturgy (Hammond p. 223) ne nos inducas in temptationem, neque *permittas* ullam iniquitatem in nos dominari.

A consideration of this liturgical evidence, of the passages from Tertullian and Cyprian (above pp. 64, 65), of the fact that neither of these two glosses occurs in any known Greek text of the N.T., and that only one of them is found in any known Latin text of the N.T., and lastly of the analogy of other additions to and adaptations of the Prayer, seems to me to prove that they made their way from the Liturgies into (or towards) the text of the N.T., and not vice versa. The further fact that these glosses occur in writers who are separated from each other in time and in circumstance, and that they are found in Liturgies belonging to different families, shews very clearly that they must be due to very early liturgical usage.

Note on an English Version of this clause in the King's Book (1543).

The *Institution of a Christian Man*, 1537, often called the *Bishops' Book*, has on the clause *And leade us not into temptation* the following comment: 'For the more playne declaration of the sixth petition we thinke it convenient that all byshops and preachers shall instructe and teache the people...that our Savior Jesus Christ teacheth us not in this sixth peticion, to praye unto god our father, that we shulde be clerely without al temptation, but that he wol not suffre us to be led into temptation.... Sayncte Paule sayth, The trewe and faythfull god wol not suffre us to be tempted above that we maye beare, but he wol turne temptation to our profit, that we maye susteyn it and overcome it.' This exposition is substantially repeated in the *Necessary Erudition of any Christian Man*, 1543, often called the *King's Book.* But here the petition in the Prayer itself is *And lette us not be ledde into temptation.* The history of the clause in Tertullian and Cyprian curiously repeats itself, though the explanation of the history may be quite different in the two epochs. I do not know that this gloss is found in any other English Version of the Prayer.

VII.

ἀλλὰ ῥῦσαι ἡμᾶς ἀπὸ τοῦ πονηροῦ (St Matthew).

In a discussion of the interpretation of this clause three distinct questions require investigation: (1) the meaning of the prepositions *ἀπό* and *ἐκ* after *ῥύεσθαι* and kindred verbs; (2) the origin, meaning and use of the term *ὁ πονηρός*; (3) the evidence as to the gender of *ἀπὸ τοῦ πονηροῦ* to be derived from (i) the Gospels, (ii) the Epistles, (iii) early Christian literature, (iv) the earliest Versions.

Frequent reference will be made to the friendly controversy of two great scholars, who have since then passed away. It was opened by Canon Cook's *Protest against the change in the last petition of the Lord's Prayer...a letter to the Bishop of London*, dated four days after the publication on May 17, 1881, of the Revised Version of the New Testament. Bishop Lightfoot's three letters in answer to Canon Cook appeared in the *Guardian* on the 7th, 14th, and 21st of the following September[1]. Canon Cook replied by a full statement of his case in a *Second Letter* dated 26 November, 1881[2]. It would be indeed unbecoming to praise the learning of the two disputants: but, as I shall have occasion more than once to criticise Canon Cook's arguments, I may perhaps be allowed to pay a respectful tribute to the chastened and almost pathetic earnestness with which the veteran scholar pleaded his cause. Yet even such masters of the reaper's craft have left a few ears for humbler gleaners to gather.

1. *The prepositions ἀπό and ἐκ after ῥύεσθαι.*

When used with full accuracy *ἀπό*, the correlative of *πρός*,

[1] While this is passing through the press I learn that Bp Lightfoot's three letters are being reprinted in the third edition of his volume *On a Fresh Revision*.

[2] Canon Cook's protest had the enthusiastic support of Dean Burgon, *The Revision Revised*, p. 214 ff.

denotes motion *from*, emphasising the idea of *direction*; ἐκ, the correlative of εἰς, denotes motion *out of*, emphasising the idea of *emergence*. Thus, for example, the two prepositions are used correctly in the following verse of the Apocalypse (xxi. 2): καὶ τὴν πόλιν τὴν ἁγίαν Ἰερουσαλὴμ καινὴν εἶδον καταβαίνουσαν ἐκ τοῦ οὐρανοῦ ἀπὸ τοῦ θεοῦ[1]. When then ἀπό is used with a verb meaning *deliverance*, it properly implies nothing more than that the threatened danger has been averted. A person has been in the neighbourhood of peril, and has been withdrawn unharmed. The preposition ἐκ following a verb of this class properly expresses the further notion that the person delivered has been brought out of the very area of danger itself. Instances of this full meaning are: Ps. xxxiii. 20 (LXX.) πολλαὶ αἱ θλίψεις τῶν δικαίων, καὶ ἐκ πασῶν αὐτῶν (Hebr. וּמִכֻּלָּם) ῥύσεται αὐτούς[2]: and again, Jude 5 Κύριος λαὸν ἐκ γῆς Αἰγύπτου σώσας. But as a matter of fact is this distinction invariably or commonly observed in the LXX. and in the New Testament? The answer with regard to the usage of the former is of primary importance. It must however be remarked that statistics as to the phenomena of the LXX., in the present condition of the text and of the available apparatus, can only be looked upon as approximate and provisional.

It is probably due to a sense of the distinction pointed out above that the translators of the LXX. and the writers of the N.T. alike avoid the construction φυλάσσειν ἐκ, and, with the single exception of Ps. cxxxix 5, always associate with this verb the preposition ἀπό[3]. Avoidance of, not emergence out of, danger is the essential idea of this word. The choice therefore of this preposition is a natural one.

But the case is different when we take the ambiguous verb

[1] Comp. Lc. ii. 4, Jn. i. 44, 45, 46, vii. 17, xi. 1, 1 Thess. ii. 6, 2 Cor. v. 6, 8 (ἐκδημοῦμεν ἀπὸ τοῦ κυρίου...ἐκδημῆσαι ἐκ τοῦ σώματος), Apoc. xvi. 17. The contrast between ἀπὸ νεκρῶν (Lc. xvi. 30, Matt. xiv. 2, xxvii. 64) and ἐκ νεκρῶν (Lc. xvi. 31 and always elsewhere) is very instructive. The ἐκ implies a certain relation to the other dead: it hints at the thought of an ἀπαρχή.

[2] Comp. Ps. cxxiii. 7.

[3] The passages are (*a*) Deut. xxiii. 9, Josh. vi. 18, Ps. xvii. 24, cxx. 7, cxl. 9, Jer. ix. 4, Mic. vii. 5 (in all these places the Hebr. verb is שמר), Ezek. xxxiii. 8, Sir. xii. 11, xxii. 13, 26, xxxv. 22, xxxvii. 8; (*b*) Lc. xii. 15, 2 Thess. iii. 3, 1 Jn. v. 21.

ῥύεσθαι, to deliver. Here taking all the occurrences of *ῥύεσθαι*, without distinguishing them according to the Hebrew word represented, the verb is followed by *ἐκ* 30 times; by *ἐκ χειρός*[1] (or *ἐκ τῶν χειρῶν*) 20 times; while only 10 instances of *ἀπό* are found[2].

A more exact view of the facts of the case is gained if the various constructions of the verb נצל (Niphal, Piel, Hiphil, Hophal), and their several equivalents in the LXX., are investigated. For, while *ῥύεσθαι* is used to represent several Hebrew verbs (גָּאַל, הוֹשִׁיעַ, חִלֵּץ, מִלֵּט, פִּלֵּט), it occurs about 80 times as the translation of parts of נצל. The results attained are as follows.

1. מִיַּד פ״ (1) Of living creatures, chiefly persons[3]:

(*a*) *ἐκ χειρός*. Gen. xxxii. 12*, xxxvii. 21*, 22*, Ex. iii. 8*, xviii. 9*, 10*, Deut. xxv. 11*, xxxii. 39*, Josh. ix. 26*, xxii. 31, xxiv. 10*, Judg. vi. 9, viii. 34, ix. 17, 1 Sam. iv. 8*, vii. 3*, 14 (*ἀφείλοντο*), xii. 11*, xiv. 48*, xvii. 37*, 2 Sam. xii. 7, 2 Kings xviii. 29*, 33, 34*, 35*, 2 Chron. xxxii. 13 (*σῶσαι*, so *vv.* 14, 15), 17*, Ps. xxii. 21*b*, xxxi. 16, lxxxii. 4, xcvii. 10, cxliv. 7*b*, 11*, Is. xxxvi. 18, 19, 20, xliii. 13*, Jer. xv. 21*, xx. 13*, xxi. 12*, xxii. 3*, xlii. 11 (*σώζειν*), Ezek. xiii. 21, 23, xxxiv. 27*, Dan. viii. 4*, 7* (Theod.), Hos. ii. 12*, Zech. xi. 6*.

(*b*) *ἐκ*. 2 Kings xvii. 39*, Prov. vi. 5 (*σώζῃ*: but the LXX. diverges from the Hebrew).

(*c*) *ἀπό*. Ex. ii. 19, Numb. xxxv. 25*, Dan. viii. 7 (LXX.).

[1] I have noticed *ἀπὸ χειρός* only in 2 Esdr. viii. 31 (*ἐρρύσατο ἡμᾶς ἀπὸ χειρὸς ἐχθροῦ*).

[2] Job xxxiii. 17, Ps. xvi. 13, xvii. 30, 49, xxxviii. 9, xlii. 1, cxix. 2, Prov. ii. 12, (xi. 4 v.l.), Ezek. xxxvii. 23, 1 Macc. xii. 15.

[3] In passages marked with an asterisk the verb *ἐξαιρεῖσθαι* is used. In all other cases when a verb other than *ῥύεσθαι* is used, the verb is noted.

In the prayer of Esther (iv. 16), which only exists in the Greek, there occurs the petition *ῥῦσαι ἡμᾶς ἐκ χειρὸς τῶν πονηρευομένων καὶ ῥῦσαί με ἐκ τοῦ φόβου μου*. The resemblance of the prayer, which is perhaps based on some Greek Jewish formula, to the Lord's Prayer is to be noted. Fritzsche (*Libri Apocryphi* p. 51) gives besides the above the following reading: *ῥῦσαι ἡμᾶς ἐκ χειρὸς τῶν πονηρευομένων ἐφ' ἡμᾶς καὶ ἐξελοῦ με, κύριε, ἐκ χειρὸς τοῦ φόβου μου*. Comp. Jer. xx. 13 הִצִּיל...מִיַּד מְרֵעִים (LXX. *ἐξείλατο...ἐκ χειρὸς πονηρευομένων*).

(2) Of things:

ἐκ. Is. xlvii. 14*. Compare Job v. 20,

פְּדְךָ מִמָּוֶת......מִידֵי חָרֶב׃

ῥύσεταί σε ἐκ θανάτου...ἐκ χειρὸς σιδήρου λύσει σε.

2. מִכַּף פ״ (1) Of living creatures:

(*a*) *ἐκ χειρός.* 2 Sam. xiv. 16, xxii. 1* (= Ps. xviii. 1), 2 Kings xx. 6 (*σώσω*), 2 Chron. xxxii. 11 (*σώσει*), Is. xxxviii. 6.

(*b*) *ἀπὸ χειρός.* 2 Esdr. (= Ezra) viii. 31.

(*c*) *ἐκ χειρὸς ἀπό.* 2 Sam. xix. 10,

הַמֶּלֶךְ הִצִּילָנוּ מִכַּף אֹיְבֵנוּ וְהוּא מִלְּטָנוּ מִכַּף פְּלִשְׁתִּים׃

ὁ βασιλεὺς Δαυεὶδ ἐρύσατο ἡμᾶς ἐκ χειρὸς ἀπὸ πάντων[1] *τῶν ἐχθρῶν ἡμῶν, καὶ αὐτὸς ἐξείλατο ἡμᾶς ἐκ χειρὸς ἀλλοφύλων.*

(2) Of things:

Hab. ii. 9. לְהִנָּצֵל מִכַּף רָע׃

τοῦ ἐκσπασθῆναι ἐκ χειρὸς κακῶν.

3. מִן פ״ (1) Of living creatures:

(*a*) *ἐκ.* 1 Sam. xvii. 35 (*ἐξέσπασα ἐκ τοῦ στόματος αὐτοῦ*), 2 Sam. xxii. 18, 49, 1 Chron. xvi. 35*, Ps. xviii. 18, xxxi. 16, lix. 2*, 3, lxix. 15*b*, cxlii. 7, cxliii. 9*, Ezek. xxxiv. 10 (*ἐξελοῦμαι...ἐκ τοῦ στόματος αὐτῶν*), Amos iii. 12 (*ὅταν ἐκσπάσῃ ὁ ποιμὴν ἐκ στόματος τοῦ λέοντος δύο σκέλη*), Mic. v. 5.

(*b*) *ἀπό.* Ps. xviii. 49*b*, Prov. ii. 12 (*ἵνα ῥύσηταί σε ἀπὸ ὁδοῦ κακῆς καὶ ἀπὸ ἀνδρὸς λαλοῦντος μηδὲν πιστόν*). Prov. ii. 16 is altogether transformed in the LXX.

(*c*) *ἐκ χειρός.* Ps. xxxiv. 18. Comp. Ex. xviii. 4,

וַיַּצִּלֵנוּ מֵחֶרֶב פַּרְעֹה׃

ἐξείλατό με ἐκ χειρὸς Φαραώ[2].

[1] The phrase however has probably arisen from a misreading of מכף as מכל, and a subsequent conflation of the two readings.

[2] In Gen. xxxi. 16 (*ἣν ἀφείλατο ὁ θεὸς τοῦ πατρὸς ἡμῶν*), the simple genitive involves a change of construction (Hebr. מֵאָבִינוּ).

(2) Of things:

(*a*) *ἐκ*. Ex. vi. 6, Josh. ii. 13*, 1 Sam. xxvi. 24*, Ps. xxxiii. 19, xxxiv. 5, 18, 20, li. 16, liv. 9, lvi. 14, lxxxvi. 13, xci. 3 (*ῥύσεται ἐκ παγίδος θηρευτῶν, καὶ ἀπὸ λόγου ταραχώδους*), cvii. 6, cxix. 43 (*περιέλῃς*), cxliv. 7 (הַצִּילֵנִי מִמַּיִם רַבִּים מִיַּד בְּנֵי נֵכָר׃ *ἐξελοῦ με καὶ ῥῦσαί με ἐξ ὑδάτων πολλῶν, ἐκ χειρὸς υἱῶν ἀλλοτρίων*), Prov. x. 2, xxiii. 14, Amos iv. 11 (*ἐξεσπασμένος ἐκ πυρός*, ‖ Zech. iii. 2).

(*b*) *ἀπό*. Ps. xxii. 21*a*, xxxix. 9, lxix. 15*a* (*σῶσον*), xci. 3*b* (see just above), cxx. 2, Prov. ii. 12*a* (see above, 3(*b*)), xi. 4 (*δικαιοσύνη ῥύσεται ἀπὸ θανάτου*: the clause is not in B), Ezek. xxxiv. 12 (*ἀπελάσω...ἀπὸ παντὸς τόπου*). In Jon. iv. 6 (*σκιάζειν αὐτῷ ἀπὸ τῶν κακῶν αὐτοῦ*) the LXX. clearly connected לְהַצִּיל with צֵל which occurs in the earlier part of the verse.

4. מִפְּנֵי פ״ Is. xx. 6, לְהִנָּצֵל מִפְּנֵי מֶלֶךְ = *σωθῆναι ἀπὸ βασιλέως*.

5. מֵעִם פ״ Deut. xxiii. 16 (the wording is changed in the LXX.).

6. מִתַּחַת יַד פ״ Ex. xviii. 10 (omitted in the LXX.).

To pass to another important point, the prepositions *ἀπό* and *ἐκ* are often interchanged in the parallel clauses of poetical passages. Thus, for example,

Ps. xxi. (Heb. xxii.) 21, 22

ῥῦσαι ἀπὸ ῥομφαίας (מֵחֶרֶב) *τὴν ψυχήν μου,*
καὶ ἐκ χειρὸς (מִיַּד) *κυνὸς τὴν μονογενῆ μου·*
σῶσόν με ἐκ στόματος (מִפִּי) *λέοντος,*
καὶ ἀπὸ κεράτων (מִקַּרְנֵי) *μονοκερώτων τὴν ταπείνωσίν μου.*

Ps. xxxiv. (Heb. xxxv.) 10

ῥυόμενος πτωχὸν ἐκ χειρὸς στερεωτέρων αὐτοῦ (מֵחָזָק מִמֶּנּוּ),
καὶ πτωχὸν καὶ πένητα ἀπὸ τῶν διαρπαζόντων αὐτόν (מִגֹּזְלוֹ).

Ps. lxviii. (Heb. lxix.) 15

σῶσόν με ἀπὸ πηλοῦ (מִטִּיט), *ἵνα μὴ ἐνπαγῶ·*

ῥυσθείην ἐκ τῶν μισούντων με (מִשֹּׂנְאַי)

καὶ ἐκ τοῦ βάθους τῶν ὑδάτων (מִמַּעֲמַקֵּי מָיִם).

Ps. cxxxix. (Heb. cxl.) 1

ἐξελοῦ με, κύριε, ἐξ ἀνθρώπου (מֵאָדָם) *πονηροῦ,*

ἀπὸ ἀνδρὸς (מֵאִישׁ) *ἀδίκου ῥῦσαί με.*

Comp. xvii. 49, xc. 3, cxiv. 8, Sir. li. 2—5.

Further, *ἀπό* is sometimes used where reference is made to a deliverance from some adverse power which is already overwhelming its victim. Thus Ps. xxxviii. 9 *ἀπὸ πασῶν τῶν ἀνομιῶν μου* (מִכָּל־פְּשָׁעַי) *ῥῦσαί με.* Jer. xlix. (xlii. Heb.) 17 *οὐκ ἔσται αὐτῶν οὐδεὶς σωζόμενος ἀπὸ τῶν κακῶν* (מִפְּנֵי הָרָעָה) *ὧν ἐγὼ ἐπάγω ἐπ' αὐτούς.* Ezek. xxxiv. 12 (comp. Zech. viii. 7) *καὶ ἀπελάσω* (וְהִצַּלְתִּי) *αὐτὰ ἀπὸ παντὸς τόπου* (מִכָּל־הַמְּקוֹמוֹת) *οὗ διεσπάρησαν ἐκεῖ.* xxxvii. 23 *καὶ ῥύσομαι* (וְהוֹשַׁעְתִּי) *αὐτοὺς ἀπὸ πασῶν τῶν ἀνομιῶν αὐτῶν* (מִכֹּל מוֹשְׁבֹתֵיהֶם) *ὧν ἡμάρτοσαν ἐν αὐταῖς.*

Conversely, in the phrases *ἐκ θανάτου* (e.g. Ps. xxxii. 19, lv. 14) and *ἐξ ἀπωλείας* (Sir. li. 2, 12), the stricter meaning of *ἐκ* cannot be maintained. It seems in such cases to emphasise either the extremity and imminence of the danger or the completeness of the deliverance vouchsafed.

A review of the whole investigation seems to justify the following conclusions:

(1) In regard to the Hebrew verb נצל, it is more often used of deliverance from living creatures than from impersonal dangers; further, the genius of the language, loving simplicity and picturesque statement, explains the fact that the phrase 'from the hand of' is the favourite complement. As to the Greek equivalents, the literal translation of the Hebrew phrase—*ἐκ χειρός*—is the most common; and further *ἐκ*, being nearer than *ἀπό* to *ἐκ χειρός*, is most often chosen to render the Hebrew מִן.

It is clear also that the phrases both in Hebrew and in Greek—מִיַּד, מִכַּף, ἐκ χειρός, ἐκ, ἀπό—are used, though in different proportions which appear in the list of references given above, in reference to both *persons* and *things*.

(2) The primary distinction between ἐκ and ἀπό, according to which the former applies to dangers already experienced, the latter to dangers which only threaten, is not observed in the LXX.

An examination of the passages in which ῥύεσθαι and kindred verbs are used in the N. T. naturally follows an investigation into the usage of the LXX.

ἐξαιρεῖν: a verb used, it should be noticed, upwards of 70 times in the LXX. to translate הִצִּיל.

(i) ἐκ χειρός. Acts xii. 11 ὁ κύριος...ἐξείλατό με ἐκ χειρὸς Ἡρῴδου καὶ πάσης τῆς προσδοκίας τοῦ λαοῦ τῶν Ἰουδαίων. Some 'Western' authorities add ἐκ before πάσης. The ἐκ χειρός is here used in its strictest sense. The Apostle was already in the tyrant's grasp (ἐπέβαλεν...τὰς χεῖρας *v.* 1, πιάσας *v.* 4; comp. John vii. 30, 44, x. 39; 2 Cor. xi. 32 f.); 'the expectation of the people' already encircled him.

(ii) ἐκ. (*a*) Acts vii. 10 ἐξείλατο αὐτὸν [τὸν Ἰωσήφ] ἐκ πασῶν τῶν θλίψεων αὐτοῦ. Compare Ps. xxiv. 22, xxxiii. 7, 18. The preposition is clearly used in its full sense.

(*b*) Acts xxvi. 17 ἐξαιρούμενός σε ἐκ τοῦ λαοῦ καὶ ἐκ τῶν ἐθνῶν. Comp. 1 Chron. xvi. 35 ἐξελοῦ ἡμᾶς ἐκ τῶν ἐθνῶν. Jer. i. 7 f. (the latter passage throws no light on the question of construction). Guided by e.g. Acts xxiii. 27, 2 Cor. xi. 25 f. we here also give the full sense to ἐκ.

(*c*) Gal. i. 4 ὅπως ἐξέληται ἡμᾶς ἐκ τοῦ αἰῶνος τοῦ ἐνεστῶτος πονηροῦ. ἀπό in place of ἐκ has very slight support. The discussion of this passage must be reserved. See p. 115 ff.

λυτροῦσθαι. (*a*) 1 Pet. i. 18 ἐλυτρώθητε ἐκ τῆς ματαίας ὑμῶν ἀναστροφῆς πατροπαραδότου. Here obviously 'the vain manner of life' had held men within its grasp[1].

[1] On the other hand comp. Hermas *Vis.* iv. 1. 7. At the approach of the beast,

(*b*) Tit. ii. 14 ὃς ἔδωκεν ἑαυτὸν ὑπὲρ ἡμῶν ἵνα λυτρώσηται ἡμᾶς ἀπὸ πάσης ἀνομίας καὶ καθαρίσῃ ἑαυτῷ λαὸν περιούσιον. 'Iniquity' had been no merely menacing power. It had actually subjected men to its despotic rule. This is clear from iii. 3 ἦμεν γάρ ποτε καὶ ἡμεῖς κ.τ.λ. ἀπό therefore cannot imply a more or less distant danger. It seems to differ from ἐκ in that, laying less stress on the power from which deliverance is vouchsafed, it leaves more room for the thought of the deliverance itself[1].

ῥύεσθαι. (i) ἐκ χειρός. Luke i. 74 τοῦ δοῦναι ἡμῖν ἀφόβως ἐκ χειρὸς ἐχθρῶν ῥυσθέντας λατρεύειν αὐτῷ. (Comp. *v.* 71 σωτηρίαν ἐξ ἐχθρῶν ἡμῶν καὶ ἐκ χειρὸς πάντων τῶν μισούντων ἡμᾶς). The song is built up on O. T. thoughts and expressions. To this phrase in particular many parallels may be found in the O.T. e.g. Judg. ii. 18, viii. 34, 1 Sam. iv. 3, xii. 10, Ps. xvii. 18, 21, 49, xxx. 16, lviii. 2, lxiii. 2, cv. 10, cxlii. 9. The whole context shews that 'the enemies' were tyrannous powers under which the Israel of God actually mourned.

(ii) ἐκ. (*a*) Rom. vii. 24 τίς με ῥύσεται ἐκ τοῦ σώματος τοῦ θανάτου τούτου; The thought is of a captivity (αἰχμαλωτίζοντά με *v.* 23) and a slavery (δουλεύω...νόμῳ ἁμαρτίας *v.* 25) of which 'the body of this death' (comp. 'the body of sin' vi. 6) is the sphere. The preposition ἐκ has its full force.

(*b*) 2 Cor. i. 10 ὃς ἐκ τηλικούτου θανάτου ἐρύσατο ἡμᾶς καὶ ῥύσεται. The ἐκ points to the nearness of the enemy:—αὐτοὶ ἐν ἑαυτοῖς τὸ ἀπόκριμα τοῦ θανάτου ἐσχήκαμεν (*v.* 9).

(*c*) Col. i. 13 ὃς ἐρύσατο ὑμᾶς ἐκ τῆς ἐξουσίας τοῦ σκότους καὶ μετέστησεν κ.τ.λ. The full sense of ἐκ is clear.

(*d*) 1 Thess. i. 10 Ἰησοῦν τὸν ῥυόμενον ἡμᾶς ἐκ τῆς ὀργῆς τῆς ἐρχομένης. ἀπό is an apparently 'Western' reading which passed over into the 'Syrian' text. We find in St Paul's writings a double conception of the Divine wrath. There will be a *future* and final outpouring of it. Thus Rom. ii. 5, v. 9 (σωθησόμεθα δι'

the type of the great tribulation which should be, ἠρξάμην ἐρωτᾶν τὸν κύριον ἵνα με λυτρώσηται ἐξ αὐτοῦ. Deliverance from any experience of the monster's power is obviously the point of the request.

[1] Contrast Ps. cxxix. 8 καὶ αὐτὸς λυτρώσεται τὸν Ἰσραὴλ ἐκ πασῶν τῶν ἀνομιῶν αὐτοῦ.

αὐτοῦ ἀπὸ τῆς ὀργῆς); comp. Matt. iii. 7 *φυγεῖν ἀπὸ τῆς μελλούσης ὀργῆς*. There is also a *present* anticipatory manifestation. Thus Rom. i. 18, iii. 5, xii. 19, Eph. v. 6 (*ἔρχεται ἡ ὀργὴ τοῦ θεοῦ ἐπὶ τοὺς υἱοὺς τῆς ἀπειθίας*), Col. iii. 6, 1 Thess. ii. 16 (*ἔφθασεν δὲ ἐπ' αὐτοὺς ἡ ὀργὴ εἰς τέλος*). Between the two conceptions St Paul himself supplies the connecting link:—*θησαυρίζεις σεαυτῷ ὀργὴν ἐν ἡμέρᾳ ὀργῆς καὶ ἀποκαλύψεως δικαιοκρισίας τοῦ θεοῦ* (Rom. ii. 5). The deliverance is a present reality; the full revelation of the nature of the danger lies in the future[1]. The general subject of these Epistles to Thessalonica—the second coming of Christ—(note especially 1 Thess. v. 2, 2 Thess. i. 6—10, ii. 8), the special reference in the immediate context to this great expectation (*ἀναμένειν*[2] *τὸν υἱὸν αὐτοῦ ἐκ τῶν οὐρανῶν*) seem together to shew that *ἡ ὀργὴ ἡ ἐρχομένη* is the *future* exhibition of wrath against sin. In this case *ἐκ* may most naturally be taken to point to the completeness of the deliverance. 'He brings us clean out of the reach of future judgment[3].'

(*e*) 2 Tim. iii. 11 *καὶ ἐκ πάντων με ἐρύσατο ὁ κύριος*. The enumeration of dangers actually experienced which precedes these words indicates the force of the *ἐκ*.

(*f*) 2 Tim. iv. 17, 18 *καὶ ἐρύσθην ἐκ στόματος λέοντος. ῥύσεταί με ὁ κύριος ἀπὸ παντὸς ἔργου πονηροῦ*... The passage will demand fuller notice later on. For the present it may be sufficient to call attention to the fact that here only in the N. T. are the prepositions *ἐκ* and *ἀπό* following *ῥύεσθαι* contrasted with each other. The *ἐκ* is used in its fullest meaning, the phrase being a proverbial expression for extreme and hopeless danger. It is an echo of the language of the O. T. Compare Ps. xxi. 22, *σῶσόν με ἐκ στόματος λέοντος, καὶ ἀπὸ κεράτων μονοκερώτων τὴν ταπείνωσίν μου*. See also Amos iii. 12, Zech. ix. 7, Ezek. xxxiv. 10, Dan. vi. 20, 22, 1 Macc. ii. 60. The fierceness of the definite danger in the past, a wonderful deliverance out of which had

[1] Comp. *ὁ καὶ τῆς μελλούσης ἀποκαλύπτεσθαι δόξης κοινωνός* (1 Pet. v. 1). There is a present participation in that which shall hereafter be revealed.

[2] *ἀναμένειν* a *ἅπαξ λεγ.* in the N.T.—to await a final consummation—is best illustrated by Aesch. Eum. 243 *ἀναμένω τέλος δίκης*.

[3] Comp. the Ancient Homily (the so called 2nd Ep. of Clement), ch. vi. *ποιοῦντες γὰρ τὸ θέλημα τοῦ Χριστοῦ εὑρήσομεν ἀνάπαυσιν· εἰ δὲ μήγε, οὐδὲν ἡμᾶς ῥύσεται ἐκ τῆς αἰωνίου κολάσεως*.

been vouchsafed, inspires St Paul with trust for the future. But when the reference is to unknown evils which the future may bring, the clear and pointed *ἐκ* naturally gives place to *ἀπό*. For here it is not so much the possible dangers on which the Apostle's mind dwells as on the certainty of deliverance.

(*g*) 2 Pet. ii. 9 *οἶδεν Κύριος εὐσεβεῖς ἐκ πειρασμοῦ ῥύεσθαι.* The reading *πειρασμῶν* has some support (א, with some cursives and versions). The reference to the history of Lot shews that the full sense here attaches to the preposition.

(iii) *ἀπό*. (*a*) Matt. vi. 13 *ῥῦσαι ἡμᾶς ἀπὸ τοῦ πονηροῦ.*

(*b*) Rom. xv. 30 f. *παρακαλῶ δὲ ὑμᾶς...συναγωνίσασθαί μοι ἐν ταῖς προσευχαῖς ὑπὲρ ἐμοῦ πρὸς τὸν θεόν, ἵνα ῥυσθῶ ἀπὸ τῶν ἀπειθούντων ἐν τῇ Ἰουδαίᾳ.* St Paul asks for his friends' intercession that in the visit to Jerusalem, which he hopes soon to make (*v.* 25) he may not *fall into the hands* of his Jewish enemies. The use of *ἀπό* is therefore obviously natural.

(*c*) 2 Thess. iii. 1, 2 *προσεύχεσθε, ἀδελφοί, περὶ ἡμῶν...ἵνα ῥυσθῶμεν ἀπὸ τῶν ἀτόπων καὶ πονηρῶν ἀνθρώπων.* This passage is an exact parallel to that discussed immediately above.

(*d*) 2 Tim. iv. 18 quoted and commented on above.

σώζειν. (i) *ἐκ.* (*a*) John xii. 27 *πάτερ, σῶσόν με ἐκ τῆς ὥρας ταύτης. ἀλλὰ διὰ τοῦτο ἦλθον εἰς τὴν ὥραν ταύτην.* At first sight the words *ἐκ τῆς ὥρας* and *εἰς τὴν ὥραν* seem to imply that the Lord speaks of Himself as having already entered upon 'the hour,' and that He asks to be brought safely through it. Such an interpretation in such a context appears unnatural. The key to the meaning lies in *ἀλλὰ διὰ τοῦτο*. The *ἀλλά* implies a contrast between the prayer *σῶσον ἐκ τῆς ὥρας ταύτης* and the consciousness of a purpose (*διὰ τοῦτο*). The *διὰ τοῦτο* is explained by the context; it points back to the thought of the fruitfulness of death (*v.* 24). The remembrance of the purpose, if we may so put it, corrects the prayer. This is substantially Chrysostom's interpretation *in loco*, *οὕτω τετάρακται ὡς καὶ ἀπαλλαγὴν ζητεῖν, εἴ γε ἐνῆν διαφυγεῖν. ταῦτα τῆς ἀνθρωπίνης φύσεως τὰ ἀσθενήματα...τῆς ταραχῆς τοῦτο ἀναγκαζούσης λέγειν, τὸ ἐναντίον λέγω.* Thus the prepositions *ἐκ* and *εἰς* represent the Lord as just passing within the shadow of the Cross. The *ἐκ* emphasises the idea of close proximity. 'Rescue me even now from full entrance into the hour of sorrow and death.' Comp. Matt. xxvi. 39.

(*b*) Hebr. v. 7 *δεήσεις τε καὶ ἱκετηρίας πρὸς τὸν δυνάμενον σώζειν αὐτὸν ἐκ θανάτου...προσενέγκας*. Here too the preposition *ἐκ* seems to express the nearness of the adverse power. It should be remembered that the phrase *ἐκ θανάτου* with *ῥύεσθαι, ἐξαιρεῖσθαι κ.τ.λ.* had become stereotyped in the LXX., where *ἐκ*, recalling the fuller phrase *ἐκ χειρός*, conforms with the Hebrew personification of Death. See Ps. xxxii. 19, lv. 14, cxiv. 8, Prov. x. 2, Job xxxiii. 30, Hos. xiii. 14 (*ἐκ χειρὸς ᾅδου ῥύσομαι καὶ ἐκ θανάτου λυτρώσομαι αὐτούς*). The parallels from the O. T. would not of themselves require us to reject the interpretation, 'to bring safely through and out of death'; but what is in itself the more natural meaning of the words, seems also to harmonise best with the unambiguous words of Matt. xxvi. 39.

(*c*) Jas. v. 20 *ὁ ἐπιστρέψας ἁμαρτωλὸν ἐκ πλάνης ὁδοῦ αὐτοῦ σώσει ψυχὴν αὐτοῦ ἐκ θανάτου.* This is no doubt the common O. T. use of the phrase *ἐκ θανάτου.*

(*d*) Jude 5 *Κύριος λαὸν ἐκ γῆς Αἰγύπτου σώσας.* The full meaning of *ἐκ* is here necessary.

(ii) *ἀπό.* (*a*) Matt. i. 21 *αὐτὸς γὰρ σώσει τὸν λαὸν αὐτοῦ ἀπὸ τῶν ἁμαρτιῶν αὐτῶν.* See the note on Tit. ii. 14, p. 78. Here the personal act of the Saviour is that on which the main emphasis rests.

(*b*) Acts ii. 40 *σώθητε ἀπὸ τῆς γενεᾶς τῆς σκολιᾶς ταύτης.* There is an instructive passage in Numb. xvi. bearing on the use of the phrase *σωθῆναι ἀπό.* In *v.* 21 Jehovah, as if He would destroy the whole people, bids Moses and Aaron go forth from their midst: *ἀποσχίσθητε ἐκ μέσου*[1] *τῆς συναγωγῆς ταύτης* (מִתּוֹךְ הָעֵדָה הַזֹּאת). On the other hand, when in answer to the intercession of Moses and Aaron Israel is spared and commanded to depart from the neighbourhood of Korah, the phraseology is changed: *ἀναχωρήσατε κύκλῳ ἀπὸ* (מִסָּבִיב לְ׳׳) *τῆς συναγωγῆς Κορέ* (*v.* 24), *ἀποσχίσθητε ἀπὸ* (מֵעַל) *τῶν σκηνῶν τῶν ἀνθρώπων* (*v.* 26, so *v.* 27). In the first command the idea expressed by the preposi-

[1] Comp. Is. lii. 11 (2 Cor. vi. 17), Jer. li. (xxviii.) 6, 45 (Apoc. xviii. 4).

tion is that of a disentanglement, an exodus; in the latter that of removal. In the passage from the Acts, the Greek in itself does not decide whether those addressed were themselves included in the *γενεὰ σκολιά*. Certain expressions in the Apostle's speech (*προσπήξαντες ἀνείλατε* v. 23; *γινωσκέτω πᾶς οἶκος Ἰσραὴλ...ὃν ὑμεῖς ἐσταυρώσατε* v. 36; comp. iii. 13 ff., 19, iv. 27 *σὺν ἔθνεσιν καὶ λαοῖς Ἰσραήλ*) seem to suggest that they were so included. The *ἀπό* however simply emphasises the idea of removal and escape.

(*c*) Rom. v. 9 *σωθησόμεθα δι' αὐτοῦ ἀπὸ τῆς ὀργῆς*. Here the *ἀπό* expresses the thought *εἰς κρίσιν οὐκ ἔρχεται* (John v. 24). See above p. 78 f. the note on 1 Thess. i. 10.

τηρεῖν. This verb in the N. T. is followed by *ἐκ* alone.
(*a*) Jn. xvii. 15 *ἐρωτῶ...ἵνα τηρήσῃς αὐτοὺς ἐκ τοῦ πονηροῦ*. The passage must be reserved for discussion later on (p. 109 ff.).

(*b*) Apoc. iii. 10 *κἀγώ σε τηρήσω ἐκ τῆς ὥρας τοῦ πειρασμοῦ τῆς μελλούσης ἔρχεσθαι ἐπὶ τῆς οἰκουμένης ὅλης, πειράσαι τοὺς κατοικοῦντας ἐπὶ τῆς γῆς*. The parallel in St John's Gospel (*σῶσόν με ἐκ τῆς ὥρας ταύτης* xii. 27, see above p. 80) suggests that the preposition here does not imply any actual participation in this 'temptation'; and this presumption is increased when we note the close similarity between this passage and the Lord's words recorded in Luke xxi. 35 f., *ἐπεισελεύσεται γὰρ ἐπὶ πάντας τοὺς καθημένους ἐπὶ πρόσωπον πάσης τῆς γῆς. ἀγρυπνεῖτε δὲ ἐν παντὶ καιρῷ δεόμενοι ἵνα κατισχύσητε ἐκφυγεῖν ταῦτα πάντα τὰ μέλλοντα γίνεσθαι*.

φυλάττειν. The only preposition which follows this verb is *ἀπό*.

(*a*) (*b*). In two passages a Hebraistic form of prohibition and warning is borrowed from the LXX. (where *φυλάξαι ἀπό* = שְׁמֹר (הִשָּׁמֵר) מִן; see Deut. xxiii. 9, Josh. vi. 18, Mic. vii. 5). In both these places the idea of complete avoidance is conveyed without any suggestion that the evil has been a dominating power. The two passages are:

Luke xii. 15 *ὁρᾶτε καὶ φυλάσσεσθε ἀπὸ πάσης πλεονεξίας*.

1 John v. 21 *τεκνία, φυλάξατε ἑαυτὰ ἀπὸ τῶν εἰδώλων*.

(*c*) 2 Thess. iii. 3 *ὁ κύριος...ὑμᾶς...φυλάξει ἀπὸ τοῦ πονηροῦ*. The discussion of this passage must be reserved (p. 112 ff.).

The constructions after the following verbs are specially worthy of note, inasmuch as each of these verbs in itself implies a definite state, deliverance out of which is secured.

ἐλευθεροῦν.

Rom. vi. 18, 22 *ἐλευθερωθέντες ἀπὸ τῆς ἁμαρτίας* (*v.* 17 *ἦτε δοῦλοι τῆς ἁμαρτίας*).

viii. 2 *ἠλευθέρωσέν σε* [*με*] *ἀπὸ τοῦ νόμου τῆς ἁμαρτίας καὶ τοῦ θανάτου* (vii. 23 *αἰχμαλωτίζοντά με* [*ἐν*] *τῷ νόμῳ τῆς ἁμαρτίας*).

viii. 21 *ἡ κτίσις ἐλευθερωθήσεται ἀπὸ τῆς δουλείας τῆς φθορᾶς* (*v.* 20 *τῇ γὰρ ματαιότητι ἡ κτίσις ὑπετάγη*).

Compare:

Rom. vii. 3 *ἐλευθέρα ἐστὶν ἀπὸ τοῦ νόμου* (*v.* 1 *δέδεται*).

1 Cor. ix. 19 *ἐλεύθερος γὰρ ὢν ἐκ πάντων πᾶσιν ἐμαυτὸν ἐδούλωσα.* Had the Apostle used the verb (*ἐλευθερωθεὶς ἐκ*...), he would have referred to an emancipation from a previous state of bondage. The actual phrase employed (*ἐλεύθερος ὢν ἐκ*...) shews that he wishes to emphasise the *completeness* of his freedom. This interpretation is confirmed by the fact that *πᾶσιν* (interpreted by what follows) shews that *πάντων* is masculine. Comp. vi. 12 (*ὑπό τινος*), vii. 23 (*δοῦλοι ἀνθρώπων*).

λύειν. (1) *ἀπό.* (*a*) Luke xiii. 15, 16 *οὐ λύει τὸν βοῦν αὐτοῦ... ἀπὸ τῆς φάτνης; ...οὐκ ἔδει λυθῆναι ἀπὸ τοῦ δέσμου τούτου;*

In the latter clause there is a slightly-supported variant *ἐκ.*

(*b*) 1 Cor. vii. 27 *λέλυσαι ἀπὸ γυναικός;*

(2) *ἐκ.* (*a*) Apoc. i. 5 *τῷ...λύσαντι ἡμᾶς ἐκ τῶν ἁμαρτιῶν ἡμῶν.* There is however some authority for *ἀπό.* Cf. Ps. cxxix. 8 *λυτρώσεται...ἐκ....*

(*b*) Apoc. xx. 7 *λυθήσεται ὁ Σατανᾶς ἐκ τῆς φυλακῆς αὐτοῦ.*

μετανοεῖν. (1) *ἀπό.* Acts viii. 22 *μετανόησον οὖν ἀπὸ τῆς κακίας σου ταύτης.* Comp. Hebr. vi. 1 *μετανοίας ἀπὸ νεκρῶν ἔργων.*

(2) *ἐκ.* Apoc. ii. 21 *οὐ θέλει μετανοῆσαι ἐκ τῆς πορνείας αὐτῆς.* So ix. 20 f., xvi 11[1].

[1] The construction of the following verbs also is worth remark: (1) *ἀγοράζειν* (*a*) *ἀπό* Apoc. xiv. 3, 4 (*ἀπὸ τῆς γῆς...ἀπὸ τῶν ἀνθρώπων*). (*b*) *ἐκ* Apoc. v. 9 (*ἐκ*

The preceding investigation leads to a clear result. On the one hand it shews that the distinction which has been drawn on *a priori* grounds between *ἀπό* and *ἐκ* after verbs expressing *deliverance, rescue,* &c. does not exhaust the matter. Indeed this theoretical distinction is but the point of departure for actual differences. *ἀπό,* the more colourless of the two prepositions, simply implies *removal from* the danger or adverse power, whether the person rescued has or has not been actually within its grasp. The mind is therefore left more free to dwell on the thought of the deliverer. On the other hand *ἐκ* is used when it is desired to emphasise the idea that the person rescued has been actually within the grasp of the enemy. Further however, through its greater sharpness and vividness of meaning it directs attention to the danger itself, and serves to bring out into special prominence either the imminent nature of the peril or the completeness of the deliverance.

The prepositions are therefore in many cases interchangeable. They express the same thing seen from two somewhat different points of view. As they had been both used in the LXX. to represent מִן, so they both stood ready to translate the Aramaic preposition (for we have seen the strongest reasons for believing that the Lord's Prayer existed originally in Aramaic) in the clause of the Prayer under discussion. The Apostles were obliged by the conditions of translation into Greek to give one or other of two slightly differing shades of meaning to what in the language in which the Lord first taught the Prayer was colourless. No doctrinal question is involved in the choice between the prepositions; for, to apply to the particular case the general conclusion stated above, while *ἀπὸ τοῦ πονηροῦ* lays the main stress on the thought of the deliverer and the fact of deliverance itself, *ἐκ τοῦ πονηροῦ* emphasises either the nearness and greatness of the

πάσης φυλῆς). So *ἐξαγοράζειν* Gal. iii. 13 (*ἐκ τῆς κατάρας*). (2) *ἀπέχεσθαι* (=to abstain) (*a*) simple genitive Acts xv. 20, 28 (*τῶν ἀλισγημάτων...εἰδωλοθύτων*). The construction in *v.* 29 is very instructive *ἐξ ὧν διατηροῦντες ἑαυτούς*. (3) *καθαρίζειν* always with *ἀπό* 2 Cor. vii. 1, Heb. ix. 14, 1 Jn. i. 7, 9. Comp. Acts xx. 26. So *δικαιοῦσθαι* Rom. vi. 7. (4) *μετατίθεσθαι* is followed by *ἀπό* in Gal. i. 6. (5) *χωρίζεσθαι* (*a*) *ἀπό* Acts i. 4 (*ἀπὸ Ἱεροσ.*), xviii. 2 (*ἀπὸ τῆς Ῥώμης*), Rom. viii. 35, 39, 1 Cor. vii. 10, Hebr. vii. 26. (*b*) *ἐκ* Acts xviii. 1 (*ἐκ τῶν Ἀθηνῶν*).

danger, or the completeness of the deliverance from Satan's assaults.

2. *The origin and use of the term ὁ πονηρός as applied to Satan.*

In investigating the origin and the meaning of the term ὁ πονηρός as applied to Satan, it will be convenient to keep two points as distinct as possible, viz. (*a*) the development of the conception which is expressed by the term; (*b*) the history and use of the term itself.

An adequate discussion of the first of these points would presuppose a consistent theory as to the composition and date of the different Books of the Old Testament, and a comprehensive study alike of the religious education of Israel as seen in the light of the religious thought of other Semitic peoples, and of later Jewish literature in its several branches. To such encyclopaedic knowledge I certainly lay no claim. But though fulness of treatment is altogether out of the question, some light may be thrown on the term under consideration by a sketch, however tentative and fragmentary, of the growth of this element in Jewish belief. It must however be premised that in such an attempt to summarise we must necessarily neglect any traces of divergences of thought among different schools, and be content to follow the main stream of opinion.

The method of divine revelation often lies in the absorption of some popular belief which is afterwards purified and spiritualised by a process of coordination. Within the confines of the Old Testament we can watch the growth of the conception of God, and we do not fear to admit that there were prehistoric elements out of which the religion of Israel came[1]. Still less need we hesitate to allow that, in the gradual working out of the conception of evil, Israel both in early and in later times borrowed largely from the ideas current among neighbours and conquerors, and learned both slowly and partially to harmonise these conceptions with the growing knowledge of a righteous, all-sovereign, spiritual God.

[1] Mr Aubrey Moore's Essay on *The Christian idea of God* in *Lux Mundi* p. 71.

The reserve of the Old Testament on the subject of super-human powers of evil is remarkable[1]. There is the mysterious riddle of 'Azazel' in the ceremonies of the Day of Atonement. There is the conception of creatures half animal, half supernatural, haunting desolate places (הַשְּׂעִירִם Lev. xvii. 7, לִילִית Is. xxxiv. 14), with which the Arabian Jinn should perhaps be compared[2]. Again, there is the bold figure drawn from the associations of earthly monarchy, according to which Jehovah is described as surrounded by His court (Isaiah vi.), a court which has its Doeg as well as its David, its treacherous spies as well as its faithful retainers (1 Kings xxii. 19 ff., Job i.; comp. Ps. lxxviii. 49, 1 Chron. xxi. 1). There is the narrative of the Fall in Gen. iii., a narrative which stands alone, and on which the possible allusions to it in other Books of the Old Testament (Job xxxi. 33, Hos. vi. 7, Is. xliii. 27 (?)) throw no light. Such are in the main the Old Testament ideas on the subject of super-human powers of evil. It is sufficient for our present purpose to note the absence in the Old Testament of any attempt to give them unity or cohesion.

Here as elsewhere the period of the exile had a lasting influence on Jewish thought. On the one hand, Babylonian demonology left its traces on the belief of the Jews. On the other, the Persian conception[3] of the two rival empires of good and evil doubtless helped forward the process by which something of coordination and even of unity was given to the divergent ideas of Israel as to adverse spiritual powers.

I give some indications from later Jewish literature of this latter tendency. In the Book of Enoch, for example, which was composed, roughly speaking, in the century before the Gospel era, though in its present form it may incorporate sections of later date, the angelology is very complicated. In the first part great stress is laid on the sin of the angels (Gen. vi. 2 f.) and the

[1] Comp. Oehler *Theology of the O. T.*, Eng. Tr., ii. p. 288 ff. I have found some useful hints in an article by C. H. Toy on *Evil Spirits in the Bible* in the *Journal of Biblical Literature*, Andover, Mass., Vol. ix. 1890 Pt. 1.

[2] Prof. Robertson Smith *The Religion of the Semites* p. 113 ff.

[3] Compare Dr Liddon's Sermon on *the Inspiration of Selection*: 'Its later literature may betray affinities, however we explain them, with Persian modes of thought.'

corruption of men which followed. Among these fallen spirits, though Semjazu is called their chief (cc. 6, 10), Azazel has the most conspicuous place as the depraver of mankind (c. 8), and afterwards (cc. 54, 55) appears as he who with all his hosts shall be judged by the Elect One of God. Further, it is remarkable that in the 'Parables' of a later part of the Book the problem is carried a stage further back, and behind the fallen angels there are seen spiritual tempters who led them astray.

In the Book of Wisdom (ii. 23 f.) the unity of evil in the personal enemy of God is emphasised. 'God created man for incorruption (ἐπ' ἀφθαρσίᾳ), and made him the image of His own Person (τῆς ἰδίας ἰδιότητος, v. l. ἀϊδιότητος); nevertheless through envy of the devil (φθόνῳ δὲ διαβόλου) death entered into the world, and they who are on the devil's side (οἱ τῆς ἐκείνου μερίδος ὄντες) make proof of it.'

Again, in what appears to be a Jewish portion of the Sibylline Oracles (iii. 36—92), the date of which is probably about 30 B.C.[1], Beliar appears as the great embodiment of the power of evil, who 'leads astray faithful and elect Hebrews and lawless men and others who have not yet heard the word of God.' But the flaming vengeance of God 'burns up Beliar and all the proud ones who put their trust in him.' Here Belial (or Beliar) is the Antichrist (comp. *Test. xii. Patriar.*, Levi 18 ὁ Βελίαρ δεθήσεται ὑπ' αὐτοῦ, Dan 5 αὐτὸς ποιήσει πρὸς τὸν Βελίαρ πόλεμον, Benj. 3 καταργήσει Βελίαρ καὶ τοὺς ὑπηρετοῦντας αὐτῷ, see below, p. 88 note)[2]. So, when the idea of Antichrist had taken a still more definite form, Belial and Antichrist are again identified. In the Judaeo-Christian writing, *the Ascension of Isaiah* (c. iv), Belial is the returning Nero. 'There shall descend Berial the mighty angel, king of this world, over which he ruleth since its creation, and he shall descend from his firmament in the form of a man, of the king of iniquity, the matricide—he is the king of this world—and he shall persecute the plant which the

[1] Friedlieb (p. xxvi), for reasons which seem convincing, places the date of this section just before the battle of Actium. This is the view of the majority of critics (Schürer *The Jewish People* Eng. Trans. Div. ii. Vol. iii. p. 283 f.).

[2] Note 2 Cor. vi. 15 τίς δὲ συμφωνία Χριστοῦ πρὸς Βελίαρ; In the *Testaments* Belial appears as the tempter of individual men in e.g. *Is.* 7, *Dan* 1, 4, *Aser* 1, *Joseph* 7, *Ben.* 6, 7.

twelve Apostles of the Chosen One planted. This angel Berial in the form of the king aforesaid shall come, and with him shall come all the armies of this world, and shall obey him in all things which he willeth.... He shall act and speak like the Chosen One, and shall say, 'I am God most high, and before me was there not any'...And after a thousand three hundred and thirty and two days the Lord shall come with His Angels and with the armies of the saints from the seventh heaven, and shall drag Berial into Gehenna and his armies withal[1].' In Antichrist Satan takes flesh and dwells among men. As this conception becomes more definite and concrete, it points with increasing clearness to the growth of the twofold conception of the unity of evil and its concentration in a person.

Again, an approach at any rate to this conception is indicated by two expressions which meet us in the New Testament. Of these the first, *ὁ ἄρχων τῶν δαιμονίων* (Matt. ix. 34, xii. 24; Mc. iii. 22; Lc. xi. 15), though it has more applications than one in Jewish writings[2], yet certainly implies the thought of an ordered polity of evil. The second, 'the God *or* Prince of this age *or* world' (2 Cor. iv. 4, John xii. 31, xiv. 30, xvi. 11; comp. Eph. ii. 2, vi. 12)[3], is doubtless to be connected with the conception of

[1] *Ascensio Isaiae*, ed. Dillmann, p. 18 f.

[2] Lightfoot, *Hor. Hebr.* on Lc. xi. 15, notes that "among the Jews we may observe three devils called the *chief* or *prince of the devils:* (1) 'The Angel of death'... (2) The devil Asmodeus...(3) Beelzebub."

[3] See the commentators on these passages, especially Meyer on 2 Cor. iv. 4, and the articles in Levy *Neuhebr. Wörterbuch* on שטן and שר. Phrases kindred to this are common in the *Testaments;* thus, *ὁ ἄρχων τῆς πλάνης* Sym. 2, Jud. 19; *ὁ ἄρχων ὑμῶν ἐστὶν ὁ Σατανᾶς* Dan 5. Notice the terms in which the victory of Messiah is described in Lev. 18, Jud. 25, Dan 5 f. In quoting these passages thus I am assuming the integrity of the book and that it represents the views of some early Judaeo-Christians (comp. Bp Lightfoot *Galatians* p. 307). On the other hand Schnapp holds that to an original pre-Christian Jewish document there have been added (a) apocalyptic passages by a Jewish interpolator, (b) references to the Lord's Person and work by a Christian interpolator. The effect of this theory would be rather to throw backward the date of passages which criticism allows to belong to the Jewish original document and to make them primary evidence for pre-Christian Jewish beliefs. The Christian interpolations, if such they are, bear in themselves evidence of an early date. In regard to the general subject of this note it is right to quote Edersheim's verdict (*Life and Times* ii. p. 755), 'We note that with the exception of the word *Satan*, none of the names given to the great enemy in the New Testament occurs in Rabbinic writings. More important still, the latter *contain no*

Antichrist, and like it witnesses to the existence of the belief that evil is gathered up into the person of a usurping spirit.

It remains briefly to discuss one remarkable conception of later Jewish teaching, which found expression in the Yetser ha Ra of the Rabbis. There were implanted in man at creation, it was held, a good and an evil impulse. Two points about this theory are worthy of note for our present purpose. In the first place there was at least a tendency to personify both these impulses in man[1]. Secondly we must distinguish, as far as date is concerned, the conception itself, and the formulas which embody it. For the latter an artificial interpretation of Gen. ii. 7 (the two 'י' in וייצר) was utilised by Rabbinic teachers. The good impulse is יצר טוב, the evil יצר רע. The idea itself was probably of much earlier date. We find traces of it in the Fourth Book of Esdras[1]. Against the error involved in this belief, viz., that God implanted evil in man at creation, much of the New Testament teaching on the subject of evil may be taken as a protest. There the absolute and eternal antagonism of God and evil is always emphasised, and the earnestness of this insistence was probably one important factor in the process which gave currency to the expression 'the evil one.'

Thus, to sum up, Jewish thought, as we catch glimpses of it in writings separated in time and place, was working towards the supreme ethical and spiritual contrast between good and evil, God and the devil, as well as towards the sure hope of the final and complete victory of good and of God, to which the Apostles and the Lord Himself, as His words are preserved for us by the Apostles, have set their seal.

We pass on to the second point, the proper meaning of the term ὁ πονηρός.

The word πονηρός is one of a large class of adjectives with the suffix -ρο-. It appears to be formed on the false analogy of such words as τολμη-ρό-ς, and is clearly a word of artificial, and therefore comparatively late, formation. Adjectives of this group, at least in a large number of instances, correspond with English

mention of a kingdom of Satan. In other words, the power of evil is not contrasted with that of good, nor Satan with God. The devil is presented rather as the enemy of man, than of God and of good. This marks a fundamental difference.'

[1] See the additional note p. 101.

adjectives in *-some* (e.g. toilsome, wearisome), and *-ful* (e.g. painful, fearful). When the root idea has a passive as well as an active side, the meaning of the adjective bifurcates. Thus ὀκνηρός 'fearful' has the sense of (1) timid: in Thuc. i. 142 ὀκνηρότεροι is set over against θρασύνοντες: (2) terrible—a rarer use: compare Soph. *O. T.* 834 ἡμῖν μέν, ὦναξ, ταῦτ' ὀκνηρά. The case is the same with πονηρός. The quasi-passive sense (i.e. 'he who endures labours') is seemingly rare, and early fell out of use. Thus in Hesiod (Frag. 43. 5) Hercules is called πονηρότατος καὶ ἄριστος.

The active sense (i.e. causing labour to others) is the basis of the common moral signification of the word.

In primitive society toil was of two kinds. Men fought, and they tilled the ground. Hence πόνος without any qualification came to mean 'fighting' (e.g. Hom. *Il.* vi. 77, Herod. iv. 1). On the other hand, when ἔργα (as in the title of Hesiod's poem, with which it is worth while to compare 1 Cor. iii. 9[1]), without further definition, meant *farming operations*, πόνος naturally signified *labour spent on the soil.* The brightest trait in the dream of a past golden age was that the soil brought forth fruit of its own accord, and needed no πόνος to be spent on it. The word πονηρός is according to this view primarily an agricultural term, and γῆ πονηρά would mean *soil requiring immoderate labour* i.e. *worthless soil.* Thus the idea of the word, if this account of its history be true, is that of intrinsic, absolute badness.

In later times at Athens the word acquired (*a*) a social, and (*b*) a quasi-political sense.

In the social sphere it was applied, by lovers of past days, to worthless citizens who had lost, or who never possessed, true patriotism, innovators, who stood to the true breed in the same relation as counterfeit coin to money rightly stamped and ringing true. This is the sense which the word bears in Aristophanes' picture of his times: see *Ranae* 731,

τοῖς δὲ χαλκοῖς καὶ ξένοις καὶ πυρρίαις
καὶ πονηροῖς κἀκ πονηρῶν εἰς ἅπαντα χρώμεθα
ὑστάτοις ἀφιγμένοισιν, οἷσιν ἡ πόλις πρὸ τοῦ
οὐδὲ φαρμακοῖσιν εἰκῇ ῥᾳδίως ἐχρήσατ' ἄν.

Here the notion is not of mischief but of irredeemable badness.

[1] Bp Lightfoot *Ordination Addresses* p. 214.

This social sense rapidly passed into a political sense. The word was used at Athens to denote the utterly worthless knave 'which Strepsiades aspired to become under the lessons of the sophist, and which the Aristophanic Cleon already is' (Prof. Jebb's note on Theophrastus' character of the φιλοπόνηρος). In this sense the word is used by Aristotle in the *Politics*, e.g. vi. 8 δοκεῖ δ' εἶναι τῶν ἀδυνάτων τὸ εὐνομεῖσθαι...πόλιν...πονηροκρατουμένην, viii. 11 πονηρόφιλον ἡ τυραννίς. In such a connexion the notion of 'mischievous' 'doing harm' naturally became attached to the word. But the thought is an accidental accretion, and is not of the essence of the meaning of the word. Thus when Chrysostom (v. 419), among ancient Christian writers, says that πονηρία is so called because it always brings trouble (πόνους)[1], and when, among moderns, Archbishop Trench (*Synonyms* p. 316) defines ὁ πονηρός as 'the active worker out of evil,' they start far down the stream of usage, and seem to overlook its earlier wanderings[2].

With this history and these associations the word passed into the Greek Bible.

In the LXX. it is used as the constant equivalent of the Hebrew רע. The root רעע signifies 'to break.' The Qal is used eight times, and in one of these passages viz. Jer. xi. 16 (וְרָעוּ דָּלִיּוֹתָיו) it has a passive sense, 'are broken.' It is probably from the intransitive use of the Qal that the commoner sense of רעע and of the participial adjective רע comes. 'To be broken,' 'to be vitiated or spoiled,' 'to be bad' is a natural and easy gradation. From this point of view it is not hard to see how this word is often used in reference to *sorrow* e.g. Gen. xxi. 12, 1 Sam. i. 8. This account is further confirmed by the use of the Hiphil. In Ps. xliv. 3, lxxiv. 3, Jerem. xxxi. 27, the Hiphil means not 'to make to break' but 'to make to be broken' i.e., 'to break.' Thus רע exactly answers to πονηρός. In the case of the Hebrew and the Greek word alike the notion of mischief, injuriousness, is

[1] Very cognate is Chrysostom's comment on Matt. vi. 13 κατ' ἐξοχὴν δὲ οὕτως ἐκεῖνος καλεῖται, διὰ τὴν ὑπερβολὴν τῆς κακίας, καὶ ἐπειδὴ μηδὲν παρ' ἡμῶν ἀδικηθεὶς ἄσπονδον πρὸς ἡμᾶς ἔχει τὸν πόλεμον. Here the point is the devil's malice.

[2] Comp. Origen's definition of πονηρία quoted p. 139.

often the particular side of evil which is contemplated[1]. But both primarily signify *utter, complete, essential badness.*

In the New Testament, so far at least as our Lord's sayings in the Gospels are concerned, the word *πονηρός* must be regarded as the equivalent of the Aramaic adjective which is reproduced for us by the Syriac Versions in the word ܒܝܫ. This adjective is of special importance, inasmuch as we may say with little short of certainty that it is the word originally employed by our Lord in the Lord's Prayer. Its exact meaning can be ascertained by a reference on the one hand to some passages of the Hebrew Bible, on the other to Syriac usage. In Hebrew the verb באש is used in the Qal literally of that which has a vile smell, e.g. Ex. vii. 18, 21; in the Niphal, Hiphil, and Hithpael it refers metaphorically to what is utterly abhorrent, e.g. 1 Sam. xiii. 4, Ex. v. 21, 1 Chron. xix. 6. Two nouns belonging to this root are used to denote worthless fruit or weeds in Is. v. 4 (Wherefore when I looked that it should bring forth grapes, brought it forth wild grapes? (בְּאֻשִׁים)) and Job xxxi. 40 (Let thistles grow instead of wheat, and cockle (בָאְשָׁה) instead of barley), passages which illustrate the use of *πονηρός* (translating the Syriac ܒܝܫ) in Matt. vii. 17. The corresponding adjective occurs once only in the Hebrew Bible, viz. Ezra iv. 12 (They are building the rebellious and bad (בִּאוּשְׁתָּא, LXX. *πονηράν*) city). Turning to the Syriac, the verb ܒܐܫ is used impersonally in the sense of 'to be evil in the eyes of'; in the Aphel it means 'to illtreat,' and is used to translate *κακοῦν* in Acts vii. 19, xii. 1. The adjective itself is characteristically used (see Payne Smith *Syr. Thes.*) of

[1] Dr Hatch's account of the word, *Essays in Biblical Greek* p. 77 ff., differs essentially from mine. Yet he writes at the beginning of his article 'The connotation of *πονηρός* in Classical Greek is probably best shown by Arist. *Eth. N.* 7. 11. p. 1152 *a*, where Aristotle, speaking of the *ἀκρατής*, says that what he does is wrong, and that he acts as a free agent, but that he is not wicked in himself, *ἑκὼν μὲν...πονηρὸς δ' οὔ· ἡ γὰρ προαίρεσις ἐπιεικής· ὥσθ' ἡμιπόνηρος. καὶ οὐκ ἄδικος· οὐ γὰρ ἐπίβουλος.*' This appears to me to be important evidence in confirmation of my view.

The proper Latin equivalent of *πονηρός* viz. *malus* has the same significance. There was however a tendency, for reasons which I shall point out later on (see p. 163 f.), to substitute for *malus*, when used of Satan, a compound word, *malignus* (=mali-genus).

death, a wound, a metal with alloy. Thus the Aramaic word, which πονηρός renders in the Gospels, expresses the notion not of harmfulness but of intrinsic worthlessness and hatefulness.

In the New Testament the Greek word is used of the diseased eye (Matt. vi. 23, opposed to ἁπλοῦς *v.* 22; the best commentary is perhaps vii. 3 ff.), of worthless fruit (Matt. vii. 17). In Matt. xiii. 49 οἱ πονηροί are parallel to τὰ σαπρά (comp. vii. 17). πονηρός stands in the same relation to φαῦλος (Jn. iii. 19, 20) as ἀγαθός does to καλός. Thus πονηρός is frequently the opposite to ἀγαθός Matt. v. 45 (comp. vii. 11), xii. 34 f., xx. 15, xxii. 10, Rom. xii. 9. The καρδία πονηρὰ ἀπιστίας (Heb. iii. 12) is at the extreme pole from καρδία καλὴ καὶ ἀγαθή (Lc. viii. 15); συνείδησις πονηρά from συνείδησις ἀγαθή (Acts xxiii. 1, 1 Tim. i. 5, 19, 1 Pet. iii. 16, 21; once καλὴ συνείδησις Heb. xiii. 18) and καθαρὰ συνείδησις (1 Tim. iii. 9, 2 Tim. i. 3)[1].

A further point is reached when we note that the word πονηρός in Jewish literature is specially used in connexion with supernatural powers of evil. Here no doubt the conception of activity in evil is often included in the associations of the word. But I believe that the primary sense of *essential badness* is still the main thought. Thus the words πνεῦμα πονηρόν are employed in the description of Saul's frenzy (πνεῦμα κυρίου ἀπέστη ἀπὸ Σαοὺλ καὶ ἔπνιγεν αὐτὸν πνεῦμα πονηρὸν (רוּחַ־רָעָה) παρὰ κυρίου...ἀφίστατο ἀπ' αὐτοῦ τὸ πνεῦμα τὸ πονηρόν (1 Sam. xvi. 14, 23). 'Evil angels' (ἄγγελοι πονηροί) are described in Ps. lxxviii. 49 as the ministers of divine vengeance upon apostate Israel. Asmodeus in Tobit (iii. 8) is τὸ πονηρὸν δαιμόνιον[2]. In the New Testament

[1] πονηρὰ ἔργα is found in Jn. iii. 19, vii. 7, 1 Jn. iii. 12, Col. i. 21. Commonly the deep root of evil deeds is contemplated (see especially Jn. iii. 19, 20). On the other hand ἀγαθά and καλά are both used frequently of good works, for the outward attractiveness of such works is often the point (see e.g. 1 Pet. ii. 12, Jn. x. 32). In 1 Thess. v. 21 πᾶν εἶδος πονηρόν is opposed to τὸ καλόν, where εἶδος makes all the difference. The phrase ὀφθαλμὸς πονηρός (Mc. vii. 22; comp. Deut. xv. 9, Prov. xxiii. 6, Ecclus. xxxiv. 13, &c.) no doubt implied the *baneful* glance of envy. But the phrase ὀφθαλμὸς ἀγαθός (Ecclus. xxx. 10 ἐν ἀγαθῷ ὀφθαλμῷ δόξασον τὸν κύριον, 12) used of the healthful, cheerful, look of content suggests that the true idea is that of the sickly, jaundiced eye of envy. Comp. *Pirqe Aboth* v. 29. Hebrew wisdom says that 'envy is the rottenness of the bones' (Prov. xiv. 30; comp. *Testaments* Sym. 3).

[2] Comp. Joseph. *de B. Jud.* vii. 6. 3 τὰ γὰρ καλούμενα δαιμόνια, ταῦτα δὲ πονηρῶν

the phrase *πνεύματα πονηρά* is common (Matt. xii. 45, Lc. vii. 21, viii. 2, xi. 26, Acts xix. 12 ff.; comp. *τὰ πνευματικὰ τῆς πονηρίας* Eph. vi. 12), as it is in the *Testaments of the xii Patriarchs* (e.g. Sym. 4, 6, Levi 5, 18, Aser 6 &c.).

We are now in a position to give a reasonable account of the origin and meaning of the expression *ὁ πονηρός*. St Matthew puts it into our Lord's mouth for the first time either in the Sermon on the Mount (v. 37, 39, vi. 13) or, if the masculine interpretation of these passages be denied, at least in xiii. 19 (*ἔρχεται ὁ πονηρός*), without a word of comment or explanation. The use of the phrase in the Gospels and in the Epistles leads us to suppose that it was one on which the Lord set the seal of His authority, not a chance expression in the apostolic rendering of the Lord's words. Further, it is clear that the phrase was current and in familiar use, at least in Christian circles, by the time the Gospel according to St Matthew was written.

The expression, we may venture to say, is the resultant of three converging influences. (1) We have remarked the tendency in Jewish thought to ascribe a unity to the conception of supernatural evil. (2) We have seen that the word *πονηρός* was characteristically used in reference to these spiritual powers[1]. (3) Once more, our Lord came to proclaim with a distinctness unknown before the supreme and perfect goodness of the Father in Heaven. In the teaching of Christ and His Apostles the Father is *ὁ ἀγαθός* (Matt. xix. 17, Mc. x. 18, Lc. xviii. 19, comp. probably 1 Pet. iii. 13), *ὁ ἀληθινός* (1 John v. 20, John xvii. 3). It was now possible and needful in the development of religious thought that men should learn that to the All-good is opposed the one who is absolutely evil[2]. It is the conception which is emphasised especially in St John's writings—*ἐν τῇ ἀληθείᾳ οὐκ ἔστηκεν, ὅτι οὐκ ἔστιν*

ἐστιν ἀνθρώπων πνεύματα, τοῖς ζῶσιν εἰσδυόμενα κ.τ.λ. This is said to be the only reference to demoniacal possession 'in the later pre-Christian Jewish period' (Toy's article in the *Journal of Biblical Literature* p. 29).

[1] The phrase *ὁ πονηρὸς ἄρχων* (Barn. iv. 13) exactly illustrates this stage of the history.

[2] This thought is strikingly brought out by Tertullian (*de Patientia* v.), Cum Deus optimus, diabolus e contrario pessimus, ipsa sui diversitate testantur neutrum alteri facere, ut nobis non magis a malo aliquid boni quam a bono aliquid mali editum videri possit.

ἀλήθεια ἐν αὐτῷ (viii. 44); *ἀπ' ἀρχῆς ὁ διάβολος ἁμαρτάνει* (1 John iii. 8). When the supreme contrast is thus made plain, it is not hard to see that the impersonal notion of malignity and mischief satisfies neither the expression itself nor the conditions of the divine teaching in which it lies embedded[1].

To sum up, while the expression, we may believe, first became current in the teaching of Christ and Christianity, it was not a sudden creation: the past in respect both of language and of theological conception had prepared the way for it.

The following are the passages (1) in the New Testament; (2) in early Christian literature, where *ὁ πονηρός* is used of Satan. I have not hesitated to include those passages where the incontrovertible evidence of accidence is unattainable.

(1) *New Testament.*

(*a*) Synoptic Gospels: only St Matthew.

v. 37. *ἔστω δὲ ὁ λόγος ὑμῶν ναὶ ναί, οὒ οὔ· τὸ δὲ περισσὸν τούτων ἐκ τοῦ πονηροῦ ἐστίν.*

Chrysostom, taking the words to refer to all oaths, gives the masculine interpretation of *ἐκ τοῦ πονηροῦ.*

v. 39. *ἐγὼ δὲ λέγω ὑμῖν μὴ ἀντιστῆναι τῷ πονηρῷ.*

Here again Chrysostom maintains a reference to Satan. *οὐκ εἶπε μὴ ἀντιστῆναι τῷ ἀδελφῷ, ἀλλὰ τῷ πονηρῷ· δεικνὺς ὅτι ἐκείνου κινοῦντος ταῦτα τολμᾶται* (vii. 234 E). It is difficult to resist Chrysostom's conclusion, and for these reasons. (1) The use of abstract terms seems alien to the spirit of the Sermon on the Mount; all there is concrete. Hence it is unlikely that *τῷ*

[1] I am altogether without the knowledge which is necessary for the discussion of the question how near Rabbinic teaching approached to this term *ὁ πονηρός*. I only offer one or two desultory remarks. (1) Bp Lightfoot quotes three passages from Rabbinic writings in which the name 'the evil one' is applied to Satan. Canon Cook (*Second Letter* p. 30) demurs to the force of these quotations for the conclusive reason that the word in each case is not רע but רשע. (2) In the Hebrew Bible רע, like *πονηρός* in the LXX., is used of adverse spiritual powers. The phrase יצר הרע is an important witness to a tendency to specialise the word. (3) In his article on יצר (*Chald. Wört.*) Levy refers to a remarkable passage, Suc. 52[a], where it is said that יצר הרע has seven names, the first of these being 'the evil one' (רע Gen. viii. 21). (4) I do not suppose that there is in the Rabbinic writings more than an approximation to the name 'the evil one.' Comp. Edersheim *Life and Times* ii. p. 755 quoted above p. 88 n.

πονηρῷ is neuter. (2) If however the gender is masculine, the reference is probably to Satan; for throughout this discourse Christ uses the language of paradox: He puts truths in their extreme and absolute form. Further, *ἀλλ' ὅστις*...seems to imply that a different person is spoken of from the one referred to in the previous clause. Otherwise *ἐάν δέ σε ῥαπίζῃ* (or the like) would have been the natural form of the sentence. (3) Canon Cook (*Second Letter* p. 17) condemns Chrysostom's exegesis as 'in direct opposition to the plainest injunctions of Scripture.' He probably refers to such words as *ἀντίστητε δὲ τῷ διαβόλῳ* (James iv. 7). But is not the A.V. as unscriptural as Chrysostom? For 'the plain injunction of Scripture' is *ἀποστυγοῦντες τὸ πονηρόν* (Rom. xii. 9). The fact is that, whether the word is masculine or neuter, the reference is to violence and persecution, and not to moral evil. Persecution is traced to Satan (e.g. Apoc. ii. 10); the Passion of Christ is notably so (see p. 108). It is the history of the Passion which supplies the clearest comment on the words. Christ's rebuke of St Peter when he smote the High-priest's servant together with the last miracle of healing is equally in point, whether the masculine or the neuter rendering be adopted. But the words of Christ which St Luke records, *ἀλλ' αὕτη ἐστὶν ὑμῶν ἡ ὥρα καὶ ἡ ἐξουσία τοῦ σκότους* (xxii. 53, comp. Col. i. 13, Acts xxvi. 18), i.e. the chosen opportunity of treacherous men and behind it the tyranny of Satan, seem to strengthen very greatly the case for the masculine rendering. Compare Jude 9. At first sight this interpretation of the passage seems to bring it into collision with 1 Pet. v. 9 (*ᾧ ἀντίστητε κ.τ.λ.*). But the thought of the Gospel is 'Do not be careful to withstand Satan's violence'; the thought of the Epistle is, 'Satan will try to make you traitors through persecution; stand firm against the tempter.' The contradiction therefore is only verbal.

vi. 13 *ῥῦσαι ἡμᾶς ἀπὸ τοῦ πονηροῦ.*

xiii. 19 *ἔρχεται ὁ πονηρός* (= *ὁ Σατανᾶς* Mc., *ὁ διάβολος* Lc.).

xiii. 38 *τὰ δὲ ζιζάνιά εἰσιν οἱ υἱοὶ τοῦ πονηροῦ.*

The masculine interpretation here is as old as Irenaeus (iv. 66. 2): see p. 160.

(*b*) St Paul's Epistles.

2 Thess. iii. 3 *πιστὸς δέ ἐστιν ὁ κύριος, ὃς στηρίξει ὑμᾶς καὶ φυλάξει ἀπὸ τοῦ πονηροῦ.* See below, p. 112 ff.

Gal. i. 4 *ὅπως ἐξέληται ἡμᾶς ἐκ τοῦ αἰῶνος τοῦ ἐνεστῶτος πονηροῦ.* The passage is discussed below, p. 115 ff.

Eph. vi. 16 *ἐν ᾧ δυνήσεσθε πάντα τὰ βέλη τοῦ πονηροῦ [τὰ] πεπυρωμένα σβέσαι.* Comp. *τὰς μεθοδίας τοῦ διαβόλου* (*v.* 11).

(*c*) St John's writings.

John xvii. 15 *ἐρωτῶ...ἵνα τηρήσῃς αὐτοὺς ἐκ τοῦ πονηροῦ.*

1 John ii. 13, 14 *νενικήκατε τὸν πονηρόν.* Comp. John xvi. 33 *ἐγὼ νενίκηκα τὸν κόσμον.*

1 John iii. 12 *οὐ καθὼς Καὶν ἐκ τοῦ πονηροῦ ἦν καὶ ἔσφαξεν τὸν ἀδελφὸν αὐτοῦ*[1]. Comp. John viii. 44.

1 John v. 18 f. *ὁ γεννηθεὶς ἐκ τοῦ θεοῦ τηρεῖ αὐτόν, καὶ ὁ πονηρὸς οὐχ ἅπτεται αὐτοῦ...ὁ κόσμος ὅλος ἐν τῷ πονηρῷ κεῖται.*

(*d*) There are three passages in which there is evidence that in some forms of the text the phrase 'the evil one' was introduced.

Matt. xiii. 38 f. The Old Syriac reads: 'The tares are the children of the evil one (ܕܒܝܫܐ), and *the sower he is the evil one* (ܒܝܫܐ).

Acts x. 38. The Vulgate Syriac in translating the phrase *πάντας τοὺς καταδυναστευομένους ὑπὸ τοῦ διαβόλου* represents the last words by ܡܢ ܒܝܫܐ.

For the Syriac Versions see p. 154 ff.

Matt. xiii. 28 (*ἐχθρὸς ἄνθρωπος τοῦτο ἐποίησεν*). Origen in a Homily on Ps. xxxvi. (Hom. ii. § 4), as it is preserved in the translation of Rufinus, says, 'Sed et Dominus in Evangelio diabolum non dixit peccatorem tantummodo, sed malignum vel malum, et cum docet in oratione, vel dicit: Sed libera nos a malo. Et alibi, *malus homo fecit, sive malignus.*' This implies the reading *ὁ πονηρός* or *πονηρὸς ἄνθρωπος*. The words however may be a slip of memory[2].

[1] This passage seems to underlie Theophilus *ad Autol.* ii. 29 *ἡνίκα ἑώρα [ὁ Σατανᾶς] τὸν Ἄβελ εὐαρεστοῦντα τῷ θεῷ, ἐνεργήσας εἰς τὸν ἀδελφὸν αὐτοῦ τὸν καλούμενον Καὶν ἐποίησεν ἀποκτεῖναι τὸν ἀδελφὸν αὐτοῦ τὸν Ἄβελ.* This treatise, it will be remembered, contains 'the earliest quotation of St John's Gospel by name which has been preserved' (Bp Westcott *Canon* p. 228).

[2] Compare Esther vii. 6 *ἄνθρωπος ἐχθρὸς Ἀμὰν ὁ πονηρὸς οὗτος.*

(2) *Early Christian Literature.*

Ep. Barnabas ii. 10 ἵνα μὴ ὁ πονηρὸς παρείσδυσιν πλάνης ποιήσας ἐν ἡμῖν ἐκσφενδονήσῃ ἡμᾶς ἀπὸ τῆς ζωῆς ἡμῶν.

xix. 11 εἰς τέλος μισήσεις τὸν πονηρόν. The reading however is doubtful. (1) *Documentary evidence.* Of the two oldest MSS. *Cod. Sinaiticus* (א) omits the article; *Cod. Constantinopolitanus* (C) has τό. The other Greek MSS., which, as they seem to be derived from a common archetype (Gebhardt *Proleg.* p. x.), are represented by a common symbol (G), have τόν. The Latin Version[1] (L) is clear for the masculine (malus odiosus tibi erit in perpetuum). Gebhardt's general view (p. xxxvii.) is 'Multo saepius in veris quam in falsis L cum G convenit, ita ut his ambobus haud raro codicum א et C consensum postponendum esse duxerim.' In this passage the omission in א before πον- slightly favours τόν. On the whole therefore the evidence of the MSS. leans towards τόν. (2) *Internal evidence.* (*a*) ἀγρυπνοῦντες...ἐπὶ τὸ πονηρόν (xx. 2) is, I think, the only certain instance of τὸ πονηρόν in Barnabas. (*b*) On the one hand the neuter gains some probability from iv. 1 μισήσωμεν τὴν πλάνην τοῦ νῦν καιροῦ, iv. 10 μισήσωμεν τελείως τὰ ἔργα τῆς πονηρᾶς ὁδοῦ, xix. 2 μισήσεις πᾶν ὃ οὐκ ἔστιν ἀρεστὸν τῷ θεῷ, μισήσεις πᾶσαν ὑπόκρισιν. But on the other hand the antithesis suggested by the words (ἀγαπήσεις τὸν ποιήσαντά σε) at the beginning of the chapter (xix. 2) distinctly favours the masculine τόν. Further, while the certain use of ὁ πονηρός in ii. 10 is a strong argument, there is nothing in the context to suggest a reminiscence of St Paul's words ἀποστυγοῦντες τὸ πονηρόν (Rom. xii. 9). The lines of evidence therefore appear to converge in favour of τόν[2].

[1] The date of this Version is uncertain. On the one hand traces of the influence of the Vulgate are wanting. On the other it does not appear to have been known to Jerome. Gebhardt (p. lv.) approves the general conclusion 'eam ante seculi vii exitum conscriptam esse credas; verisimile vero videtur eam multo antiquiorem esse.'

[2] Dr Taylor (*Expositor*, Third Series, vol. iii. p. 408) argues in favour of the reading τό. But (1) his view that μισήσεις τὸ πονηρόν is an 'abbreviated form' of μισήσεις πᾶσαν ὑπόκρισιν καὶ πᾶν ὃ μὴ ἀρεστὸν τῷ κυρίῳ (*Didaché* iv.), a phrase which Barnabas (inverting the order of the clauses) has already incorporated (xix. 2), seems unnatural; (2) he appears to neglect the angelology of Barnabas; see the passages quoted below p. 99 n.

xxi. 3 *ἐγγὺς ἡ ἡμέρα ἐν ᾗ συναπολεῖται πάντα τῷ πονηρῷ.* Compare *The Ecclesiastical Canons* 14. In this passage the interpretation, as in the passage just discussed, the reading is doubtful. The Latin Version has the equally ambiguous 'cum malo.' The following considerations favour the masculine. (1) Just above it is said, *ὁ ἐκεῖνα* (i.e. the deeds of 'the evil way') *ἐκλεγόμενος μετὰ τῶν ἔργων αὐτοῦ συναπολεῖται.* Here there is the same combination of the masculine and the neuter. A common destruction of the worker and his works is spoken of. (2) This interpretation of a clause at the end of the description of 'the evil way' corresponds with the opening definition *ἡ τοῦ μέλανος ὁδός*[1]. (3) There is an earlier passage (xv. 5) which would be decisive if the reading were beyond dispute: *ὅταν ἐλθὼν ὁ υἱὸς αὐτοῦ καταργήσει τὸν καιρὸν τοῦ ἀνόμου καὶ κρινεῖ τοὺς ἀσεβεῖς καὶ ἀλλάξει τὸν ἥλιον καὶ τὴν σελήνην καὶ τοὺς ἀστέρας κ.τ.λ.* In G however we find *αὐτοῦ* in place of *τοῦ ἀνόμου*, the word being perhaps repeated from *ὁ υἱὸς αὐτοῦ* just before. Cod. א provokingly omits the word altogether. L has 'tempus iniquitatis.' The *τοῦ ἀνόμου* of C, which was long ago conjectured by Bp Fell, seems to explain the variations. It is supported by xviii. 2 *ὁ μέν ἐστιν κύριος...ὁ δὲ ἄρχων καιροῦ τοῦ νῦν τῆς ἀνομίας*, a passage which probably suggested the emendation of L. Compare iv. 9 *ἐν τῷ ἀνόμῳ καίρῳ.* If *τοῦ ἀνόμου* is thought the best supported reading, it is almost conclusive in favour of the masculine interpretation of *τῷ πονηρῷ*[2].

[1] Happily we are saved from a discussion of gender by the other passage in Barnabas where the term occurs, *ἵνα· μὴ σχῇ παρείσδυσιν ὁ μέλας* (iv. 9). This remarkable name is probably of Hebrew origin (see Harnack's note), but it serves here to emphasise the contrast: *ἡ ὁδὸς τοῦ φωτός* (xix. 1), *ἐφ' ἧς ... εἰσὶν τεταγμένοι φωταγωγοὶ ἄγγελοι θεοῦ.* It should be considered in connexion with the baptismal custom of turning to the west and renouncing Satan: compare Cyril of Jerusalem *Catech.* xix. *Myst.* i. 4 (*ἀποτάσσεσθε τῷ σκοτεινῷ ἐκείνῳ καὶ ζοφερῷ ἄρχοντι*).

[2] The following passages in the Epistle should be noted: *ἡμερῶν οὖν οὐσῶν πονηρῶν καὶ αὐτοῦ τοῦ ἐνεργοῦντος* (L. contrarius) *ἔχοντος τὴν ἐξουσίαν* (ii. 1); *ἵνα μήποτε ...ὁ πονηρὸς ἄρχων λαβὼν τὴν καθ' ἡμῶν ἐξουσίαν ἀπώσηται ἡμᾶς ἀπὸ τῆς βασιλείας τοῦ κυρίου* (iv. 13); *ἄγγελος πονηρὸς ἐσόφιζεν αὐτούς* (ix. 4); *ἐφ' ἧς δὲ ἄγγελοι τοῦ Σατανᾶ* (xviii. 1). A parallel can be found in Jewish Apocalyptic literature to (a) the *neuter*, 4 Esdras vi. 27, Delebitur enim malum et extinguetur dolus, a passage found in the Syriac, the Aethiopic (iv. 32), the Arabic (malum cor recedet ab iis), the Armenian Versions; comp. viii. 53; (b) the *masculine*; *Assumptio Moyseos* x. 1, Et tunc parebit regnum illius in omni creatura illius et tunc *Zabulus* finem habebit, et

Letter of the Churches of Vienne and Lyons (Eus. *H. E.* v. 1) *δυνάμενοι διὰ τῆς ὑπομονῆς πᾶσαν τὴν ὁρμὴν τοῦ πονηροῦ εἰς ἑαυτοὺς ἑλκύσαι*[1]. See below, p. 132.

Clementine Homilies (*a*) *Epist. Clem. ad Jac.* i. *ἐπὶ τοῦ ἐνεστῶτος πονηροῦ τὸν ἐσόμενον ἀγαθὸν ὅλῳ τῷ κόσμῳ μηνύσας βασιλέα.* See below, p. 116.

(*b*) *ib.* iv. *δικαίως συνενθυμήθητί μοι, πότε σου τῆς συμμαχίας χρείαν ἔχει ὁ χριστός, νῦν ὅτε ὁ πονηρὸς κατὰ τῆς αὐτοῦ νύμφης πόλεμον ἤρατο, ἢ εἰς τὸν ἐπιόντα χρόνον ὅτε νικήσας βασιλεύσει;*

(*c*) Hom. xix. 2 *καὶ ὁ Πέτρος· ἀδύνατόν ἐστί μοι φωνὴν τοῦ ἐμοῦ ἀρνήσασθαι διδασκάλου, διὸ καὶ ὁμολογῶ εἶναι τὸν πονηρόν κ.τ.λ.* See below, p. 133.

It may be suggested that the connexion of the word *ὁ πονηρός* with sayings of our Lord in the last of these passages from the 'Clementines' (see p. 133), together with the fact that the term is used by St Matthew alone among the Synoptists and with the use of the term in the Syriac Versions (see p. 155), is an indication that this was a usual designation for Satan in the Aramaic Gospel, oral and written, on which were based 'the Gospel according to the Hebrews' and our Gospel according to St Matthew.

Clem. Alex. *Paedagogus* (*a*) i. 7 *οὗτος* (i.e. the angel who wrestled with Jacob and who was the Paedagogus) *ἦν ὁ ἄνθρωπος ὁ ἄγων καὶ φέρων, ὁ συγγυμναζόμενος καὶ ἀλείφων κατὰ τοῦ πονηροῦ τὸν ἀσκητὴν Ἰακώβ....πτερνίζειν διδάσκων τὸν ἀνταγω-*

tristitia *cum eo* abducetur. The latter passage is obviously the closer parallel to our present passage. Compare Edersheim *Life and Times* ii. p. 441, "In the latter [the renewed earth] neither physical nor moral darkness would any longer prevail, since the *Yetser ha Ra*, or 'Evil impulse,' would be destroyed (*Yalkut* i. p. 45 c)."

[1] If Melito's treatise *τὰ περὶ τοῦ διαβόλου καὶ τῆς ἀποκαλύψεως Ἰωάννου* (Eus. *H.E.* iv. 26) had been preserved, the usage of an important school would doubtless have been made clear to us. In the *Martyrdom of Polycarp* xvii. (*ὁ δὲ ἀντίζηλος καὶ βάσκανος καὶ πονηρός, ὁ ἀντικείμενος τῷ γένει τῶν δικαίων*) there is some *slight* authority for the omission of *καὶ* before *πονηρός*. The following passage from Athenagoras *Supplicatio* c. 24 illustrates the meaning of *ὁ πονηρός* and probably implies its currency as a name for Satan, *οὗτός τε ὁ τῆς ὕλης καὶ τῶν ἐν αὐτῇ εἰδῶν ἄρχων...οὗτος δὲ ἀμελήσας καὶ πονηρὸς περὶ τὴν τῶν πεπιστευμένων γενόμενος διοίκησιν...ὁ δὲ τῆς ὕλης ἄρχων...ἐναντία τῷ ἀγαθῷ τοῦ θεοῦ ἐπιτροπεύει καὶ διοικεῖ...ὁ δὲ θεὸς τελείως ἀγαθὸς ὤν κ.τ.λ.*

νιστήν. It is possible that the clause of the Lord's Prayer is in Clement's mind.

(*b*) ii. 12. *ἤδη δὲ καὶ φανερώτατα τοῦ πονηροῦ σύμβολα οὐκ αἰσχύνονται περικείμεναι. ὡς γὰρ τὴν Εὔαν ὁ ὄφις ἠπάτησεν, οὕτω δὲ καὶ τὰς ἄλλας γυναῖκας ὁ κόσμος ὁ χρυσοῦς δελέατι προσχρώμενος τοῦ ὄφεως τῷ σχήματι ἐξέμηνεν εἰς ὕβρεις.*

(*c*) ii. 12. *ἐκχέουσιν ἑταιρικῶς τὸν πλοῦτον εἰς ὄνειδος· καὶ τοῦ θεοῦ τὰ δωρήματα ἀπειροκαλίᾳ παραχαράττουσι, ζηλοῦσαι τοῦ πονηροῦ τὴν τέχνην.*

On the passages of Tertullian where *malus* is used as a name of Satan, see below, p. 135 f.

It is probable that there are other passages even in the scanty remains of the Christian literature of the second century which have come down to us, in which this name of Satan is used. It hardly seems however to have gained a wide currency till the days of formal New Testament exegesis[1]. Justin Martyr does not mention it either in *Apol.* i. 28 (*ὁ ἀρχηγέτης τῶν κακῶν δαιμόνων ὄφις καλεῖται καὶ Σατανᾶς καὶ διάβολος*) or in *Dial.* 103[2], although in *Dial.* 125 there is an apparent allusion to the term, *προσῆλθεν αὐτῷ ὁ διάβολος, τουτέστιν ἡ δύναμις ἐκείνη ἡ καὶ ὄφις κεκλημένη καὶ Σατανᾶς, πειράζων αὐτόν...ὁ δὲ αὐτὸν κατέλυσε καὶ κατέβαλεν, ἐλέγξας ὅτι πονηρός ἐστι.* In the passages in which the name occurs it has every appearance of being a term in recognised, though not common, use.

Note on the *Yetser ha Ra* (see p. 89).

A few points in this complicated subject may be touched upon in a note. (1) On the *Yetser* see Levy *Chald. Wörterbuch* i. p. 342, *Neuhebr. u. Chald. Wörterb.* ii. p. 757 ff.; Weber *System der Altsynagogalen Palästinischen Theologie* § 54 (p. 242 ff.), comp. pp. 208 f., 216, 223 f.; Edersheim *The Life and Times of Jesus the Messiah* i. p. 52, ii. p. 757 ff. Several questions, as it will appear, suggest themselves, a full investigation of which would throw light on many points of great interest, as, for example, St Paul's doctrine of the Fall. (2) If an amateur in such studies may trust his super-

[1] Thus for *τὰς ἐνέδρας τοῦ διαβόλου* (Ignat. *Trall.* viii.) the Interpolator in the 4th century substitutes *τὰς ἐνέδρας τοῦ πονηροῦ.*

[2] Comp. Apoc. xii. 9 *ἐβλήθη ὁ δράκων ὁ μέγας, ὁ ὄφις ὁ ἀρχαῖος, ὁ καλούμενος διάβολος καὶ ὁ Σατανᾶς*, xx. 2.

ficial observation, the article is commonly present in the one case, wanting in the other (יצר הרע, יצר טוב). If so, the tendency to personification was more active in regard to the evil impulse. This is what we should have expected, since it would be felt that the good impulse would ultimately flow from God. It should be noticed that Levy and Weber represent different views as to the personification of these two impulses. 'Welche beide Triebe als Engel personificirt,' writes the former (ii. p. 258). The criticism of the latter runs thus (p. 228): 'Auch Levy *Chal. W. B.* i. 342 nennt ihn den 'bösen Engel,' aber identisch sind sie nicht. Sofern der Jezer und der Satan die gleiche gottwidrige Absicht haben, wirkt dieser durch jenen und ist in ihm die bewegende Kraft; so kann es geschehen, dass Eines für das Andere steht, ohne dass Beides zusammenfällt. Allerdings ist die Neigung, beide Begriffe zu verschmelzen, in der späteren jüdischen Theologie gewachsen. Zu *Kidduschin* (81[a]) bemerkt Raschi: Es erschien ihm Satan, welcher der Jezer hara ist.' Thus Weber admits a relative personification. (3) The passages in 4 Esdras referred to above (p. 89) are these: iv. 30 Quoniam granum seminis mali seminatum est in corde Adam ab initio, et quantum impietatis generavit usque nunc, et generat usque dum veniat area[1]. iii. 21 Cor enim malignum baiulans primus Adam transgressus et victus est, sed et omnes qui de eo nati sunt. (4) I cannot help suspecting that the conception of the *two impulses* is closely allied to the conception of the *two ways*, and that the tendency to personification in the one case is closely akin to a similar tendency in the other case. It will be remembered that in the *Didaché* and the documents which seem directly based on it there is no reference to any connexion between 'the two ways' and spiritual powers. In other documents such a reference has the appearance of being a later addition. If so, the *Didaché* presents us with 'the two ways' in a more original form. For these two points viz. (a) the connexion between the *two impulses* and the *two ways*, (b) the allied processes of personification, compare the following passages, *Test. xii. Patriarch.* Jud. 20 δύο πνεύματα σχολάζουσι τῷ ἀνθρώπῳ, τὸ τῆς ἀληθείας καὶ τὸ τῆς πλάνης· καὶ μέσον ἐστὶ τὸ τῆς συνέσεως τοῦ νοός, οὗ ἐὰν θέλῃ κλῖναι. Aser 1 δύο ὁδοὺς ἔδωκεν ὁ θεὸς τοῖς υἱοῖς τῶν ἀνθρώπων, καὶ δύο διαβούλια, καὶ δύο πράξεις, καὶ δύο τόπους (v. l. τρόπους), καὶ δύο τέλη...ὁδοὶ δύο, καλοῦ καὶ κακοῦ· ἐν οἷς εἰσὶ τὰ δύο διαβούλια ἐν στέρνοις ἡμῶν διακρίνοντα αὐτάς. ἐὰν οὖν ἡ ψυχὴ θέλῃ ἐν καλῷ, πᾶσα πρᾶξις αὐτῆς ἐστὶν ἐν δικαιοσύνῃ, κἂν ἁμάρτῃ εὐθὺς μετανοεῖ... ἐὰν δὲ ἐν πονηρῷ κλίνει τὸ διαβούλιον, πᾶσα πρᾶξις αὐτῆς ἐστὶν ἐν πονηρίᾳ, καὶ ἀπωθούμενος τὸ ἀγαθὸν προσλαμβάνει τὸ κακὸν καὶ κυριευθεὶς ὑπὸ τοῦ Βελίαρ, κἂν ἀγαθὸν πράξει, ἐν πονηρίᾳ αὐτὸ μεταστρέφει.... ὁ θησαυρὸς τοῦ διαβόλου (v. l. διαβουλίου) ἰοῦ πονηροῦ πνεύματος πεπλήρωται. The Latin Fragment published by Gebhardt in Harnack *Die Lehre &c.* p. 277: Viae duae sunt in seculo, vitae et mortis, lucis et tenebrarum. In his constituti sunt angeli duo, unus aequitatis, alter iniquitatis.

[1] Compare vii. 92 (part of the 'Missing Fragment,' ed. Prof. Bensly p. 67), Ordo primus, quoniam cum labore multo certati sunt ut vincerent cum eis plasmatum cogitamentum malum, ut non eas seducat a vita in mortem.

Barn. xviii., xix. Hermas *Mand.* vi. 1. 2 ἀλλὰ νῦν θέλω σοι, φησίν, δηλῶσαι καὶ τὰς δυνάμεις αὐτῶν, ἵνα νοήσῃς τίς αὐτῶν τίνα δύναμιν ἔχει καὶ ἐνέργειαν. διπλαῖ γάρ εἰσιν αἱ ἐνέργειαι αὐτῶν· κεῖνται οὖν ἐπὶ δικαίῳ καὶ ἀδίκῳ· σὺ οὖν πίστευε τῷ δικαίῳ, τῷ δὲ ἀδίκῳ μὴ πιστεύσῃς· τὸ γὰρ δίκαιον ὀρθὴν ὁδὸν ἔχει, τὸ δὲ ἄδικον στρεβλήν... ἀρέσκει μοι, φημί, κύριε, ταύτῃ τῇ ὁδῷ πορεύεσθαι. πορεύσῃ, φησί, καὶ ὃς ἂν ἐξ ὅλης καρδίας ἐπιστρέψῃ πρὸς κύριον, πορεύσεται ἐν αὐτῇ. ἄκουε νῦν, φησί, περὶ τῆς πίστεως· δύο εἰσὶν ἄγγελοι μετὰ τοῦ ἀνθρώπου, εἷς τῆς δικαιοσύνης καὶ εἷς τῆς πονηρίας. The whole passage should be studied. (5) Dr C. Taylor (*Sayings of the Jewish Fathers* p. 144) assumes without question that the teaching about *Yetser* was current in our Lord's time, and conjectures that the original form of ἀπὸ τοῦ πονηροῦ may have been מיצר הרע. The evidence of the Syriac Versions is sufficient to disprove this latter conjecture. But the two passages which Dr Taylor quotes from the Targum bring the phrase into a closer connexion with the word which I suppose that the Lord actually used: '"Lest mine enemy say, I have prevailed against him" (Ps. xiii. 5) becomes in the Targum, "Lest יצרא בישא say, &c." "They shall bear thee up in their hands, lest thou stumble against [יצרא בישא which is like] a stone" (Ps. xci. 12).'

3. *Is ἀπὸ τοῦ πονηροῦ masculine or neuter?*

(i). Evidence derived from the Gospels.

(*a*) *The Baptism and the Temptation.*

No sooner has the Lord been publicly set apart for the ministry by the heavenly voice and the gift of the Holy Spirit, than He enters the field of conflict with the devil. Gathering up humanity into Himself, 'He gathered up that ancient and primeval quarrel against the serpent[1].' The Temptation was no casual and accidental parenthesis in the Lord's life: it was essential to its reality and, if we may say so, to its completeness. The Temptation was an epitome of His whole life[2].

The Lord's Prayer is the Prayer of redeemed humanity taught to men by the Son of Man. We should expect to find reflected here something of what, as He learned by suffering, is most characteristic of human life. We feel that the remembrance of the pain endured in this necessary conflict inspires the words.

[1] Iren. v. xxi. 2 Non autem Dominus antiquam illam et primam adversus serpentem inimicitiam in semetipso recapitulatus fuisset...si ab alio venisset patre.

[2] οἱ διαμεμενηκότες μετ' ἐμοῦ ἐν τοῖς πειρασμοῖς μου (Luke xxii. 28).

Every clause of the Prayer, I believe, stands forth with greater sharpness and clearness of meaning when seen in the light of the Lord's Temptation.

Our Father which art in heaven: The proclamation of the Heavenly Sonship is in order of time the preface, and in the subtleties of the spiritual conflict the occasion, of the Temptation. 'And lo, a voice out of the heavens, saying, This is my beloved Son, in whom I am well pleased.' 'If thou art the Son of God, command that these stones become bread.... If thou art the Son of God, cast thyself down.'

Hallowed be thy name. Thy kingdom come. The two earliest petitions in the Prayer seem closely linked with the temptation which stands last in St Matthew's record. The refusal to fall down and worship the tempter and the vindication of God's exclusive right to worship were a complete hallowing of the Name. The devil's offer of the possession of all the kingdoms of the world and the glory of them appealed to the desire for the cessation of conflict, which inspires the prayer for the coming of the divine kingdom.

Thy will be done, as in heaven, so on earth. In the Lord's firm resistance of the temptation to claim the letter of a divine promise, in His recognition of the limits of the divine purpose concerning Him, we can discern a perfect doing of the will of the Father on earth on the part of Him who 'in the beginning...was with God.'

Give us this day our daily bread. 'And when he had fasted forty days and forty nights, he afterward hungered. And the tempter came and said unto him, If thou art the Son of God, command that these stones become bread.' Lack of daily bread was the ἀφορμή of the tempter in the first assault.

And forgive us our debts, as we also have forgiven our debtors. It is most true that temptation begat no sin in Christ to need forgiveness. But it is worthy of remark that He came straight to the conflict with Satan, after He had received what to other men was βάπτισμα μετανοίας εἰς ἄφεσιν ἁμαρτιῶν (Mc. i. 4).

And bring us not into temptation. The word which St Mark (i. 12) uses to express the action of the Spirit—καὶ εὐθὺς τὸ πνεῦμα αὐτὸν ἐκβάλλει εἰς τὴν ἔρημον—denotes, not indeed compulsion, but a constraining influence. 'In the days of his flesh' the Son of Man shrank back from the strain and horror of the lonely conflict. He 'suffered being tempted.' Therefore as He Himself in the later hour of a severer struggle besought His Father that 'the cup might pass from Him,' He permitted and taught His disciples to pray that their Father in Heaven would spare them the perilous honour of temptation.

But deliver us from—the evil one or *evil.* Which of these two renderings is more natural? May we not ask which necessarily follows from a consideration of the Prayer regarded from the point of view of Christ's Temptation? It is difficult to imagine that the analogy between the two breaks down in the last clause, and that the prominence of the tempter in the history has no counterpart in the Prayer[1].

(*b*) *The Lord's Prayer.* It has been sometimes urged that it is inconceivable that a Prayer which begins with an appeal to God as Father, should end with a petition for deliverance from the devil. The assumption is that according to this interpretation the thought of the devil is suddenly and violently dragged into an alien context. The comparison of the Prayer with the circumstances of the Lord's Temptation will have gone far to break the force of this argument.

A more detailed examination of the clauses of the Prayer will, if I mistake not, shew clearly that underlying the whole there is the conception of the supreme conflict. The representation of the devil in the New Testament is of one who parodies the character and work of God. God realises the ideal in all His relations to men. As Father, as Guide, as King, He is ὁ ἀλη-

[1] A friend has pointed out to me that Dean Plumptre in his Commentary on St Matthew in Bp Ellicott's *New Test. Commentary for English Readers* makes the parallel between the facts of the Temptation and the last two clauses an argument for the masculine rendering of ἀπὸ τοῦ πονηροῦ. The feeling of this analogy underlies a passage of Dionysius of Alexandria quoted below, p. 139 f. The point was indeed touched upon by Bp Lightfoot in the second of his three letters to the *Guardian*: "Nor is it an insignificant fact that only two chapters before the Evangelist has recorded how the Author of this prayer found Himself face to face with temptation (iv. 1, 3) and was delivered from the 'Evil One.'"

θινός. In all these directions the devil opposes God by imitating Him[1].

Our Father which art in heaven. Contrast οἱ υἱοὶ τοῦ πονηροῦ (Matt. xiii. 38), ὑμεῖς ἐκ τοῦ πατρὸς τοῦ διαβόλου ἐστέ (John viii. 44), υἱὲ διαβόλου (Acts xiii. 10). So 1 John iii. 10 φανερά ἐστιν τὰ τέκνα τοῦ θεοῦ καὶ τὰ τέκνα τοῦ διαβόλου. To realize absolutely our relation to the True Father is to be rescued from the habitual authority of the False: πᾶς ὁ γεγεννημένος ἐκ τοῦ θεοῦ οὐχ ἁμαρτάνει...καὶ ὁ πονηρὸς οὐχ ἅπτεται αὐτοῦ (1 John v. 18).

Hallowed be thy name. Contrast in the symbolism of the Apocalypse ὀνόματα (v. l. ὄνομα) βλασφημίας belonging to the Beast who is the representative of the Dragon's power (xiii. 1, xvii. 3). Compare Apoc. ix. 11, xiv. 11 (contrast xiv. 1 τὸ ὄνομα αὐτοῦ καὶ τὸ ὄνομα τοῦ πατρὸς αὐτοῦ).

Thy kingdom come. Contrast ὁ ἄρχων τοῦ κόσμου τούτου (John xii. 31, xiv. 30, xvi. 11, comp. Eph. ii. 2); ὁ θεὸς τοῦ αἰῶνος τούτου (2 Cor. iv. 4), opposed to ὁ βασιλεὺς τῶν αἰώνων (1 Tim. i. 17); so αἱ ἀρχαί, αἱ ἐξούσιαι, οἱ κοσμοκράτορες [contrast ὁ παντοκράτωρ] τοῦ σκότους τούτου (Eph. vi. 12), ὁ μέν ἐστιν κύριος ἀπὸ αἰώνων καὶ εἰς τοὺς αἰῶνας, ὁ δὲ ἄρχων καιροῦ τοῦ νῦν τῆς ἀνομίας (Barn. xviii.). In the imagery of the Apocalypse Satan has his throne (ὅπου ὁ θρόνος τοῦ Σατανᾶ ii. 13), just as he has his worship (συναγωγὴ τοῦ Σατανᾶ ii. 9, iii. 9) and, if the word be allowed, his 'theology' (τὰ βαθέα τοῦ Σατανᾶ, ὡς λέγουσιν ii. 24).

Thy will be done, as in heaven, so on earth. Before the will of the True Father and King the lusts of the False will give way. Compare ὑμεῖς ἐκ τοῦ πατρὸς τοῦ διαβόλου ἐστὲ καὶ τὰς ἐπιθυμίας τοῦ πατρὸς ὑμῶν θέλετε ποιεῖν (John viii. 44). Contrast the oneness of the divine will with the manifoldness of the lusts of the evil one; comp. 1 Pet. iv. 2 τὸ μηκέτι ἀνθρώπων ἐπιθυμίαις ἀλλὰ θελήματι θεοῦ τὸν ἐπίλοιπον ἐν σαρκὶ βιῶσαι χρόνον. Eph. ii. 3 τὰ θελήματα τῆς σαρκός.

Forgive us our debts. Contrast Apoc. xii. 10 ὁ κατήγωρ τῶν ἀδελφῶν ἡμῶν, ὁ κατηγορῶν αὐτοὺς ἐνώπιον τοῦ θεοῦ ἡμῶν ἡμέρας καὶ νυκτός.

Bring us not into temptation, but deliver us from the evil one,

[1] Varie diabolus aemulatus est veritatem. Adfectavit illam aliquando defendendo concutere (Tert. *adv. Prax.* i.).

or *evil.* These two petitions alone in the Prayer are connected together. The key to the interpretation lies in the *ἀλλά.* The mutual relation of the two petitions may be presented thus:

μὴ εἰσενέγκῃς ἡμᾶς εἰς πειρασμόν
ῥῦσαι ἡμᾶς ἀπὸ τοῦ πονηροῦ.

In the New Testament the devil is consistently represented as the tempter. Comp. Matt. iv. 3 ὁ πειράζων εἶπεν αὐτῷ[1]. 1 Thess. iii. 5 μή πως ἐπείρασεν ὑμᾶς ὁ πειράζων[2]. 1 Cor. vii. 5 ἵνα μὴ πειράζῃ ὑμᾶς ὁ Σατανᾶς. Apoc. ii. 10 μέλλει βάλλειν ὁ διάβολος ἐξ ὑμῶν εἰς φυλακὴν ἵνα πειρασθῆτε. 1 Tim. vi. 9 (compared with iii. 7, 2 Tim. ii. 26). Nor does Jas. i. 14 (ἕκαστος δὲ πειράζεται ὑπὸ τῆς ἰδίας ἐπιθυμίας) conflict with this view of the general drift of New Testament teaching. The Apostle there wishes to vindicate the ways of God to men. In the matter of temptation he throws the responsibility on the man himself: the man's will is the offender—τὰς ἐπιθυμίας τοῦ πατρὸς ὑμῶν θέλετε ποιεῖν (John viii. 44). The question of the final source of temptation lies outside the scope of the passage.

When then it is noticed that the two clauses in each of their several parts correspond to, and are set over against, each other, the presumption in favour of the masculine rendering of τοῦ πονηροῦ becomes very strong; and a review of the Prayer itself confirms the verdict based on the consideration of its relation to the Lord's own experience.

(c) *The Ministry and the Passion.* The Lord's life is the best commentary on the Lord's Prayer. St John explains the purpose of the Incarnation in the words: εἰς τοῦτο ἐφανερώθη ὁ υἱὸς τοῦ θεοῦ ἵνα λύσῃ τὰ ἔργα τοῦ διαβόλου (1 John iii. 8). The life in its activities of ministry is briefly summarised by St Peter thus: διῆλθεν εὐεργετῶν καὶ ἰώμενος πάντας τοὺς καταδυναστευομένους

[1] Ipse a diabolo temptatus praesidem et artificem temptationis demonstravit (Tert. *de Orat.* viii.). Gregory of Nyssa (*de Orat. Dom.* v.) strangely exaggerates this view when he suggests that πειρασμός is one of Satan's names.

[2] Resch (p. 233) compares the *agraphon* in Hom. Clem. iii. 55, τοῖς δὲ οἰομένοις ὅτι ὁ θεὸς πειράζει, ὡς αἱ γραφαὶ λέγουσιν, ἔφη, ὁ πονηρός ἐστιν ὁ πειράζων. He thinks that the mode of expression resembles the style of the Synoptic Gospels. Bp Westcott on the other hand doubts the genuineness of this saying (*Introduction to the Study of the Gospels* p. 457 n.).

ὑπὸ τοῦ διαβόλου (Acts x. 38)[1]. With this general description of the whole Ministry the Lord's words as to one of His miracles should be compared: 'Ought not this woman...whom Satan had bound (*ἣν ἔδησεν ὁ Σατανᾶς*), lo, these eighteen years, to have been loosed from this bond (*λυθῆναι ἀπὸ τοῦ δέσμου τούτου*) on the day of the sabbath' (Luke xiii. 16)? It is not easy to believe that any who so remembered the Lord's words and works, and so shaped the record of that remembrance, would have hesitated as to the meaning of the disputed clause in the Prayer.

But it is when we turn to the story of the Passion that the evidence becomes clearest. The visit of Judas to the chief priests was due to the promptings of Satan (Luke xxii. 3). It was in obedience to the same inspiration that the traitor rose from the table to head his Master's enemies (John xiii. 2, 27). The Lord Himself interpreted the crisis of redemption in three different ways as the ineffectual coming, the judgment, the expulsion, of 'the prince of this world' (John xii. 31, xiv. 30, xvi. 11). Now He met face to face 'the tyranny of darkness' (*ἡ ἐξουσία τοῦ σκότους* Luke xxii. 53, comp. Col. i. 13 *ἐρύσατο ἡμᾶς ἐκ τῆς ἐξουσίας τοῦ σκότους*, Acts xxvi. 18, Eph. vi. 12).

Christ's interpretation of His sufferings is repeated by the Apostolic teachers. St Paul views the cross of shame as the triumphal car on which the Conqueror exhibits the vanquished 'principalities and powers' (Col. ii. 15). The writer to the Hebrews (ii. 14 f.) unfolds the paradox that through death, the devil's tool, the Lord brought the devil to nought and set his captives free.

Two passages however, imbedded in the history of the Passion, demand closer investigation. The view of the Passion insisted on above throws light on both of them.

(i). The first passage is from St Luke's Gospel (xxii.), 'Ye are they which have continued with me in *my temptations;* and I appoint unto you *a kingdom,* even as *my Father* appointed unto me (*vv.* 28, 29)....Simon, Simon, behold, *Satan asked to have you* (*ὁ Σατανᾶς ἐξῃτήσατο ὑμᾶς*), that he might sift you as wheat; but *I made supplication* for thee (*ἐγὼ δὲ ἐδεήθην περὶ σοῦ*), that thy faith fail not (*vv.* 31, 32)....And he came out, and went, as his custom

[1] The Syriac Vulgate here translates *τοῦ διαβόλου* by ܒܝܫܐ (the-evil-one). See below, p. 155.

was, unto the mount of Olives (*v.* 39)....And when he was at the place, he said unto them, *Pray that ye enter not into temptation* (*προσεύχεσθε μὴ εἰσελθεῖν εἰς πειρασμόν v.* 40)....He kneeled down and prayed, saying, *Father*, if thou be willing, remove this cup from me: nevertheless *not my will, but thine, be done* (*μὴ τὸ θέλημά μου ἀλλὰ τὸ σὸν γινέσθω vv.* 41, 42)....Why sleep ye? rise and *pray, that ye enter not into temptation*' (*προσεύχεσθε, ἵνα μὴ εἰσέλθητε εἰς πειρασμόν, v.* 46).

The scene, it is true, shifts from the upper room to the Garden; yet there is an irresistible sense of unity about the history. The brief interval of time which separates the first of the words quoted above from the last does not affect the close *nexus* of the thoughts. The language of the Evangelists[1] seems designed to emphasise the relation between the Lord's Prayer and the Lord's teaching on the evening of the betrayal. This parallel will to many minds establish beyond a doubt the masculine interpretation of *ἀπὸ τοῦ πονηροῦ*.

(ii). The other passage is from the true Oratio Dominica (John xvii. 15): 'I pray not (*οὐκ ἐρωτῶ*) that thou shouldest take them from (*ἵνα ἄρῃς...ἐκ...*) the world, but that thou shouldest keep them from the evil one' (*ἵνα τηρήσῃς αὐτοὺς ἐκ τοῦ πονηροῦ*). The reference of *ἐκ τοῦ πονηροῦ* to the devil seems to be certain for the following four reasons[2]. (1) The form of the sentence: *οὐκ ...ἐκ τοῦ κόσμου ἀλλὰ...ἐκ τοῦ πονηροῦ*. The usage of St John (*ὁ ἄρχων τοῦ κόσμου τούτου* xii. 31, xiv. 30, xvi. 11, *ὁ κόσμος ὅλος ἐν τῷ πονηρῷ κεῖται* 1 John v. 19) seems to indicate decisively the contrast intended—from the tyrant's power, not from the region which the tyrant claims as his. (2) The preceding context (*vv.* 11, 12): 'Holy Father, keep (*τήρησον*) them in thy name which thou hast given me....While I was with them, I kept (*ἐτήρουν*) them in thy name which thou hast given me; and I guarded them (*ἐφύλαξα*), and not one of them perished, but the son of perdition; that the scripture might be fulfilled.' The last clause is the

[1] It is important to observe that (*a*) St Matthew has the same phrase here (xxvi. 42 *γενηθήτω τὸ θέλημά σου*) as in the Lord's Prayer: St Luke omits this clause in xi. 2. (*b*) in the language of Syria different 'voices' of the same verb are equivalent respectively to *εἰσενέγκαι* and *εἰσελθεῖν* (see p. 61 f.).

[2] Canon Cook (*Second Letter* p. 81) points out that Chrysostom gives the neuter interpretation here—*τουτέστιν, ἀπὸ τῆς κακίας* (x. 664 B, so viii. 483).

connecting link with an earlier passage. 'I speak not of you all: I know whom I have chosen: but that the scripture may be fulfilled, He that eateth my bread lifted up his heel against me.... So when he had dipped the sop, he taketh and giveth it to Judas, the son of Simon Iscariot. And after the sop, then *entered Satan into him*' (xiii. 18, 26 f.). All the Apostles were safely kept by their Master save one. He fell a victim to the devil's power. For the future the Lord prays that those whom He leaves behind may still be kept from the great enemy, who had made one of their number his own. (3) The parallels in the Epistle:

GOSPEL.	EPISTLE.
While I was with them, *I kept* (ἐτήρουν) them in thy name...and I *guarded* (ἐφύλαξα) them, and not one of them perished, but the son of perdition.	*He that was begotten of God* (ὁ γεννηθεὶς ἐκ τοῦ θεοῦ) *keepeth* (τηρεῖ) him and *the evil one* toucheth him not (ὁ πονηρὸς οὐχ ἅπτεται αὐτοῦ).... My little children, *guard* (φυλάξατε) yourselves from idols. v. 18, 21.
I have given them *thy word;* and *the world* hated them, because they are not of *the world*, even as I am not of *the world.* I pray not that thou shouldest take them from *the world*, but that thou shouldest *keep* them from *the evil one* (ἐκ τοῦ πονηροῦ). They are not of *the world*, even as I am not of *the world.* xvii. 12—15. *I have overcome the world.* xvi. 33.	I have written unto you, young men, because ye are strong, and the *word of God* abideth in you, and ye *have overcome the evil one* (τὸν πονηρόν). Love not *the world*, neither the things that are in *the world.* ii. 14, 15.

(4) The parallel in St Luke xxii. 31, 32:

ST JOHN.	ST LUKE.
While I was with them, I kept them....I guarded them....*I pray* (ἐρωτῶ)...that thou shouldest keep them from *the evil one.*	Simon, Simon, behold *Satan* asked to have you, that he might sift you as wheat; but *I made supplication* (ἐδεήθην) for thee.

But if, as these arguments appear to prove, ἐκ τοῦ πονηροῦ is masculine, is it possible to disconnect the prayer which the Lord taught as the typical Christian prayer from the prayer which He Himself prayed? Is not the one the best guide to a true understanding of the other? And indeed, however great the difference as to surroundings and form of expression, there are striking points of contact between the two prayers. The same great spiritual realities lie at the root of both.

Our Father which art in heaven.	Father (*vv.* 1, 5, 21, 24), Holy Father (*v.* 11), Righteous Father (*v.* 25).
Hallowed be thy name.	I manifested thy name (*v.* 6). Keep them...I kept them, in thy name which thou hast given me (*vv.* 11, 12). I made known unto them thy name (*v.* 26)[1].
Thy kingdom come.	Glorify thy Son, that the Son may glorify thee: even as thou gavest him authority over all flesh... (*vv.* 1, 2).
Thy will be done, as in heaven, so on earth.	I glorified thee on the earth, having accomplished the work which thou hast given me to do...the glory which I had with thee before the world was (*vv.* 4, 5). I am no more in the world, and these are in the world (*v.* 11). Even as thou, Father, art in me, and I in thee, that they also may be in us: that the world may believe... (*v.* 21).
Bring us not into temptation, but deliver us from the evil one (ἀπὸ τοῦ πονηροῦ).	I kept them...I guarded them (*v.* 12). ...I pray...that thou shouldest keep them from the evil one (ἐκ τοῦ πονηροῦ) (*v.* 15).

The above table indicates some of the resemblances. No such mechanical arrangement however can lay bare the one spirit which quickens both prayers.

The conjecture might be hazarded that in the Gospel and Epistle of St John we have a Johannine form of the clause of the Lord's Prayer under discussion, in which τήρησον or φύλαξον (comp. 2 Thess. iii. 3 φυλάξει ἀπὸ τοῦ πονηροῦ) takes the place of

[1] Comp. πάτερ, δόξασόν σου τὸ ὄνομα (John xii. 27). Chrysostom commenting on the Lord's Prayer says: τὸ γάρ, ἁγιασθήτω, τοῦτό ἐστιν, δοξασθήτω (vii. 250 c).

ῥῦσαι, and the preposition ἐκ the place of the ἀπό of the Synoptists[1].

But, however this may be, the evidence derived from the Gospels themselves—the account of the Temptation, the Lord's Prayer, the history of the Ministry and especially of the Passion—seems without any shadow of uncertainty to warrant the conclusion that Christ taught His Church in the Lord's Prayer to pray for deliverance from the assaults of the devil.

(ii). Evidence derived from the Epistles.

Reasons have been given for thinking that in the earliest days as now the Lord's Prayer was in familiar use. The Apostolic writers who so used it would sometimes consciously, sometimes unconsciously, mould their language after the model of its words. But the indications which suggest frequency of use are also proofs that as yet the Prayer had no such stereotyped form as it assumed a little later. Without this warning a slight variation of phrase in the Apostolic writings might throw us off our guard, and we might pass by unnoticed what is in truth little else than a quotation of one of the petitions of the Prayer.

We proceed to discuss certain possible references in the Epistles to the last clause of the Lord's Prayer.

(1) 2 Thess. iii. 1 ff. *τὸ λοιπὸν προσεύχεσθε, ἀδελφοί, περὶ ἡμῶν...ἵνα ῥυσθῶμεν ἀπὸ τῶν ἀτόπων καὶ πονηρῶν ἀνθρώπων, οὐ γὰρ πάντων ἡ πίστις. πιστὸς δέ ἐστιν ὁ κύριος, ὃς στηρίξει ὑμᾶς καὶ φυλάξει ἀπὸ τοῦ πονηροῦ* We ask two questions—What is the interpretation of the last clause? How far may a reference to the Lord's Prayer be considered certain?

In regard to the first question, St Paul certainly uses the phrase 'the evil one' in *πάντα τὰ βέλη τοῦ πονηροῦ τὰ πεπυρωμένα* (Eph. vi. 16, comp. *τὰς μεθοδίας τοῦ διαβόλου* v. 11, and contrast *τὰ πνευματικὰ τῆς πονηρίας* v. 12). In the present passage the context clearly points to the masculine. For here we have a good instance of that dovetailing of ideas and phrases familiar to the student of St Paul:

[1] The investigation into the usage of the Greek Bible (p. 71 ff.) has shewn that these two prepositions are interchangeable.

οὐ γὰρ πάντων ἡ πίστις.	*πιστὸς δέ ἐστιν ὁ κύριος.*
ἵνα ῥυσθῶμεν ἀπὸ	*στηρίξει ὑμᾶς καὶ φυλάξει ἀπὸ*
τῶν ἀτόπων καὶ πονηρῶν ἀνθρώπων.	*τοῦ πονηροῦ.*

The correlation of clauses would be impaired if the *personal* agency of evil men were made to balance *abstract* evil[1] (τὸ πονηρόν Rom. xii. 9). Moreover in St Paul's mind the thought of evil men lay very near the thought of the evil one, their inspirer and instigator[2]. Thus in this Epistle (ii. 9), 'He whose coming is according to the working of Satan'; again, 'Even Satan fashioneth himself into an angel of light; it is no great thing therefore if his ministers also fashion themselves as ministers of righteousness' (2 Cor. xi. 14 f.); 'The spirit that now worketh in the sons of disobedience' (Eph. ii. 2). Again, the choice of words favours the masculine interpretation—στηρίξει and φυλάξει taken together[3] are more appropriate if the enemy is a person. The metaphor is drawn from war. Compare πρὸς τὸ δύνασθαι ὑμᾶς στῆναι πρὸς τὰς μεθοδίας τοῦ διαβόλου...ἵνα δυνηθῆτε ἀντιστῆναι...στῆναι. στῆτε οὖν (Eph. vi. 11, 13, 14), ὁ ἀντίδικος ὑμῶν διάβολος...ᾧ ἀντίστητε στερεοὶ τῇ πίστει (1 Pet. v. 8 f.), ἀντίστητε δὲ τῷ διαβόλῳ (James iv. 7). Once more, the position of the phrase in the Epistle is remarkable. The Apostle begins what he means to be the concluding paragraph of the letter with τὸ λοιπόν (iii. 1). The paragraph, it will be noticed, corresponds with the closing sentences of the first letter to Thessalonica. In it there are four main thoughts: (1) A request for prayer on the Apostle's behalf (*vv.* 1, 2): so 1 Thess. v. 25. (2) The assurance—πιστὸς δέ ἐστιν ὁ κύριος: so 1 Thess. v. 24 (πιστὸς ὁ καλῶν ὑμᾶς). (3) An expression of trust —ἃ παραγγέλλομεν καὶ ποιεῖτε καὶ ποιήσετε. (4) A benediction— ὁ δὲ κύριος κατευθύναι κ.τ.λ.: so 1 Thess. v. 23 αὐτὸς δὲ ὁ θεὸς τῆς εἰρήνης ἁγιάσαι ὑμᾶς. Here then the Apostle had meant, it

[1] St Paul starts in *v.* 1 with the idea of help and hindrance in work. Comp. ἐνέκοψεν ἡμᾶς ὁ Σατανᾶς (1 Thess. ii. 18).

[2] Comp. the Jewish Prayer (Berakoth 16 *b*): 'May it be thy will, O Lord our God...to deliver us from the shameless, and from shamelessness; from the evil man, and from evil hap, from evil *yeçer*, from evil companion, from evil neighbour, and from Satan the destroyer' (Dr Taylor, *Sayings of the Jewish Fathers* p. 142). For similar prayers in the Christian Liturgies see below, p. 144.

[3] Contrast παρακαλέσαι ὑμῶν τὰς καρδίας καὶ στηρίξαι ἐν παντὶ ἔργῳ καὶ λόγῳ ἀγαθῷ (ii. 17; 1 Thess. iii. 2, 13).

would seem, to close. But the reference in *ἃ παραγγέλλομεν* (*v.* 4) may be misunderstood: it needs further definition. Hence yet another paragraph is added (iii. 6—16; comp. Phil. iii. 1 f., iv. 8). Thus, according to St Paul's intention when he wrote the words, the assurance *φυλάξει ἀπὸ τοῦ πονηροῦ* would have stood at the very end of the Epistle. If we adopt the masculine interpretation, we find a parallel in a similar prophecy of victory over the devil at the close of the greatest Epistle of the next group—*ὁ δὲ θεὸς τῆς εἰρήνης συντρίψει τὸν Σατανᾶν ὑπὸ τοὺς πόδας ὑμῶν ἐν τάχει* (Rom. xvi. 20). Among the Epistles of the First Captivity the 'Ephesian' Epistle ends with the picture of the Christian soldier equipped in 'the whole armour of God,' able to 'stand against the wiles of the devil[1].'

But may the words *φυλάξει ἀπὸ τοῦ πονηροῦ* be taken as a direct reference to the clause of the Lord's Prayer? It is hard to refuse an affirmative answer. If St Paul had written *ῥύσεται ἀπὸ τοῦ πονηροῦ*, the reference would have been beyond dispute. As it is, even if we put aside the quite possible supposition that a current version of the Lord's Prayer had *φύλαξον* in place of *ῥῦσαι*, we may account for St Paul's substitution of *φυλάξει* by the fact that *ῥυσθῶμεν* had been used just above and that *φυλάξει* harmonises better than *ῥύσεται* with *στηρίξει*[2].

(2) 2 Cor. xii. 7 f. *ἐδόθη μοι σκόλοψ*[3] *τῇ σαρκί, ἄγγελος Σατανᾶ...ὑπὲρ τούτου τρὶς τὸν κύριον παρεκάλεσα ἵνα ἀποστῇ ἀπ' ἐμοῦ.* The remembrance of the Lord's thrice repeated prayer in Gethsemane perhaps inspires the *τρὶς...παρεκάλεσα.* Further, as *ἀποστῆναι* in the New Testament is only used of persons[4], the subject of *ἀποστῇ* is *ἄγγελος Σατανᾶ* (comp. Matt. xxv. 41, Apoc.

[1] Comp. 1 Pet. v. 8 f.; 1 John v. 18 ff.

[2] The Antiochenes however do not support the masculine. Chrys. passes over the word. Theod. of Mops. paraphrases—'ab omni discedentes inconvenienti actu.'

[3] The passages where the word occurs in the LXX., viz. Numb. xxxiii. 55, Ezek. xxviii. 24 (*σκόλοψ πικρίας καὶ ἄκανθα ὀδύνης*), Hos. ii. 6, seem to shew that it bears the later (Alexandrian) sense of *thorn* (not *stake*). See especially Field *Otium Norvicense* iii. p. 115.

[4] Lc. ii. 37, iv. 13, viii. 13, xiii. 27, Acts v. 38, xii. 10 (*ἀπέστη ὁ ἄγγελος*), xv. 38, xix. 9, xxii. 29, 1 Tim. iv. 1, 2 Tim. ii. 19, Heb. iii. 12. The rendering of the Syriac Vulgate connects together Luke iv. 13, the interpolated clause in Luke xi. 4, and 2 Cor. xii. 8. But the Syriac word used is a very common one.

xii. 7, 9, Barn. xviii. 1). The parallel in Luke iv. 13 (*ὁ διάβολος ἀπέστη ἀπ' αὐτοῦ*) is remarkable, and we possibly have here one of the links which connect St Paul's Epistles with the Pauline Gospel. However that may be, St Paul tells of a prayer of his for deliverance from the power of Satan, and it is a plausible conjecture that the Lord's Prayer was in his mind.

(3) Gal. i. 3 f. *Ἰησοῦ Χριστοῦ, τοῦ δόντος ἑαυτὸν ὑπὲρ* (v. l. *περὶ*) *τῶν ἁμαρτιῶν ἡμῶν ὅπως ἐξέληται ἡμᾶς ἐκ τοῦ αἰῶνος τοῦ ἐνεστῶτος πονηροῦ κατὰ τὸ θέλημα τοῦ θεοῦ καὶ πατρὸς ἡμῶν.*

Two interpretations may be given of the words *τοῦ αἰῶνος τοῦ ἐνεστῶτος πονηροῦ*, and in either case a reference to the Lord's Prayer seems to me probable. The ideas common to this passage and the Prayer are—our Father, the will, forgiveness, rescue from evil (or the evil one).

(i) The words may be translated, 'the present age, evil as it is,' *πονηροῦ* being emphatically added to describe its character[1], a kind of tertiary predicate. When it is remembered that *ἐξελέσθαι* in the LXX. shares with *ῥύσασθαι* the duty of representing הצּיל (comp. p. 73), and so might well be a translation of the Aramaic word meaning 'deliver' in the last clause of the Lord's Prayer, and further that 'this age' and 'this world' are represented in the New Testament as being under the dominion of Satan (2 Cor. iv. 4, Eph. ii. 2, vi. 12, John xii. 31, xiv. 30, xvi. 11, 1 John v. 19), the conclusion that here there is an indirect reference to the Lord's Prayer becomes probable. The emphatic *πονηροῦ* finds thus an explanation,—the character of the age corresponds to the character of its god, its ruler. The general sense will be illustrated by John xii. 31, xvi. 11, Col. i. 13, ii. 15, Heb. ii. 14.

(ii) But is it not more natural to take the words *τοῦ ἐνεστῶτος πονηροῦ* together as defining to whom or to what the age belongs? For such a genitive compare Eph. ii. 2 *κατὰ τὸν αἰῶνα τοῦ κόσμου τούτου* (where the idea of the personal evil power comes out in the next clause *κατὰ τὸν ἄρχοντα κ.τ.λ.*), Barnabas xv. 5 *ἐλθὼν ὁ*

[1] Comp. Eph. v. 16 *ἐξαγοραζόμενοι τὸν καιρόν, ὅτι αἱ ἡμέραι πονηραί εἰσι*, Barn. ii. 1 *ἡμερῶν οὖν οὐσῶν πονηρῶν καὶ αὐτοῦ τοῦ ἐνεργοῦντος ἔχοντος τὴν ἐξουσίαν*, viii. 6. Contrast Barn. x. 11 *ὁ δίκαιος καὶ ἐν τούτῳ τῷ κόσμῳ περιπατεῖ καὶ τὸν ἅγιον αἰῶνα ἐκδέχεται.* For the construction in this case compare 1 Pet. i. 18 *ἐλυτρώθητε ἐκ τῆς ματαίας ὑμῶν ἀναστροφῆς πατροπαραδότου.*

υἱὸς αὐτοῦ καταργήσει τὸν καιρὸν τοῦ ἀνόμου (on the reading see p. 99). The converse is found in 2 Cor. iv. 4 *ὁ θεὸς τοῦ αἰῶνος τούτου*. Further, it is important to observe that not only in St Paul's Epistles but also in the rest of the New Testament and, I believe, in other early Christian writings the literal equivalent (*οὗτος ὁ αἰών*) of the Hebrew phrase הָעוֹלָם הַזֶּה is used; the word *ἐνεστώς* does not occur, so far as I have observed, in this connexion.

If this construction of the words be adopted two questions arise, (*a*) What is the gender of *πονηροῦ*? (*b*) What is the exact force of *ἐνεστῶτος*?

(*a*) What is the gender of *τοῦ...πονηροῦ*? The neuter is of course possible. But there are weighty arguments against it. The masculine interpretation is implied in a passage of the Clementines, *Epist. Clem. ad Jac.* i., referred to by Bp Lightfoot on Gal. i. 4, *οὗτος αὐτὸς* (sc. *Πέτρος*) *διὰ τὴν ἄμετρον πρὸς ἀνθρώπους στοργὴν σαφῶς, δημοσίᾳ, ἐπὶ τοῦ ἐνεστῶτος πονηροῦ, τὸν ἐσόμενον ἀγαθὸν ὅλῳ τῷ κόσμῳ μηνῦσαι βασιλέα, μέχρις ἐνταῦθα τῇ Ῥώμῃ γενόμενος κ.τ.λ.* 'At all events,' writes the Bishop, 'a possible interpretation is thus suggested.' But I venture to think this 'possible interpretation' becomes probable in the light of two considerations. 'This age' in the New Testament is never connected with mere abstract evil, but always with the tyranny of a personal evil spirit. Such too, at least generally, is the usage of sub-Apostolic writers. Again, this passage must be taken in connexion with other passages in St Paul's writings where reference to the Lord's Prayer is probable.

(*b*) Is the probability, which may be claimed for the masculine interpretation, disturbed by the presence of the word *ἐνεστῶτος*? What is the exact force of the word? It is commonly taken in a temporal sense, *present*. Thus Bp Lightfoot says of the passage in the Clementines that the writer "appears to have interpreted the words 'from the æon, the dominion, of the present evil one.'" The word *ἐνεστώς* has, it is true, this meaning; but I believe it is used in a strictly temporal sense only when the context, as in the Clementines (*τὸν ἐσόμενον*), defines the meaning. Thus Rom. viii. 38 (*οὔτε ἐνεστῶτα οὔτε μέλλοντα*), 1 Cor. iii. 22. Compare Polyb. xviii. 38. 5 (to which Bp Lightfoot refers) *ὁ γὰρ προειρη-*

μένος ἀνὴρ κατὰ τὸν πατέρα μέν, ἔτι νεὸς ὢν...ὁμοίως δὲ κατὰ τὸν ἐνεστῶτα βασιλέα. This temporal sense however is secondary, and the primary thought is rather of imminence, often of some threatening power[1]. Compare e.g. Lycurg. 148. 32 ὁ νῦν ἐνεστηκὼς ἀγών (where the addition of νῦν is to be noticed), Plutarch *Lucull.* 13 ὃν αὐτὸς ἐνστησόμενον τῇ φυγῇ μετὰ νεῶν ἀπεστάλκει, and (in the Greek Bible) 1 Macc. xii. 44 πολέμου μὴ ἐνεστηκότος ἡμῖν, 2 Macc. iii. 17 τὸ κατὰ καρδίαν ἐνεστὸς ἄλγος, vi. 9 τὴν ἐνεστῶσαν ταλαιπωρίαν, 3 Macc. i. 16 βοηθεῖν τῇ ἐνεστώσῃ ἀνάγκῃ, 1 Cor. vii. 26 διὰ τὴν ἐνεστῶσαν ἀνάγκην, 2 Thess. ii. 2 ἐνέστηκεν ἡ ἡμέρα τοῦ κυρίου, 2 Tim. iii. 1, Heb. ix. 9; so Ep. Clem. 55 λοιμικοῦ τινος ἐνστάντος καιροῦ. In the passage under consideration this appears to be the meaning. The word points to the imminence of, the besetment of men by, the evil one. The following passages will be the best commentary, Ps. cviii. 6 διάβολος στήτω ἐκ δεξιῶν αὐτοῦ, Zech. iii. 1 καὶ ὁ διάβολος εἱστήκει ἐκ δεξιῶν αὐτοῦ τοῦ ἀντικεῖσθαι αὐτῷ, Eph. ii. 2 τοῦ πνεύματος τοῦ νῦν ἐνεργοῦντος ἐν τοῖς υἱοῖς τῆς ἀπειθίας, 1 Tim. v. 14 μηδεμίαν ἀφορμὴν διδόναι τῷ ἀντικειμένῳ (*v.* 15 ὀπίσω τοῦ Σατανᾶ), 1 John v. 19 ὁ κόσμος ὅλος ἐν τῷ πονηρῷ κεῖται. Compare also the idea suggested by Col. ii. 15 ἀπεκδυσάμενος τὰς ἀρχὰς καὶ τὰς ἐξουσίας.

To sum up, in the light of other passages St Paul's meaning here seems to be that Christ died 'to rescue us from the age of the evil one who besetteth us'; and, if this be his meaning, his words are probably a reminiscence of the Lord's Prayer.

(4) Col. i. 12 ff. εὐχαριστοῦντες τῷ πατρὶ τῷ ἱκανώσαντι ἡμᾶς εἰς τὴν μερίδα τοῦ κλήρου τῶν ἁγίων ἐν τῷ φωτί, ὃς ἐρύσατο ἡμᾶς ἐκ τῆς ἐξουσίας τοῦ σκότους καὶ μετέστησεν εἰς τὴν βασιλείαν τοῦ υἱοῦ τῆς ἀγάπης αὐτοῦ, ἐν ᾧ ἔχομεν τὴν ἀπολύτρωσιν, τὴν ἄφεσιν τῶν ἁμαρτιῶν.

In this passage four of the leading thoughts of the Lord's Prayer are found side by side—'the Father,' 'who delivered us out of the power of darkness,' 'the kingdom,' 'the forgiveness of our sins.' It can hardly be urged that this is a mere coincidence. The Prayer had worked itself into the Apostle's mind and habit

[1] The word is used of a logical difficulty which confronts a line of argument in Plato *Phaedo* 77 B (ἔτι ἐνέστηκεν ὃ νῦν δὴ Κέβης ἔλεγε).

of thought, and the reminiscence, even though it be unintentional, is full of significance.

Two questions arise:

First, is the reference in *ἡ ἐξουσία τοῦ σκότους* necessarily to the personal power of evil? Such an interpretation, it would appear, is clearly required by the antithesis—*ἐκ τῆς ἐξουσίας τοῦ σκότους, εἰς τὴν βασιλείαν τοῦ υἱοῦ.* Further, a passage from the companion Epistle is strongly on the same side: *πρὸς τὰς ἀρχάς, πρὸς τὰς ἐξουσίας, πρὸς τοὺς κοσμοκράτορας τοῦ σκότους τούτου* (Eph. vi. 12). Compare also Acts xxvi. 18 *τοῦ ἐπιστρέψαι ἀπὸ σκότους εἰς φῶς καὶ τῆς ἐξουσίας τοῦ Σατανᾶ ἐπὶ τὸν θεόν.* These parallels seem to establish a reference to Satan.

Secondly, could St Paul have written, 'He *delivered* us from the power of darkness,' if he had understood the Lord's Prayer to *ask for* deliverance from Satan? For is not the assertion of an emancipation in the past wholly incompatible with the remembrance of a petition for deliverance? Here we touch upon an objection which has been most strongly and confidently urged against the masculine interpretation of the clause in the Prayer. Such an interpretation, it is argued, misrepresents the position of the Christian man. He has been rescued, he has been brought clean out of the range of Satan's power. He has no need to ask for what is his already.

The passage of St Paul which we are considering itself shews that such an argument proves too much. St Paul speaks of the transference of men into the kingdom as a thing already achieved, an act of the Father in the past (*μετέστησεν*). How then, we might ask, can Christian men pray 'Thy kingdom come'?

The answer depends on an appreciation of the difference between a state which is ideal or potential, and a state which is actual. It is possible to conceive of the 'consummation of the ages' (*συντέλεια τῶν αἰώνων*) as already attained; it was reached when the Lord died and rose again (Hebr. ix. 26). On the other hand 'the consummation of the age' (*ἡ συντέλεια τοῦ αἰῶνος*) is still future. The Lord's return will usher it in (Matt. xiii. 39, 40, 49, xxiv. 3, xxviii. 20). So in one sense the Lord's work is complete (*τετέλεσται* Jn. xix. 30); the victory is won (e.g. Jn. xvi. 33, Col. ii. 15, Heb. ii. 14); the reconciliation of all things to God is achieved (Col. i. 20). In another sense the results of the victory have still to be made good (1 Cor. xv. 25 ff.); in 'the regeneration, the restoration of all things' we see a goal still unattained (Matt. xix. 28, Acts iii. 21). And with this twofold view of the work of the Redeemer there corresponds a twofold view of the position of the Christian man. St Paul can say *ἀπεθάνετε*, yet in the same breath *νεκρώσατε οὖν τὰ μέλη τὰ ἐπὶ τῆς γῆς* (Col. iii. 3, 5); *ἐσώθημεν* (Rom. viii. 24), yet *σωθησόμεθα* (Rom. v. 10); *συνεζωοποίησεν τῷ χριστῷ...καὶ συνήγειρεν καὶ συνεκάθισεν ἐν τοῖς ἐπουρανίοις ἐν Χριστῷ Ἰησοῦ* (Eph. ii. 5 f.), yet *ἐν αὐτῷ ἐδιδάχθητε...ἀνανεοῦσθαι τῷ πνεύματι τοῦ νοὸς ὑμῶν, καὶ ἐνδύσασθαι τὸν καινὸν ἄνθρωπον* (Eph. iv. 23); *ἔχομεν τὴν ἀπολύτρωσιν* (Eph. i. 7), yet *ἐσφραγίσθητε εἰς ἡμέραν ἀπολυτρώσεως* (Eph. iv. 30, cf. Rom. viii. 23). And in the same way there are two different ways of speaking of the relation of Christian men to Satan. St John, for example, writes in his Epistle *νενικήκατε τὸν πονηρόν* (ii. 13, 14), *ὁ πονηρὸς οὐχ ἅπτεται αὐτοῦ* (v. 18). St Paul, speaking from a different point of view, summons men to a conflict which will tax all their powers (Eph. vi. 11—17, compare Jas. iv. 7, 1 Pet. v. 9), and encourages them with the *hope* of God's speedy victory over the enemy (Rom. xvi. 20).

There is nothing strange then if St Paul translated his remembrance of the prayer for deliverance into the declaration of a past emancipation. The prayer for deliverance is only possible because the deliverance is ideally an accomplished fact.

(5) 2 Tim. iv. 16 ff. *ἐν τῇ πρώτῃ μου ἀπολογίᾳ οὐδείς μοι παρεγένετο...ὁ δέ κύριός μοι παρέστη καὶ ἐνεδυνάμωσέν με, ἵνα δι' ἐμοῦ τὸ κήρυγμα πληροφορηθῇ καὶ ἀκούσωσιν πάντα τὰ ἔθνη, καὶ ἐρύσθην ἐκ στόματος λέοντος. ῥύσεταί με ὁ κύριος ἀπὸ παντὸς ἔργου πονηροῦ καὶ σώσει εἰς τὴν βασιλείαν αὐτοῦ τὴν ἐπουράνιον· ᾧ ἡ δόξα εἰς τοὺς αἰῶνας τῶν αἰώνων, ἀμήν.* Here in the close juxtaposition of *ἀπὸ παντὸς ἔργου πονηροῦ* and *εἰς τὴν βασιλείαν αὐτοῦ* the reference to two clauses of the Lord's Prayer seems clear. But is not the passage equally decisive for the neuter interpretation? To answer this question some discussion of the whole passage is necessary.

ἐρύσθην ἐκ στόματος λέοντος. The phrase is evidently derived from the Old Testament. Comp. *Δανιὴλ...ἐρρύσθη ἐκ στόματος λεόντων* (1 Macc. ii. 60), *σῶσόν με ἐκ στόματος λέοντος* (Ps. xxi. 22); so Amos iii. 12, Dan. vi. 20, 27. It is possible however that an expression drawn from this source may have a particular application, and may refer to Satan. The absence of the article does not imply that the danger was vague, but rather tends to emphasise its character[1]. If then this reference be allowed, we should have a close parallel in 1 Pet. v. 8 *ὁ ἀντίδικος ὑμῶν διάβολος ὡς λέων ὠρυόμενος περιπατεῖ ζητῶν καταπιεῖν*. In this latter passage the words in the context *τὰ αὐτὰ τῶν παθημάτων* (*v.* 9), *ὀλίγον παθόντας* (*v.* 10, cf. i. 6) shew that persecution, not temptation to sin, is here regarded as the devil's work. Two figures are employed to describe Satan as the persecutor of the Church. On the one hand the Apostle uses the image of the unsatisfied savagery of the lion, an image not uncommon in the Old Testament (Ps. xxi. 14, Jer. ii. 15, Ezek. xxii. 25, Zeph. iii. 3). On the other, using the name *διάβολος* and the term *ὁ ἀντίδικος*, which elsewhere in the New Testament retains its proper meaning of an 'opponent at law[2],' he seems to describe the devil as prompting false accusations against 'the Brethren' before ruling powers (comp. ii. 12, iii. 16 ff., iv. 14 ff.). Thus the two ideas of savage attack and of accusation before rulers are common to 2 Tim. iv. 16 ff. and 1 Peter v. 8[3].

[1] Comp. e.g. *ἐν υἱῷ* (Hebr. i. 2), *ἐν πάθει ἀληθινῷ* (Ignat. *Eph.* i.).

[2] Matt. v. 25, Lc. xii. 58, xviii. 3. In Classical Greek the word *ἀντίδικος* is used of a party in a lawsuit, whether the plaintiff or more properly the defendant. It is only in a poetical passage (Aesch. *Ag.* 41 *Πριάμου μέγας ἀντίδικος, Μενέλαος ἄναξ ἠδ' Ἀγαμέμνων*) that the word seems at first sight to bear a more general sense, and even here its primary meaning gives force to the passage. In the LXX. it is used four times as equivalent to words connected with the root ריב (1 Sam. ii. 10, Is. xli. 11, Jer. l. 34, li. 36). In Prov. xviii. 17 it is used to translate רֵעַ, but the metaphor is a judicial one. Thus the usage of the Greek Bible is consistently in favour of the strict rendering.

[3] Comp. *οἱ φαῦλοι δαίμονες, ἐχθραίνοντες ἡμῖν καὶ τοὺς τοιούτους δικαστὰς ἔχοντες ὑποχειρίους καὶ λατρεύοντας, ὡς οὖν ἄρχοντας δαιμονιῶντας, φονεύειν ἡμᾶς παρασκευάζουσι* (Justin *Ap.* ii. 1, so *Ap.* i. 5): *ὁ δὲ ἀντίζηλος καὶ βάσκανος καὶ πονηρός, ὁ ἀντικείμενος τῷ γένει τῶν δικαίων ... ὑπέβαλε ... Νικήτην ... ἐντυχεῖν τῷ ἄρχοντι* (*Mart. Polyc.* ch. xvii.). The use of the figure of a lion to describe Satan may not have been unknown among the Jews. Justin Martyr, in his exposition of two passages of the Psalms, is very probably following traditional exegesis, though it is possible that in the former of these passages he is rather thinking of 1 Pet. v. 8. In *Dial.* ch. 103 he is commenting on the words *ἤνοιξαν ἐπ' ἐμὲ τὸ στόμα αὐτῶν ὡς λέων ὁ ἁρπάζων*

Persecution is traced to Satan's working notably in the case of our Lord's Passion. And in Apostolic and post-Apostolic times the same explanation of persecution prevailed[1]. If this interpretation be adopted, a fuller force is given to the words *ὁ κύριός μοι παρέστη καὶ ἐνεδυνάμωσέν με*[2]. Chrysostom characteristically glides from the interpretation commonly quoted as his (*λέοντα τὸν Νέρωνά φησι*: so Eus. *H. E.* ii. 22[3]) into that which I have suggested as possible. After explaining 'every evil work' as equivalent to 'every sin' he adds *καὶ γὰρ καὶ τοῦτο, τὸ δυνηθῆναι μέχρις αἵματος ἀντικαταστῆναι πρὸς τὴν ἁμαρτίαν καὶ μὴ ἐνδοῦναι, ἑτέρου λέοντός ἐστι ῥύσασθαι* (v. l. *ῥυσθῆναι*), *τοῦ διαβόλου.*

If Satan is referred to, as I have suggested, in the earlier clause, it is quite natural that the reminiscence of the Prayer in the second clause should be indirect. Further, there is, I think, some evidence that the phrase *ἀπὸ παντὸς πονηροῦ* (*ἔργου, πράγματος*) was current in Greek Jewish prayers (cf. 2 Tim.

καὶ ὠρυόμενος (Ps. xxi. 14). He applies the words to the Messiah. After saying that the lion may mean Herod, he adds *ἢ λέοντα τὸν ὠρυόμενον ἐπ' αὐτὸν ἔλεγε τὸν διάβολον.* Again, in chapter 105 he explains the words which occur later in the Psalm (*v.* 21 f.) of the Lord's Passion (*σῶσόν με ἐκ στόματος λέοντος*), and he concludes thus: He prayed *ἵνα, ἡνίκα ἡμεῖς πρὸς τῇ ἐξόδῳ τοῦ βίου γινόμεθα, τὰ αὐτὰ αἰτῶμεν τὸν θεόν, τὸν δυνάμενον ἀποστρέψαι πάντα ἀναιδῆ* [this refers to *ἐκ χειρὸς κυνός*] *πονηρὸν ἄγγελον μὴ λαβέσθαι ἡμῶν τῆς ψυχῆς.* As to Rabbinic writers, I merely transcribe a few words from Edersheim *Life and Times* ii. p. 759: 'In the time of Ezra, the object of Israel's prayer (Neh. viii. 6) was to have Satan delivered to them. After a three days' fast it was granted, and the Yetser ha Ra of idolatry, in the shape of a young lion, was delivered up to them...(Yoma, 69 b).'

[1] Compare Apoc. ii. 10 and much of the later chapters of the Book. For later times see the passages quoted above and the references given in Hagenbach *Hist. of Doctrine*, Eng. Trans., i. p. 200.

[2] Compare *ἐνδυναμοῦσθε ἐν κυρίῳ* (Eph. vi. 10) and the succeeding context. If the ordinary interpretation be adopted, Ps. cviii. 31 (*παρέστη ἐκ δεξιῶν πένητος, τοῦ σῶσαι ἐκ τῶν διωκόντων τὴν ψυχήν μου*) is an apt parallel. Comp. also *Pss. Solomon* xiii. 3 *θηρία ἐπέδραμον αὐτοῖς πονηρά, ἐν τοῖς ὀδοῦσιν αὐτῶν ἔτιλλον σάρκας αὐτῶν, καὶ ἐν ταῖς μύλαις αὐτῶν ἔθλων ὀστᾶ αὐτῶν· καὶ ἐκ τούτων ἁπάντων ἐρρύσατο ἡμᾶς κύριος.*

[3] Comp. Esther iv. 10 (xiv. 13) *δὸς λόγον εὔρυθμον εἰς τὸ στόμα μου ἐνώπιον τοῦ λέοντος* (i.e. Ahasuerus), Joseph. *Antiq.* xviii. 6. 10 *Μαρσύας δὲ τοῦ Ἀγρίππου ὁ ἀπελεύθερος πυθόμενος Τιβερίου τὴν τελευτὴν...γλώσσῃ τῇ Ἑβραίων τέθνηκεν ὁ λέων φησίν.* These passages, referred to by Grinfield, certainly support the first of Chrysostom's interpretations.

iii. 11). In the liturgical portion of the *Didaché* (x. 5) the words occur τοῦ ῥύσασθαι αὐτὴν ἀπὸ παντὸς πονηροῦ: and in an earlier passage (iii. 1) we read φεῦγε ἀπὸ παντὸς πονηροῦ. Similar phrases are found in the Liturgies; thus in that of St James, ῥυόμενος ἡμᾶς ἀπὸ παντὸς πονηροῦ πράγματος (Swainson p. 238 f., Hammond p. 32), εἰς ἀποτροπὴν παντὸς πονηροῦ πράγματος (Swainson p. 320 f., Hammond p. 52)[1]. Such phrases should be compared with the Hebrew prayers quoted by Dr Taylor, *Sayings of the Jewish Fathers*, p. 142 f.; and in their Greek form they appear to be liturgical adaptations of such passages of the LXX. as Deut. xxiii. 9 φυλάξῃ ἀπὸ παντὸς ῥήματος πονηροῦ, Job i. 1, 8 ἀπεχόμενος ἀπὸ παντὸς πονηροῦ πράγματος, Ps. cxx. 7 κύριος φυλάξει σε ἀπὸ παντὸς κακοῦ, compare Wisd. xvi. 8 σὺ εἶ ὁ ῥυόμενος ἐκ παντὸς κακοῦ. If then St Paul weaves into his words a well-known liturgical phrase, he gives it a special application. 'The Lord has rescued me from the enemy once,' we may understand him to mean, 'He will deliver me, if need be, again. One μεθοδεία διαβόλου is past; others will follow; through the help of God all will fail.'

According to this view the reference to the last petition of the Lord's Prayer is spread over the two clauses, though the key words (ῥύσεται...ἀπὸ...πονηροῦ) occur only in the second. If this explanation be accepted, the passage as a whole may be thought to support the masculine interpretation.

(6) 1 John v. 18 f. οἴδαμεν ὅτι πᾶς ὁ γεγεννημένος ἐκ τοῦ θεοῦ οὐχ ἁμαρτάνει, ἀλλ' ὁ γεννηθεὶς ἐκ τοῦ θεοῦ τηρεῖ αὐτόν, καὶ ὁ πονηρὸς οὐχ ἅπτεται αὐτοῦ.

Here ὁ γεννηθείς refers to the Eternal Son. The close connexion of this passage with Christ's prayer for His Apostles recorded by St John (xvii.) has been already pointed out (p. 110). This close connexion carries with it the probability of a reference to the Lord's Prayer.

To sum up this stage of the discussion: the references to the clause of the Prayer which I have pointed out in the Epistles are not all of them beyond dispute. But in each case probability

[1] Comp. *Test. xii. Patr.* Dan 6 διατηρήσατε οὖν ἑαυτοὺς...ἀπὸ παντὸς ἔργου πονηροῦ. For such phrases in the 'Clementine' Liturgy see below, p. 144.

has, I believe, been reached, and it must be remembered that the combined force of several probabilities far exceeds their simple aggregate. Each fresh probability not only adds to the number of probabilities, but increases the strength of each of those to which it is added. The evidence therefore derived from the Epistles confirms that derived from the Gospels and supports the masculine interpretation of *ἀπὸ τοῦ πονηροῦ*.

On the Locality in which the Lord's Prayer was given.

In St Matthew's Gospel the Lord's Prayer is embodied in a carefully framed discourse, which contains many passages which are found scattered throughout the other Synoptic Gospels. St Luke (xi. 1), on the other hand, distinctly describes the occasion on which the Prayer was given. With regard to the locality he uses a striking though indefinite expression: 'It came to pass as He was praying *in a certain place*' (*ἐν τῷ εἶναι αὐτὸν ἐν τόπῳ τινὶ προσευχόμενον*), or, as it may be perhaps more literally rendered: 'It came to pass as He was *in a certain place* praying.' Is there any possibility of identifying the locality from the context?

The incident recorded in the verses which immediately precede is the story of the two sisters, Martha and Mary. This is introduced by an equally vague term: 'And as they journeyed He entered *into a certain village*' (*εἰς κώμην τινά*). But we know from St John's Gospel (xi. 1) that the actual residence of Mary and her sister Martha was Bethany[1]. And Bethany, the same Gospel tells us (xi. 18), 'was nigh unto Jerusalem, about fifteen furlongs off.' It was on the other side of the Mount of Olives. The 'certain village' then, which for some reason St Luke does not name, was one which played an important part in the Gospel history. It was the scene of the raising of Lazarus from the dead: it was the home of our Lord during the last week before the Passion: it was the spot from which He ascended from earth to heaven.

The 'certain place' in which our Lord was praying just before He gave His Prayer to the Disciples may well have been as definite and as interesting a spot, although St Luke does not record its name. The context leads us to

[1] When we compare this passage in St John, *Λάζαρος ἀπὸ Βηθανίας ἐκ τῆς κώμης Μαρίας καὶ Μάρθας τῆς ἀδελφῆς αὐτῆς*, with the words of the same writer (i. 44), *ἦν δὲ ὁ Φίλιππος ἀπὸ Βηθσαιδά, ἐκ τῆς πόλεως* (i.e. probably Capernaum) *Ἀνδρέου καὶ Πέτρου*, we may perhaps, with Bp Westcott (*ad loc.*), regard the prepositions as contrasting their 'actual residence' with their 'true home.' But this does not seriously affect the argument. Bethany itself is called a *κώμη* by St John immediately afterwards (xi. 30).

look for it in the neighbourhood of Bethany, the Mount of Olives, and Jerusalem. May it not have been 'the garden of Gethsemane'?

The name Gethsemane occurs in Matt. xxvi. 36, *τότε ἔρχεται μετ' αὐτῶν ὁ Ἰησοῦς εἰς χωρίον λεγόμενον Γεθσημανεί*, and Mc. xiv. 32, *καὶ ἔρχονται εἰς χωρίον οὗ τὸ ὄνομα Γεθσημανεί*. The word *χωρίον* occurs seven times elsewhere in the N. T., John iv. 5, Acts i. 18, 19, iv. 34, v. 3, 8, xxviii. 7; and in every case it has the definite meaning of a parcel or plot of land belonging to a private owner. We must suppose therefore that Gethsemane was an enclosed piece of ground to which our Lord and His Disciples had some special right of entry. This is borne out by John xviii. 1, *ἐξῆλθεν σὺν τοῖς μαθηταῖς αὐτοῦ πέραν τοῦ χειμάρρου τῶν Κέδρων ὅπου ἦν κῆπος, εἰς ὃν εἰσῆλθεν αὐτὸς καὶ οἱ μαθηταὶ αὐτοῦ. ᾔδει δὲ καὶ Ἰούδας...τὸν τόπον, ὅτι πολλάκις συνήχθη Ἰησοῦς ἐκεῖ μετὰ τῶν μαθητῶν αὐτοῦ.*

When we turn to St Luke's account of the Agony we find the same vagueness about the locality as we have seen already in his Gospel: Lc. xxii. 39, *καὶ ἐξελθὼν ἐπορεύθη κατὰ τὸ ἔθος εἰς τὸ Ὄρος τῶν Ἐλαιῶν· ἠκολούθησαν δὲ αὐτῷ καὶ οἱ μαθηταί. γενόμενος δὲ ἐπὶ τοῦ τόπου εἶπεν αὐτοῖς Προσεύχεσθε μὴ εἰσελθεῖν εἰς πειρασμόν.* Is it too much to suppose that the very prayer which He bids them pray was immediately suggested by the associations of the actual locality in which He had said to them before: *ὅταν προσεύχησθε, λέγετε...Μὴ εἰσενέγκῃς ἡμᾶς εἰς πειρασμόν*? It has been already pointed out (see p. 61) that the coincidence is far more striking in the Syriac Versions, which may be taken as representing to us approximately the original form of the words: for in those Versions the two words, *εἰσελθεῖν* and *εἰσενέγκῃς*, are but the two voices, ܬܥܘܠܘܢ (Peal) and ܬܥܠܢ (Aphel) of the same verb[1]. It has also been demonstrated that other words of the Prayer were in our Lord's mind at this supreme moment (see p. 108 ff.).

To return to the word *χωρίον*. In Matt. xxvi. 36 the Latin Versions vary

[1] The want of a causative voice in the Greek language to correspond to the Aphel of the Syriac receives a parallel illustration in the case of the root ܢܦܩ, 'to go forth,' *ἐξελθεῖν*. In the following among many other passages the Aphel of this verb, 'to make to go forth,' corresponds to the Greek *ἐκβάλλειν*, a word which in the light of this correspondence will not bear the stress which is sometimes laid on it. Mt. ix. 38 *ὅπως ἐκβάλῃ ἐργάτας* ('send forth' A. V., R. V.), xii. 35 *ἐκ τοῦ ἀγαθοῦ θησαυροῦ ἐκβάλλει τὰ ἀγαθά* ('bringeth forth' A. V., R. V.), Mc. i. 12 *τὸ πνεῦμα αὐτὸν ἐκβάλλει* ('driveth him' A. V., 'driveth him forth' R. V.), i. 43 *εὐθὺς ἐξέβαλεν αὐτόν* ('sent him away' A. V., 'sent him out' R. V.), Lc. x. 35 *ἐκβαλὼν δύο δηνάρια* ('took out' A. V., R. V.), Jn. x. 4 *τὰ ἴδια πάντα ἐκβάλῃ* ('putteth forth' A. V., 'hath put forth' R. V.), Acts xvi. 37 *λάθρᾳ ἡμᾶς ἐκβάλλουσιν* ('thrust us out' A. V., 'cast us out' R. V.), Jas. ii. 25 *ἑτέρᾳ ὁδῷ ἐκβαλοῦσα* ('sent them out' A. V., R. V.). Notably in two of the above instances, Mt. ix. 38 and Mc. i. 12, commentators have frequently been misled by the apparent strength of the expression in the Greek. It is worth while to compare with the latter passage Mt. iv. 1 *ἀνήχθη...ὑπὸ τοῦ πνεύματος*, and Lc. iv. 1 *ἤγετο ἐν τῷ πνεύματι*, phrases which seem to represent two efforts to escape from the harshness of *ἐκβάλλει*.

between 'uillam' (Vulg.), 'locum' (Brix.=*f*) and 'agrum' (Bezae=*d*). In Mc. xiv. 32 it is rendered by 'praedium.' It is possible that St Luke purposely chose the vaguer word τόπος both in xi. 1 and in xxii. 40 in preference to the more definite χωρίον, which would have involved a further description of the site. In this case two alternatives would probably have presented themselves to his mind: either to give the name Gethsemane and follow it by a translation; or simply to say that the name of the place was 'Oil-press,' as in xxiii. 33 he says ὅτε ἦλθαν ἐπὶ τὸν τόπον τὸν λεγόμενον Κρανίον. But apparently he considered that he had sufficiently defined the locality by saying ἐπορεύθη κατὰ τὸ ἔθος εἰς τὸ Ὄρος τῶν Ἐλαιῶν. In the omission of the name Gethsemane his account is in harmony with that of St John, who contents himself with saying that the κῆπος was a place where 'Jesus ofttimes assembled (συνήχθη, a word suggesting gatherings for prayer or teaching) with His disciples.'

A suggestion of this kind is not capable, with the evidence at our disposal, of exact proof. It must remain as a suggestion: but I am glad to have been allowed to make it in connection with the line of argument which has been adopted in this essay. [J. A. R.]

(iii) Evidence derived from early Christian literature.

Early Christian exegesis is not infallible. It is always devout, often suggestive; yet sometimes criticism convicts it of grave mistakes. It cannot therefore of itself be taken as decisive on such a question as that under consideration. But, though not in itself decisive, it has a twofold value. It has an historical or archaeological value; for it cannot but be of the highest interest to ascertain in what sense the early generations of Christians, to many of whom Greek was a spoken language, understood the disputed clause. Again, early exegesis, so far as its verdict coincides with the conclusion which is based on a consideration of the modes of thought and expression current in the time of our Lord and His Apostles, may be regarded as supplying confirmatory evidence as to the original meaning of the disputed clause. The cogency of the primary evidence which we have already discussed will be strengthened, if we see that it harmonises with the view which prevailed at a later date. What this view was will appear all the more distinctly if we bear in mind the incidental nature of the allusion to the last petition of the Lord's Prayer in many of the passages now to be discussed.

(1) *Didaché* x. πρὸ πάντων εὐχαριστοῦμέν σοι ὅτι δυνατὸς εἶ σύ· σοὶ ἡ δόξα εἰς τοὺς αἰῶνας. μνήσθητι, κύριε, τῆς ἐκκλησίας σου τοῦ ῥύσασθαι αὐτὴν ἀπὸ παντὸς πονηροῦ καὶ τελειῶσαι αὐτὴν ἐν τῇ ἀγάπῃ σου, καὶ σύναξον αὐτὴν ἀπὸ τῶν τεσσάρων ἀνέμων, τὴν ἁγιασθεῖσαν εἰς τὴν σὴν βασιλείαν, ἣν ἡτοίμασας αὐτῇ· ὅτι σοῦ ἐστιν ἡ δύναμις καὶ ἡ δόξα εἰς τοὺς αἰῶνας.

Many questions about the *Didaché* must still be treated with great caution; none more so than the problem connected with the liturgical element in this document. As yet our knowledge of ancient Synagogue Prayers and of their relation to the earliest Christian liturgies is too slight to warrant anything more than provisional conclusions. In what follows I wish wholly to disclaim a desire to dogmatise.

The passage quoted above forms part of the Eucharistic formula, which the Didachist incorporates in his manual, and to which I have had occasion to refer more than once (see above, pp. 16 f., 33 f.). The whole thanksgiving seems to be the resultant, as I have already suggested, of two converging forces, Jewish prayers and the Lord's Prayer. The first section of this formula answers (see above, p. 34) to the clauses in the Lord's Prayer which speak of the divine Name and Kingdom and Will. The second section refers to the petition for 'daily bread.' There is nothing to correspond to the prayer for forgiveness. And thus we are brought to the last two clauses of the Prayer as those to which this thanksgiving (εὐχαριστοῦμέν σοι ὅτι κ.τ.λ.) and this prayer (μνήσθητι...πονηροῦ) refer.

I have already suggested (p. 16) that the word δυνατός thus applied absolutely to God is borrowed from Greek Jewish prayers. The whole phrase δυνατὸς εἶ σύ (where the emphatic σύ is to be noted) seems most natural if the thought of victorious conflict with the great spiritual enemy of the Church is implied. This conclusion is to some extent supported by the comparison of a petition put into Esther's mouth, but probably based on some liturgical formula [Esther iv. 16 (xiv. 19), see Fritzsch *Libri Apocryphi* p. 51]: καὶ νῦν δυνατὸς ὢν ἐπὶ πάντας εἰσάκουσον φωνῆς ἀπηλπισμένων καὶ ῥῦσαι ἡμᾶς ἐκ χειρὸς τῶν πονηρευομένων ἐφ' ἡμᾶς. Here the reference is to personal enemies. Further, this idea would be obviously in harmony with many passages of the

New Testament, such as Apoc. xii. 10 ff., xv. 3 f., xix. 1 f., Eph. vi. 10 ff., Rom. xvi. 20, Lc. xi. 22 (|| Matt. xii. 29, Mc. iii. 27).

When however we pass from the thanksgiving to the prayer which follows it, we find in the *ἀπὸ παντὸς πονηροῦ* a different interpretation of *ἀπὸ τοῦ πονηροῦ* suggested.

The Didachist has already used the same phrase, *τέκνον μου, φεῦγε ἀπὸ παντὸς πονηροῦ* (iii. 1, comp. v. 2 *ῥυσθείητε, τέκνα, ἀπὸ τούτων ἁπάντων*). Probably in both places he is repeating some current liturgical formula, either directly borrowed from, or based upon, Greek Jewish prayers. The passage will then be closely akin to 2 Tim. iv. 18 (see above, p. 121 f.). Assuming therefore, in the present state of our knowledge as to the liturgical sources of the *Didaché*, that there is a reference to the Lord's Prayer in this Eucharistic form, we conclude that, though the Didachist in the word *δυνατός* appears to hint at the thought of the great spiritual enemy, yet in the phrase *ἀπὸ παντὸς πονηροῦ*, which is probably derived from some well-known formula, he gives the neuter interpretation of the last petition of the Lord's Prayer.

(2) Ep. Clement 60. *ναί, δέσποτα, ἐπίφανον τὸ πρόσωπόν σου ἐφ' ἡμᾶς εἰς ἀγαθὰ ἐν εἰρήνῃ, εἰς τὸ σκεπασθῆναι ἡμᾶς τῇ χειρί σου τῇ κραταιᾷ καὶ ῥυσθῆναι ἀπὸ πάσης ἁμαρτίας τῷ βραχίονί σου τῷ ὑψηλῷ· καὶ ῥῦσαι ἡμᾶς ἀπὸ τῶν μισούντων ἡμᾶς ἀδίκως.* This passage is quoted by Canon Cook. 'In his notes on this passage,' he writes (*Second Letter* p. 57), 'the Bishop marks distinctly the words taken from the Old Testament; but he does not notice the striking fact that, when these words are omitted, the petition is in accordance with the closing words of the Lord's Prayer, the same phrase, *ῥῦσαι ἡμᾶς ἀπό*, "*deliver us from*," being used at the close; and further, that the power from which deliverance is craved is not that of Satan, but of *all sin* and of human enemies: presenting in a comprehensive form the sense which I have throughout maintained to be expressed by the words *τοῦ πονηροῦ*.' This position would perhaps have appeared stronger if Canon Cook had noted some words a few lines earlier in the same chapter of the Epistle which might seem to be a reference to another petition of the Prayer: *ἄφες ἡμῖν τὰς ἀνομίας ἡμῶν καὶ τὰς ἀδικίας καὶ τὰ παραπτώματα καὶ πλημμελείας.* A reference however to Trommius' Concordance seems to shew plainly enough

the ultimate source of Clement's words[1]. Compare (*a*) Gen. l. 17 *ἄφες αὐτοῖς τὴν ἀδικίαν καὶ τὴν ἁμαρτίαν αὐτῶν*, Ps. xxiv. 18 *ἄφες πάσας τὰς ἁμαρτίας μου*, Numb. xiv. 18 *ἀφαιρῶν ἀνομίας καὶ ἀδικίας καὶ ἁμαρτίας*: (*b*) Ps. xvii. 21 *ῥύσεταί με ἐξ ἐχθρῶν μου δυνατῶν καὶ ἐκ τῶν μισούντων με*, xxx. 16 *ῥῦσαί με ἐκ χειρὸς ἐχθρῶν μου*, xxxvii. 20 *ἐπληθύνθησαν οἱ μισοῦντές με ἀδίκως*, lxviii. 15 *ῥυσθείην ἐκ τῶν μισούντων με*, cv. 10 *ἔσωσεν αὐτοὺς ἐκ χειρῶν μισούντων*: (*c*) Ps. xxxviii. 9 *ἀπὸ πασῶν τῶν ἀνομιῶν μου ῥῦσαί με*, Ezek. xxxvii. 23 *ῥύσομαι αὐτοὺς ἀπὸ πασῶν τῶν ἀνομιῶν αὐτῶν ὧν ἡμάρτοσαν ἐν αὐταῖς*.

These three groups of passages put it beyond a doubt that Clement cannot be claimed as a witness in this discussion.

(3) The Ancient Homily (formerly called the Second Epistle of Clement) xviii. *καὶ γὰρ αὐτὸς πανθαμαρτωλὸς*[2] *ὢν καὶ μήπω φυγὼν τὸν πειρασμόν, ἀλλ' ἔτι ὢν ἐν μέσοις τοῖς ὀργάνοις τοῦ διαβόλου, σπουδάζω τὴν δικαιοσύνην διώκειν*.

We seem here to have a rhetorical reminiscence of the last two clauses of the Lord's Prayer[3], which perhaps had just been said in the assembly.

Besides the coincidence of ideas, the form of the sentence suggests this conclusion. There is the familiar juxtaposition of words *πειρασμόν, ἀλλά*.

It is moreover to be noticed that the preacher very frequently quotes sayings of our Lord in a form which sometimes agrees with, but sometimes diverges from, the text of our Gospels. Examples will be found in Chapters ii., iii., iv., v., vi., viii., ix., xiii. If

[1] It is remarkable that both in regard to words and thoughts Clement has at this point much in common with the Benedictus (Lc. i. 68 ff., see esp. *vv.* 71, 74, 79). Note the phrase *ἐν ὁσιότητι καὶ δικαιοσύνῃ* (Lc. i. 75, Clem. 48, 60). St Paul, it should be remembered, has the reverse order in a familiar passage (Eph. iv. 24). See note A, p. 147.

[2] Comp. *πανθαμάρτητοι* *Did.* v. 2.

[3] Shortly after the publication of Bp Lightfoot's letters on *ἀπὸ τοῦ πονηροῦ* I noticed this passage and ventured to call the Bishop's attention to it. In the letter, in which with his usual thoughtful kindness he acknowledged the suggestion, he wrote, 'I am certainly disposed to think that the preacher had the Lord's Prayer in his mind.' Later I stumbled upon the coincidence with the Lord's Prayer in the *Letter of Vienne and Lyons* noted below, and communicated it to the Bishop. From his reply I gathered that he accepted this reference also. These parts of the discussion therefore have, at least for myself, a special interest.

there are some quotations from apocryphal sources (iv., v., xii.), one phrase from our Gospels is introduced by the formula, *καὶ ἑτέρα δὲ γραφὴ λέγει* (ii.)[1].

Three leading ideas of the Lord's Prayer—the Fatherhood, the Will, the Kingdom of God—are clearly favourite thoughts with the preacher, and are associated together in his mind. Thus *ποιήσωμεν τὸ θέλημα τοῦ καλέσαντος ἡμᾶς* (ch. v.), *ποιοῦντες τὸ θέλημα τοῦ Χριστοῦ εὑρήσομεν ἀνάπαυσιν* (vi.), *ποιήσαντες τὸ θέλημα τοῦ πατρός* (viii.), *ἐκδεχώμεθα οὖν καθ' ὥραν τὴν βασιλείαν τοῦ θεοῦ* (xii.), *ἐπερωτηθεὶς...ὁ κύριος...πότε ἥξει αὐτοῦ ἡ βασιλεία* (xii.), *ἐλεύσεται ἡ βασιλεία τοῦ πατρός μου* (xii.), *ποιοῦντες τὸ θέλημα τοῦ πατρὸς ἡμῶν* (xiv.).

But whether the reference to the Lord's Prayer be conceded or not, the passage is of importance from another point of view. 'I am greatly mistaken,' wrote Canon Cook[2], 'if in any of the earliest and best of the Fathers, traces can be found, I will not say of the new interpretation of the petition, but of a condition of spirit in which Christians of all ages, in every stage of spiritual life, are found praying for deliverance from Satan.'

It is remarkable that the preacher of the earliest Christian sermon which has come down to us took a widely different view. He, like St Paul, is profoundly conscious that he has to contend against supernatural foes and that 'there is no discharge in that war.' It is of course true that the Fathers not unfrequently follow the example of St John and, taking an idealistic view of the Christian man's position, speak of Satan as already conquered[3]. This idealistic conception was perhaps all the more natural to them because they felt the contrast between the purity and peace of the persecuted Church and, on the other hand, the foulness and the inhumanity of the dominant paganism. Sometimes also—for then, as now, piety and exact thought did not always go hand in hand—we find in early Christian literature teaching on this subject not of the soberest order. Several passages in the 'Shepherd' fall under this category. Thus, 'Turn

[1] Comp. xiv. (*τὰ βιβλία καὶ οἱ ἀπόστολοι*).

[2] *A Second Letter to the Bp of London* p. 61.

[3] See, for example, the passages collected in Hagenbach *Hist. of Doctrines*, E. T., i. p. 204.

ye, ye who walk in the commandments of the devil, in hard and bitter and cruel lasciviousness, and fear not the devil, for in him there is no power against you. For I will be with you, I, the Angel of Repentance, who have dominion over him. The devil hath nought but fear, and his fear hath no force. Fear him not therefore, and he will flee from you....The threatening of the devil fear ye not at all: for he is without force like the sinew of a corpse' (*Mand.* xii. 4, 6). This strain of teaching runs through the whole book. It would however be as unfortunate to take the 'Shepherd' as a standard of the sober doctrinal conclusions of the Church in the Second Century as it would be to assume that the Pilgrim's Progress is an index of the belief of English Christians in the Seventeenth. Both books alike are illustrations of, and tended to perpetuate, certain popular fashions of religious thought. To what unbalanced expressions such popular views of the Christian position led is seen in the request for baptism put into the mouth of the heroine of a religious romance current in Tertullian's time, which, however generally inferior, is yet not without its points of resemblance to the 'Shepherd.' 'Only give me the seal,' exclaims Thecla, 'which is in Christ (i.e. Baptism), and temptation shall not touch me' (*μόνον δός μοι τὴν ἐν Χριστῷ σφραγῖδα καὶ οὐχ ἅψεταί μου πειρασμός*: *Acta Paul. et Thecl.* 25, comp. 1 Jn. v. 18).

But there are not wanting passages in early writers, even in such a writer as Hermas himself, which shew that the practical instinct of Christian humility asserted itself. One such passage from an early Christian sermon has been the starting point of this discussion. Similarly we read in the Epistle of Barnabas a warning 'lest haply, resting as those who have been called, we fall asleep in our sins, and so the evil ruler (*ὁ πονηρὸς ἄρχων*), assuming his power against us (*τὴν καθ' ἡμῶν ἐξουσίαν*), thrust us from the kingdom of the Lord' (iv. 13)[1]. Again, the revelation given to Hermas about 'the angel of evil' (*ὁ ἄγγελος τῆς πονηρίας*) is significant. 'His works are evil, overthrowing the servants of God. When therefore he cometh into thine heart, know him by his works...When anger or bitterness assaileth

[1] Comp. c. ii. (*ἡμερῶν οὖν οὐσῶν πονηρῶν καὶ αὐτοῦ τοῦ ἐνεργοῦντος ἔχοντος τὴν ἐξουσίαν*), and the passage from Athenagoras *Supplicatio* quoted above p. 100.

thee, know thou that he is within thee...When these lusts come into thine heart, know thou that the angel of evil is within thee...If a man be very faithful and yet the thought of this angel cometh into his heart, that man or woman must sin' (*Mand.* vi. 2; comp. iv. 3, 4 ff., xii. 4 f.). Hence the anxious humility which inspires such words as those of Barnabas (ii. 10), 'We ought, brethren, to be exceeding circumspect (*ἀκριβεύεσθαι*) in the matter of our salvation, lest the evil one should craftily effect an entrance issuing in error and should hurl us forth (*ἐκσφενδονήσῃ*) out of our life.' Two later writers, both of whom understand the petition under discussion to refer to Satan, may be taken as the best exponents of the combination of wise fear and chastened confidence, which was and is, I believe, the characteristic of sober Christian teaching on this subject. On the one hand Cyprian, the earliest Doctor of the Western Church, in a passage (*de Oratione Dominica*) which will call for closer investigation presently, uses the following words in reference to the closing clauses of the Lord's Prayer, 'Quando autem rogamus ne in temptationem veniamus, ádmonemur infirmitatis et imbecillitatis nostrae dum sic rogamus, ne quis se insolenter extollat, ne quis sibi superbe atque arroganter aliquid assumat, ne quis sibi aut confessionis aut passionis gloriam suam ducat...adversa cuncta quae contra nos in hoc mundo molitur inimicus; a quibus potest esse fida et firma tutela, si nos Deus liberet, si deprecantibus atque implorantibus opem suam praestet[1]'. On the other hand Cyril of Jerusalem, holding that in the Lord's Prayer we pray against the assaults of Satan, uses language (*Catechesis* xvi. 19), when speaking of the Holy Spirit as 'the ally and champion sent from God,' hardly less confident than that of the 'Shepherd': *μὴ φοβηθῶμεν τοὺς δαίμονας μήτε τὸν διάβολον· μείζων γὰρ ὁ ἡμῶν ὑπεραγωνιστής· μόνον ἀνοίξωμεν αὐτῷ τὰς θύρας.*

(4) Hermas *Mand.* xii. 6. *ἐὰν ἐπιστραφῆτε πρὸς τὸν κύριον ἐξ ὅλης τῆς καρδίας ὑμῶν...καὶ δουλεύσητε αὐτῷ ὀρθῶς κατὰ*

[1] Comp. the intensely practical tract *de Aleatoribus* 5: Quam magna et larga pietas domini fidelium, quod in futurum praescius nobis consulat, ne quis frater incautus denuo laqueis diaboli capiatur. Sollicitos esse jussit et providos adque eruditos, quoniam hostis ille antiquus circuit pulsans dei servos non uno genere temptans.

τὸ θέλημα αὐτοῦ, ποιήσει ἴασιν τοῖς προτέροις ὑμῶν ἁμαρτήμασι, καὶ ἕξετε δύναμιν τοῦ κατακυριεῦσαι τῶν ἔργων τοῦ διαβόλου. Comp. ib. 4, *ἐγὼ γὰρ ἔσομαι μεθ' ὑμῶν, ὁ ἄγγελος τῆς μετανοίας, ὁ κατακυριεύων αὐτοῦ.*

It would be wrong to assert dogmatically that the writer here has the Lord's Prayer in his mind. But the agreement of the three ideas—God's will, forgiveness, power over Satan—with three petitions of the Lord's Prayer is worth attention.

(5) The letter of the Churches of Vienne and Lyons (ap. Eus. *H. E.* v. 1 § 6). *ἀντεστρατήγει δὲ ἡ χάρις τοῦ θεοῦ, καὶ τοὺς μὲν ἀσθενεῖς ἐρρύετο· ἀντιπαρέτασσε δὲ στύλους ἑδραίους, δυναμένους διὰ τῆς ὑπομονῆς πᾶσαν τὴν ὁρμὴν τοῦ πονηροῦ εἰς ἑαυτοὺς ἑλκύσαι, οἳ καὶ ὁμόσε ἐχώρουν [αὐτῷ], πᾶν εἶδος ὀνειδισμοῦ καὶ κολάσεως ἀνεχόμενοι.*

A reference to the Lord's Prayer seems very probable (*ἐρρύετο ...τοῦ πονηροῦ*). But is *τοῦ πονηροῦ* masculine[1]? Any remaining doubt as to this point is dissipated by a study of other passages in the letter. It was 'according to a device of Satan' (*κατ' ἐνέδραν τοῦ Σατανᾶ*) that the household servants of certain Christians invented lying stories against them (§ 14). The fury of the governor and crowd and soldiers was kindled to exceeding frenzy because it was 'Satan's ambition' (*φιλοτιμουμένου τοῦ Σατανᾶ*) that some of the blasphemous slanders should be spoken even by the holy martyrs (§ 16). In the martyr Sanctus 'Christ suffered and wrought out His great glory, bringing the adversary (*τὸν ἀντικείμενον*, compare 1 Tim. v. 14 f., Zech. iii. 1) to nought' (§ 23). When Biblias had denied Christ, the devil, wishing to consummate her condemnation, brought her again to torture (§ 25). When 'the blessed ones' stood firm 'the devil invented fresh tortures' (§ 27). At a later stage of the trial Maturus and Sanctus 'endured every torment of the amphitheatre, as though they had suffered nothing heretofore, but rather had in many previous conflicts driven back the adversary' (*τὸν ἀντίπαλον*, § 38). When all was over, 'the wild and barbarous tribes incited by the Wild Beast' (*ὑπὸ ἀγρίου θηρὸς*) sought to rob the

[1] Compare the words of Eusebius (*H.E.* ii. 14) *ἡ θεία καὶ ὑπερουράνιος χάρις... ἀναπτομένην τοῦ πονηροῦ τὴν φλόγα ᾗ τάχος ἐσβέννυ.* The words just above (*ἡ μισόκαλος καὶ τῆς ἀνθρώπων ἐπίβουλος σωτηρίας πονηρὰ δύναμις*) define the meaning.

Christian of the bodies of the martyrs (§ 57). Throughout the letter the agency of the devil is traced in every detail of the persecution, and thus the reference in the earlier passage is fixed.

(6) Clementine Homilies xix. 2 (Migne *P. G.* 2 p. 424). *καὶ ὁ Πέτρος· ἀδύνατόν ἐστί μοι φωνὴν τοῦ ἐμοῦ ἀρνήσασθαι διδασκάλου, διὸ καὶ ὁμολογῶ εἶναι τὸν πονηρόν, ὅτι πολλάκις αὐτὸν ὑπάρχειν ὁ πάντα ἀληθεύσας εἴρηκε διδάσκαλος...ὅτι ἑώρακε τὸν πονηρὸν ὡς ἀστραπὴν πεσόντα ἐκ τοῦ οὐρανοῦ ἐδήλωσε...καὶ πάλιν· μὴ δότε πρόφασιν τῷ πονηρῷ. ἀλλὰ καὶ συμβουλεύων εἴρηκεν· ἔστω ὑμῶν τὸ ναί, ναί, καὶ τὸ οὔ, οὔ· τὸ δὲ περισσὸν τούτων ἐκ τοῦ πονηροῦ ἐστίν. ἀλλὰ καὶ ἐν ᾗ παρέδωκεν εὐχῇ ἔχομεν εἰρημένον· ῥῦσαι ἡμᾶς ἀπὸ τοῦ πονηροῦ.* See above p. 100.

The verdict of this passage is clear as to the interpretation of the petition of the Lord's Prayer. Canon Cook, however, questioned its validity. 'Those spurious and heretical writings lay altogether outside the scope of my argument...I should have shrunk from an attempt to introduce them into any controversy touching our Lord's teaching or the mind of the primitive Church' (*A Second Letter* p. 56). The case is materially altered when the passage from the Clementines is viewed in connexion with the body of evidence from the Apostolic and sub-Apostolic writings which we have collected and reviewed. It does not stand alone as the isolated utterance of misguided separatists. It does but state explicitly the interpretation which we have found to be implied in writings which are above the suspicion of heterodoxy. And further, the one witness outside the New Testament, whose evidence is equivocal, if it be not adverse to the interpretation maintained in this essay, becomes here of special importance. The Didaché is a document with strong Jewish affinities. Whether or no it be an adaptation of a purely Jewish manual or purely Jewish manuals, it speaks with the voice of Jewish Christians, who, at the time of its composition or shortly afterwards, were regarded as standing upon, if not outside, the extreme limits of the Catholic Church. Its evidence therefore shews that the masculine interpretation of *ἀπὸ τοῦ πονηροῦ* was not the characteristic and proper possession of the Judaising Christians.

(7) Tertullian. In two treatises, one of which is placed

among his earlier, the other among his later Montanistic writings, Tertullian discusses the last clause of the Lord's Prayer.

(*a*) *de Oratione* viii. Ne nos inducas in temptationem, id est, ne nos patiaris induci, ab eo utique qui temptat[1]. Ceterum absit ut dominus temptare videatur, quasi aut ignoret fidem cujusque aut deicere sit gestiens. Diaboli est et infirmitas et malitia...Ipse a diabolo temptatus praesidem et artificem temptationis demonstravit. Hunc locum posterioribus confirmat, Orate, dicens, ne temptemini. Adeo temptati sunt dominum deserendo, quia somno potius indulserunt quam orationi. Ergo respondet clausula, interpretans quid sit, Ne nos deducas in temptationem. Hoc est enim, Sed devehe nos a malo.

Throughout Tertullian is eager to justify God's ways to men. To the devil therefore he assigns a double part in regard to temptation. He both leads men into temptation (induci ab eo... artificem temptationis) and he tempts them (qui temptat...praesidem temptationis). It is for this reason (because, that is, the occasion of the temptation and the temptation itself are to be traced to Satan, not to God), that the explanatory clause is added, Sed devehe nos a malo. If *malo* were neuter, the addition according to Tertullian's exegesis would be without point[2].

(*b*) *de Fuga in Persecutione* ii. In legitima oratione, cum dicimus ad Patrem, Ne nos inducas in temptationem (quae autem major temptatio quam persecutio?), ab eo illam profitemur accidere a quo veniam ejus deprecamur. Hoc est enim quod sequitur, Sed erue nos a maligno, id est, ne nos induxeris in temptationem

[1] Comp. *adv. Marc.* iv. 26. Quis non sinet nos deduci in temptationem? Quem poterit temptator non timere, an qui a primordio temptatorem angelum praedamnavit? On the gloss *ne nos patiaris induci* see above p. 64 ff.

[2] Canon Cook's interpretation (*Second Letter* p. 85) of Tertullian's words seems to me to leave out of sight individual expressions (e.g. qui temptat) and the general thought which binds together the whole chapter. 'Whether [Tert's.] exegesis is right or wrong,' he writes, 'it is evident that he understands that prayer to mean, Let not Satan lead us into a position where we shall be in contact with evil and be in danger of overthrow; and when he adds that the last clause corresponds to this petition and interprets it, sc. *Sed devehe nos a malo*, his meaning must be, Instead of suffering us to be led by Satan into such contact, do Thou lead us away from *evil*, in other words, keep us out of the way of every evil which might imperil our salvation.'

permittendo nos maligno. Tunc enim eruimur diaboli manibus, cum illi non tradimur in temptationem.

A study of the whole chapter, of which the most important words are quoted above, shews that Tertullian follows here the same general line of thought as in the *de Oratione.* In both places he discusses the relation of temptation to God and to Satan, only in the later treatise he is led by circumstances to regard temptation under the special form of persecution; in both he refers to the illustration of the Disciples in the Garden; in both places he adopts the same view as to 'ne nos inducas...' In the *de Oratione* his gloss is 'ne nos patiaris induci ab eo'; in the *de Fuga* it is 'ne nos induxeris...permittendo nos maligno[1].'

Canon Cook indeed, maintaining that in the *de Oratione* Tertullian is a witness on his side, finds in his conversion to Montanism a special reason for his supposed change of mind. But in point of fact, had Montanism influenced Tertullian at all in the matter, it would have influenced him in the opposite direction. As a Montanist he claimed to be in an especial sense under the immediate guidance of the Paraclete; he and his were 'spiritual men.' Had he hesitated before, still more would he have hesitated now, to pray for deliverance from the evil one[2].

These two passages are clear as to Tertullian's interpretation of the petition of the Lord's Prayer. It remains however to collect passages in Tertullian's writings in which 'malus' even in the oblique cases is used as a name of Satan. It should be noticed that such an absolute use of the simple adjective is against the Latin idiom, which would rather require 'malus ille,' a phrase which we find in *de Cultu Fem.* ii. 5 (Christianus a malo illo adjuvabitur in aliquo?) and in Zeno of Verona *Tract.* 43 (Migne

[1] The care and sobriety of thought which mark the whole chapter are worth noting. To take a few sentences—'praecedere dei voluntatem circa fidei probationem, quae est ratio persecutionis, sequi autem diaboli iniquitatem ad instrumentum persecutionis, quae ratio est probationis....Nihil Satanae in servos Dei vivi licebit nisi permiserit Dominus.'

[2] It will be remembered that the Catholics of Asia with singular simplicity proposed that they should try upon the Montanists the effects of exorcism, a proposal which the Montanists rejected (Eus. *H.E.* v. 16, 16).

P. L. 11 p. 496, omnes sagittas illius mali). The following passages seem to be decisive as to Tertullian's usage. (*a*) *de Idololatria* xvi. Sed quoniam ita *malus* circumdedit seculum idololatria, licebit adesse in quibusdam, quae nos homini, non idolo, officiosos habent. Two early editions have 'malis' for 'malus' (see Oehler). The whole scope of the passage however is in favour of 'malus'; for the universality, not the evil, of the symbols of idolatry is the point (comp. *de Patientia* xi. quoted below). Further, compare c. xviii. Tu si diaboli pompam ejerasti, quicquid ex ea attigeris, id scias esse idololatriam: c. xxi. per quem te *malus* honori idolorum, id est idololatriae, quaerebat annectere. (*b*) *de Patientia* v. Porro cum deus optimus, diabolus e contrario pessimus, ipsa sui diversitate testantur neutrum alteri facere, ut nobis non magis *a malo* aliquid boni quam a bono aliquid mali editum videri possit...Quid primum fuerit ille angelus perditionis, malus an impatiens, contemno quaerere... [Mulier] traducem [Adam] ejus, quod *a malo* hauserat, facit: c. xi. Lata atque diffusa est operatio *mali*, multiplicia spiritus incitamenta jaculantis...Certemus igitur quae *a malo* infliguntur sustinere, ut hostis studium aemulatio nostrae aequanimitatis eludat...Undique igitur adstricti sumus officio patientiae administrandae, quaque ex parte aut erroribus nostris aut *mali* insidiis admonitionibus domini intervenimus: c. xiv. Quid ridebat Deus, quid dissecabatur *malus*, cum Job immundam ulceris sui redundantiam magna aequanimitate destringeret? Elsewhere (*Apol.* xxii., *de Test. Animae* iii., see Oehler's notes) Tertullian represents the common pagan exclamation *malum* as an unconscious reference to Satan (cf. *adv. Hermog.* xi. erit mali finis cum praeses ejus diabolus abierit in ignem). Thus the usage of the father of ecclesiastical Latin seems beyond the reach of controversy.

(8) Cyprian *de Oratione Dominica*.

In the case of Cyprian, as in that of Tertullian (see p. 27), it is of interest to collect the clauses of the Prayer.

Pater noster qui es in caelis, Sanctificetur nomen tuum, Adveniat regnum tuum, Fiat voluntas tua sicut in caelo et in terra, Panem nostrum cottidianum da nobis hodie, et dimitte nobis debita nostra sicut et nos remittimus debitoribus nostris, Et ne patiaris nos induci in temptationem, sed libera nos a malo.

Cyprian's exposition runs thus:—*Et ne patiaris nos induci in temptationem*[1]. Qua in parte ostenditur nihil contra nos *adversarium* posse, nisi Deus ante permiserit, ut omnis timor noster et devotio atque observatio ad Deum convertatur, quando in temptationibus nihil *malo* liceat, nisi potestas inde tribuatur.... Post ista omnia in consummatione orationis venit clausula universas petitiones et preces nostras collecta brevitate concludens. In novissimo enim ponimus, *Sed libera nos a malo*, comprehendentes adversa cuncta quae contra nos *in hoc mundo* molitur *inimicus;* a quibus potest esse fida et firma tutela, si nos Deus liberet, si deprecantibus atque implorantibus opem suam praestet. Quando autem dicimus, *libera nos a malo*, nihil remanet quod ultra adhuc debeat postulari, quando semel protectionem Dei adversus *malum* petamus; qua impetrata, contra omnia quae *diabolus et mundus* operantur securi stamus et tuti. Quis enim vel de seculo metus est cui in seculo Deus tutor est?

The words which I have italicised put it beyond a doubt that Cyprian's verdict, like Tertullian's, is for the masculine interpretation of *a malo*. In the last sentences indeed he speaks rather as a rhetorician than as a careful interpreter. But here the *diabolus et mundus* is explained by the *in hoc mundo...inimicus* just above[2]. The closing words are justified by their epigram[3].

The importance of the treatment of the point at issue by Tertullian and Cyprian[4] is partly literary and partly religious.

[1] On this clause see above p. 64 f.

[2] There is probably a reference to the formula of renunciation at Baptism; comp. Tert. *de Cor.* 3 (contestamur nos renuntiare diabolo et pompae et angelis ejus), Cyprian *Ep.* vi. (seculo renuntiaveramus cum baptizati sumus), *de Lapsis* 437 (qui jam diabolo renuntiaverat et seculo).

[3] Canon Cook, claiming the support of Cyprian as of Tertullian, (1) unwittingly overlooked Cyprian's comment on *ne patiaris nos induci*; (2) laying the whole stress on *adversa cuncta...a quibus*, he divorced these words from the defining clause *quae molitur inimicus*.

[4] That Cyprian's exposition was regarded as authoritative is clear from the following passage of Hilary of Poictiers (Migne *P. L.* 9 p. 943), 'De orationis autem sacramento necessitate nos commentandi Cyprianus vir sanctae memoriae liberavit. Quamquam et Tertullianus hinc volumen aptissimum scripserit; sed consequens error hominis detraxit scriptis probabilibus auctoritatem.' Hilary himself elsewhere appears to give, as do Chromatius and Pseudo-Augustine, the masculine interpretation; see above p. 67 f.

On the one hand, their evidence is clear as to the current interpretation of *a malo* when the Latin versions of the New Testament were still in the process of formation. On the other hand, they give a singularly noble expression to the feelings with which thoughtful Christian men may regard the prayer for deliverance from the spiritual enemy.

(9) Origen. In three passages of his writings, as they are preserved to us, does Origen give his interpretation of the last clause of the Lord's Prayer.

(*a*) *de Oratione* 30. The date of the treatise is doubtful, but it appears to fall within the Alexandrian period of Origen's literary activity (Bp Westcott in *D. C. Biog.* iv. p. 103). 'No writing of Origen,' says Bp Westcott (*D. C. B.* iv. p. 124), 'is more free from his characteristic faults, or more full of beautiful thoughts.'

δοκεῖ δέ μοι ὁ Λουκᾶς διὰ τοῦ Μὴ εἰσενέγκῃς ἡμᾶς εἰς πειρασμόν, δυνάμει δεδιδαχέναι καὶ τὸ Ῥῦσαι ἡμᾶς ἀπὸ τοῦ πονηροῦ. καὶ εἰκός γε πρὸς μὲν τὸν μαθητήν, ἅτε δὴ ὠφελημένον, εἰρηκέναι τὸν κύριον τὸ ἐπιτομώτερον, πρὸς δὲ τοὺς πλείονας δεομένους τρανοτέρας διδασκαλίας τὸ σαφέστερον. ῥύεται δὲ ἡμᾶς ὁ θεὸς ἀπὸ τοῦ πονηροῦ, οὐχὶ ὅτε οὐδαμῶς ἡμῖν πρόσεισιν ἀντιπαλαίων ὁ ἐχθρὸς δι' οἵων δήποτε μεθοδειῶν ἑαυτοῦ καὶ ὑπηρετῶν τοῦ θελήματος αὐτοῦ, ἀλλ' ὅτε νικῶμεν ἀνδρείως ἱστάμενοι πρὸς τὰ συμβαίνοντα.

(*b*) *Selecta in Psalmos.* Origen deals with Psalm xxxvi. in a series of Homilies. The date of these Homilies is circ. 241 A.D. (Bp Westcott *D. C. B.* iv. p. 104). They are only preserved to us in the Latin translation of Rufinus, who, as appears from the language (e.g. malignum vel malum), to some extent paraphrased the original.

(i) Hom. ii. § 4. 'Quia qui nequiter agunt, exterminabuntur; qui autem expectant Dominum, ipsi haereditate possidebunt terram.' Apparet quia nequitia alia quidem species mali est, praeter cetera peccata. Unde et hic sermo divinus alium describit peccatorem, et alium nequam, sicut et ibi simili utitur distinctione cum dicit: Contere brachium peccatoris et maligni, id est, nequam. Sed et Dominus in Evangelio diabolum non dixit peccatorem tantummodo, sed malignum vel malum, et cum docet in oratione, vel dicit: Sed libera nos a malo. Et alibi: Malus homo fecit, sive malignus. Definiunt quidam *πονηρίαν*, id est, nequitiam, spontaneam vel voluntariam esse malitiam. Aliud est enim per ignorantiam mala agere, et vinci a malo; aliud est voluntate et studio mala facere, et hoc est nequitia. Unde et merito diabolus hoc nomine *πονηρός*, id est, malignus vel nequam appellatur.

(ii) Hom. v. § 7. Venit enim ad unamquamque animam de hoc mundo exeuntem princeps hujus mundi et aereae potestates, et requirunt si inveniant in ea aliquid suum....Et singula quaeque eorum similia si invenerint, suae partis est, et sibi eam defendunt, et ad se eam trahunt....Si vero aliquis imitatus est illum qui dixit: Ecce veniet princeps mundi hujus, et in me non habet quidquam, et si se aliquis ita observavit, veniunt quidem isti peccatores et requirentes in eo quae sua sunt et non invenientes tentabunt nihilominus ad suam partem violenter eum detorquere, sed Dominus eripiet eum a peccatoribus. Et forte propterea jubemur cum quodam mysterio etiam in oratione petere dicentes: Sed libera nos a malo (comp. Justin *Dial.* 105, quoted above p. 121).

These passages, belonging as they do to different periods of Origen's life, shew that he consistently accepted the masculine interpretation of the clause. The theory of Canon Cook (*A Second Letter* pp. 30, 62) that Origen was misled here by his love for 'mystical expositions,' and that this interpretation 'was probably first introduced, as it was certainly first urged upon the Church, by Origen,' is disproved by the evidence for the general currency of the masculine interpretation which we have reviewed, and further by the fact that in the passage from the earlier treatise the interpretation is introduced by Origen, not as a novelty, but incidentally and in a matter of fact way. It is true that in the third passage quoted above he uses the phrase *cum quodam mysterio;* but the *mysterium* applies not to the interpretation itself, but to a particular application of it.

(10) The greatest of Origen's pupils was Dionysius, his successor, though not his immediate successor, as head of the Catechetical School, afterwards Bishop of Alexandria. In a fragment on Luke xxii. 46 (Migne *P. G.* 10 p. 1599) Dionysius deals thus with the last clause of the Lord's Prayer:

καὶ προσεύχεσθαι δὲ πάλιν ἐδίδασκε μὴ ἐμπεσεῖν εἰς πειρασ-

μόν· καὶ δὴ καὶ μὴ εἰσενέγκῃς ἡμᾶς εἰς πειρασμόν· τουτέστι μὴ ἐάσῃς ἡμᾶς [1 Cor. x. 13] *ἐμπεσεῖν εἰς πειρασμόν· ὅτι δὲ τοῦτο ἦν οὐ τὸ μὴ πειρασθῆναι, ῥυσθῆναι δὲ ἀπὸ τοῦ πονηροῦ, προσέθηκεν, ἀλλὰ ῥῦσαι ἡμᾶς ἀπὸ τοῦ πονηροῦ· καὶ τί διενήνοχεν, ἴσως ἐρεῖς, τὸ πειρασθῆναι καὶ τὸ εἰς πειρασμὸν ἐμπεσεῖν ἤτοι εἰσελθεῖν; ὁ μὲν γὰρ ἡττηθεὶς ὑπὸ τοῦ πονηροῦ (ἡττηθήσεται δὲ εἰ μὴ ἀγωνίζοιτο, ὑπερασπίζοι δὲ αὐτοῦ καὶ ὁ θεός), εἰς πειρασμὸν οὗτος ἐνέπεσε, καὶ εἰς πειρασμὸν εἰσῆλθεν καὶ ἔστιν ἐν αὐτῷ, καὶ ὑπ' αὐτοῦ ὥσπερ ἀχθεὶς αἰχμάλωτος· ὁ δὲ ἀντισχὼν καὶ ὑπομείνας πεπείρασται μὲν οὗτος, οὐ μὴν εἰς πειρασμὸν εἰσῆλθεν ἤτοι ἐνέπεσεν. ἀνήχθη γοῦν ὁ Ἰησοῦς ὑπὸ τοῦ πνεύματος, οὐκ εἰς πειρασμὸν εἰσελθεῖν, ἀλλὰ πειρασθῆναι ὑπὸ τοῦ διαβόλου...καὶ αὐτὸς δὲ ὁ κύριος ἐπείραζεν τοὺς μαθητάς· ὁ μὲν γὰρ πονηρὸς πειράζων εἰς τοὺς πειρασμοὺς καθέλκει, οἷα πειραστὴς κακῶν· ὁ δὲ θεὸς πειράζων παραφέρει ὡς ἀπείραστος κακῶν· ὁ γὰρ θεός, φησίν, ἀπείραστός ἐστι κακῶν· ὁ μὲν γὰρ διάβολος ἐπ' ὄλεθρον ἕλκων βιάζεται, ὁ δὲ θεὸς ἐπὶ σωτηρίαν γυμνάζων χειραγωγεῖ.* The passage is consistently in favour of the masculine interpretation. Two points may be noticed. (1) In an earlier part of this fragment Dionysius gives the neuter interpretation of 1 John v. 19, *καὶ γὰρ ἀδύνατον μάλιστα μὲν ἴσως καὶ παντὶ ἀνθρώπῳ τὸ παντελῶς ἄγευστον χαλεποῦ τινος διαβιῶναι. ὅλος γάρ, φησίν, ὁ κόσμος ἐν τῷ πονηρῷ κεῖται· καὶ τὸ πλέον τῶν ἡμερῶν τοῦ ἀνθρώπου κόπος καὶ πόνος κ.τ.λ.* This interpretation is certainly erroneous, for, whatever be the gender of *ἐν τῷ πονηρῷ*, the reference must be to moral evil. (2) In the latter part of the quotation *πειραστὴς κακῶν* cannot be, as Canon Cook translates, 'a tempter of the wicked.' The following clause shews that *κακῶν* is neuter, 'a tempter to that which is evil.' It is in fact explained by *ἐπ' ὄλεθρον* in the next sentence.

(11) The next witness is Peter, Bishop at the beginning of the next century of the same great see as Dionysius. Some Canons of this Bishop have been preserved to us dealing with the questions connected with the Lapsi. They are printed in Routh *Reliquiae Sacrae* iv. p. 23 ff. The opening words tell us that they were drawn up when the persecution, which began in the February of 303, had reached the fourth Easter. In the 9th Canon the Bishop says of those who had courted persecution

that they are to be received to communion though they had forgotten Christ's words—*μὴ προσέχουσιν αὐτοῦ τοῖς λόγοις διδάσκοντος, προσεύχεσθαι μὴ εἰσελθεῖν εἰς πειρασμόν, καὶ πάλιν ἐν εὐχῇ λέγειν τῷ πατρὶ Καὶ μὴ εἰσενέγκῃς ἡμᾶς εἰς πειρασμόν, ἀλλὰ ῥῦσαι ἡμᾶς ἀπὸ τοῦ πονηροῦ.* The interpretation of this petition is hinted at in a later passage of the same Canon, where the Bishop again refers to the warnings of Christ: *πάλιν ἀκούομεν αὐτοῦ λέγοντος Καὶ ὅταν διώκωσιν ὑμᾶς ἐν τῇ πόλει ταύτῃ, φεύγετε εἰς τὴν ἑτέραν· οὐ γὰρ θέλει αὐτομολεῖν ἡμᾶς πρὸς τοὺς διαβόλου ὑπασπιστὰς καὶ δορυφόρους ... ἀλλ' ἐκδέχεσθαι καὶ προσέχειν ἑαυτοῖς, γρηγορεῖν τε καὶ προσεύχεσθαι, ἵνα μὴ εἰσέλθωμεν εἰς πειρασμόν.* Compare the following passages of these Canons: (1) Routh *l.c.* p. 24, those who had fallen under torture should fast, like Christ before His temptation, forty days; after which they should more earnestly watch unto prayers, *καταμελετῶντες τὸ λεγόμενον ὑπὸ τοῦ κυρίου πρὸς τὸν πειράζοντα αὐτὸν ἵνα προσκυνήσῃ αὐτῷ, Ὕπαγε Σατανᾶ.* (2) p. 25 *ποθοῦντες λυτρωθῆναι ἀπὸ τῆς πικροτάτης αἰχμαλωσίας τοῦ διαβόλου.* (3) p. 38 *ἐνηχούμενοι καταπολεμῆσαι τὸν ὑπεραιρόμενον καὶ ἀντικείμενον...ὑπὲρ τῶν ἐν τῷ ἀγῶνι ἡττηθέντων ὑπὸ τῆς πολλῆς βίας τοῦ κακομηχάνου διαβόλου.* The masculine interpretation, though not explicitly asserted, is implied by the language of these Canons.

(12) The 'Clementine' Liturgy (*Apostolic Constitutions* vii. 5—15). The date of the other Liturgies and of their several parts is a matter of debate, and the problems connected with their interrelation are complicated. No such difficulties however hamper the student in an appeal to the 'Clementine' Liturgy. It stands apart from the rest. Its integrity is guaranteed by its place in the *Apostolical Constitutions.* 'It represents fairly the pre-Constantinian Liturgy of about the middle of the 3rd century' (Hammond *Liturgies* p. xxxviii), and it is probable that portions of it, as its frequent coincidence with the liturgical element in Clement's Epistle seems to indicate, reach back to a yet earlier date. Canon Cook (*A Second Letter* p. 74 ff.) rightly lays stress on the evidence which it yields; but his review of this evidence is incomplete and is not free, I venture to think, from serious misinterpretations. The best course will be to set forth with some fulness those portions which may with any plausibility be thought to bear upon the

interpretation of the last clause of the Lord's Prayer, and then to draw the deductions which they may seem to warrant. The text I have used is that in Hammond's *Liturgies*, and the references are to the pages of that book. I have however compared Hammond's text with that in de Lagarde *Constitutiones Apostolorum* (1862), and have noted one or two slight variations in the latter text, designating them by L.

(a) 'The Bidding Prayer for the Catechumens' (p. 3 f.). *ἵνα... ῥύσηται δὲ αὐτοὺς ἀπὸ πάσης ἀσεβείας, καὶ μὴ δῷ τόπον τῷ ἀλλοτρίῳ κατ' αὐτῶν.*

(b) (i) 'The Bidding Prayer for the Energumens' (p. 5). *ὅπως...ῥύσηται τοὺς αὐτοῦ ἱκέτας* (so L., v. l. *οἰκέτας*) *ἀπὸ τῆς τοῦ ἀλλοτρίου καταδυναστείας· ὁ ἐπιτιμήσας τῷ λεγεῶνι τῶν δαιμόνων καὶ τῷ ἀρχεκάκῳ διαβόλῳ, ἐπιτιμήσῃ αὐτὸς καὶ νῦν τοῖς ἀποστάταις τῆς εὐσεβείας καὶ ῥύσηται τὰ ἑαυτοῦ πλάσματα ἀπὸ τῆς ἐνεργείας αὐτοῦ* (L. *αὐτῶν*). Comp. (h) below. (ii) 'The Collect' for the same (p. 6). *μεγάλου πατρὸς υἱέ, ἐπιτίμησον τοῖς πονηροῖς πνεύμασι, καὶ ῥῦσαι τὰ ἔργα τῶν χειρῶν σου ἐκ τῆς τοῦ ἀλλοτρίου πνεύματος ἐνεργείας.*

(c) 'The Bidding Prayer' for the Penitents (p. 6 f.). *ὅπως... συντρίψῃ τὸν Σατανᾶν ὑπὸ τοὺς πόδας αὐτῶν ἐν τάχει, καὶ λυτρώσηται αὐτοὺς ἀπὸ τῆς παγίδος τοῦ διαβόλου καὶ τῆς ἐπηρείας τῶν δαιμόνων, καὶ ἐξέληται αὐτοὺς ἀπὸ παντὸς ἀθεμίτου λόγου, καὶ πάσης ἀτόπου πράξεως, καὶ πονηρᾶς ἐννοίας.*

(d) 'The Deacon's Litany' (p. 9). (i) *ὑπὲρ τῶν πρεσβυτέρων ἡμῶν δεηθῶμεν· ὅπως ὁ Κύριος ῥύσηται αὐτοὺς ἀπὸ παντὸς ἀτόπου καὶ πονηροῦ πράγματος.* (ii) *ὑπὲρ ἀλλήλων δεηθῶμεν, ὅπως ὁ Κύριος τηρήσῃ* (L. *διατηρήσῃ*) *ἡμᾶς καὶ φυλάξῃ τῇ αὐτοῦ χάριτι εἰς τέλος, καὶ ῥύσηται ἡμᾶς τοῦ πονηροῦ καὶ πάντων τῶν σκανδάλων τῶν ἐργαζομένων τὴν ἀνομίαν.*

(e) 'The Prayer of the Faithful' (p. 10). *λύτρωσαι* [*τὸ ποίμνιόν σου τοῦτο*] *πάσης ἀγνοίας καὶ πονηρᾶς πράξεως...ῥῦσαι αὐτοὺς πάσης νόσου καὶ πάσης μαλακίας, παντὸς παραπτώματος, πάσης ἐπηρείας καὶ ἀπάτης, ἀπὸ φόβου ἐχθροῦ κ.τ.λ.*

(f) 'Commemoration of the Work of Redemption' (p. 17). *ἀπέθανεν...καὶ ἐτάφη...ἵνα πάθους λύσῃ καὶ θανάτου ἐξέληται τούτους δι' οὓς παρεγένετο, καὶ ῥήξῃ τὰ δεσμὰ τοῦ διαβόλου, καὶ ῥύσηται τοὺς ἀνθρώπους ἐκ τῆς ἀπάτης αὐτοῦ.*

(g) 'Invocation' (p. 18). *ἵνα οἱ μεταλαβόντες αὐτοῦ βεβαιωθῶσι πρὸς εὐσέβειαν, ἀφέσεως ἁμαρτημάτων τύχωσι, τοῦ διαβόλου καὶ τῆς πλάνης αὐτοῦ ῥυσθῶσι, πνεύματος ἁγίου πληρωθῶσιν.*

(h) 'The Great Intercession' (p. 19). *ἔτι παρακαλοῦμέν σε... ὑπὲρ τῶν χειμαζομένων ὑπὸ τοῦ ἀλλοτρίου...ὅπως...καθαρίσῃς ἐκ τῆς* (L. om. *ἐκ τῆς*) *ἐνεργείας τοῦ πονηροῦ.*

(k) 'The Benediction' (p. 23). *εὐλόγησον τούς σοι κεκλικότας τοὺς ἑαυτῶν αὐχένας...ἁγίασον αὐτούς, φρούρησον, σκέπασον, ἀντιλαβοῦ, ῥῦσαι τοῦ ἀλλοτρίου καὶ παντὸς ἐχθροῦ.*

A review of these excerpts from the Liturgy warrants the following conclusions.

(1) Prayer for deliverance from Satan is offered, not only on behalf of those who are not in full communion with the Church, the Catechumens, the Energumens, and the Penitents, but also on behalf of the Faithful. This appears from the passages (d) (ii), (g), (k). The occurrence of a prayer of this kind in the 'Invocation' (g) is especially noteworthy.

(2) The term *ὁ πονηρός* is used of Satan[1]. The name is implied in (b) (ii) *τοῖς πονηροῖς πνεύμασι...τοῦ ἀλλοτρίου πνεύματος*. Further, there can be no doubt as to the use of the term in (h), for it is interpreted by the scope of the petition and by the words *ὑπὸ τοῦ ἀλλοτρίου*[2], and further by the parallels in (b),

[1] It is necessary to emphasise this point, for Canon Cook (*A Second Letter* p. 76) writes, 'I cannot but think it [i.e. *ὁ ἀλλότριος*] would not have been used here, had *τοῦ πονηροῦ* been then generally understood as the regular designation of Satan: that designation does not occur once in this book,' i.e. *Apost. Constit.* vii.

[2] Canon Cook (p. 76) points out (*a*) that *ὁ ἀλλότριος*, characteristic of this Liturgy, 'is not, so far as I remember, common in other ancient writings'; (*b*) that it has 'a special force,' representing 'Satan as wholly alien, in the special sense that he is without place, power, or influence within the region of which Christ is king.' He appears to me to be mistaken in the second of these positions. The word *ὁ ἀλλότριος* is rather equivalent to *ὁ ἐχθρός* which is twice used of Satan (comp. Lc. x. 19) in this Liturgy (pp. 5, 10, see (e)). This is clear from (k) *τοῦ ἀλλοτρίου καὶ παντὸς ἐχθροῦ*. This meaning, which arose when a foreigner was regarded as a natural enemy, belongs to the word *ἀλλότριος* in Classical Greek from Homer onwards. Comp. Hebrews xi. 34 (*παρεμβολὰς ἔκλιναν ἀλλοτρίων*). There is an interesting passage in Justin Martyr *Dial.* c. 30 which explains the word from one point of view and which is decisive as to the view which the early Christians held in regard to the doctrinal question involved in the use of these prayers. It runs thus: *ὅτι δὲ καὶ αἰτοῦμεν αὐτὸν οἱ πιστεύοντες εἰς αὐτόν, ἵνα ἀπὸ τῶν ἀλλοτρίων,*

where the prayer is also for the Energumens, ἀπὸ τῆς ἐνεργείας αὐτοῦ, ἐκ τῆς τοῦ ἀλλοτρίου πνεύματος ἐνεργείας[1]. This passage carries with it (d) (ii),...καὶ ῥύσηται ἡμᾶς τοῦ πονηροῦ, where the reference to the evil one is followed by a reference to evil men as in the Liturgy of St James (Hammond p. 29, Swainson p. 225) ῥῦσαι ἡμᾶς ἀπὸ παντὸς πειρασμοῦ διαβολικοῦ τε καὶ ἀνθρωπίνου[2]. The sense in which the term ὁ πονηρός is used in this Liturgy is perhaps indicated by the epithet ἀρχέκακος which twice occurs in it—ὁ ἀρχέκακος διάβολος (p. 5), ὁ ἀρχέκακος ὄφις (p. 15).

(3) There are clear references to the last petition of the Lord's Prayer interpreted as a petition for deliverance from Satan in (b) (i) (ii), (d) (ii), (g), (h), (k). Only less clear is the reference in (c), (f); the words ἵνα ῥήξῃ τὰ δεσμά in the last passage are a comment, at least from one point of view, on ῥῦσαι[3]. This interpretation of ἀπὸ τοῦ πονηροῦ becomes all the more noteworthy if my conjecture (see p. 121 f.) be true that in the Greek Jewish forms of Prayer such phrases as are found in this Liturgy itself (p. 9 ἀπὸ παντὸς ἀτόπου καὶ πονηροῦ πράγματος, p. 10 πονηρᾶς πράξεως) were common.

(13) Cyril of Jerusalem *Cat.* xxiii. *Myst.* v. § 18. ἀλλὰ ῥῦσαι

τουτέστιν ἀπὸ τῶν πονηρῶν καὶ πλάνων πνευμάτων, συντηρήσῃ ἡμᾶς, ὡς ἀπὸ προσώπου ἑνὸς τῶν εἰς αὐτὸν πιστευόντων σχηματοποιήσας ὁ λόγος τῆς προφητείας (Ps. xviii. 14) λέγει, πᾶσι φανερόν ἐστιν. ἀπὸ γὰρ τῶν δαιμονίων, ἅ ἐστιν ἀλλότρια τῆς θεοσεβείας τοῦ θεοῦ, οἷς πάλαι προσεκυνοῦμεν, τὸν θεὸν ἀεὶ διὰ Ἰησοῦ Χριστοῦ συντηρηθῆναι παρακαλοῦμεν. Justin's mode of reference to the petition (αἰτοῦμεν, παρακαλοῦμεν) suggests that he is quoting a prayer from a very early form of the Liturgy, which is substantially reproduced in later Liturgies.

[1] Compare *Lit. of St James* (Hammond p. 32, Swainson p. 239), ἀπὸ...πάσης διαβολικῆς ἐνεργείας, *Lit. of St Mark* (Hammond p. 171, Swainson p. 4) πᾶσαν σατανικὴν ἐνέργειαν καὶ ἀνθρώπων πονηρῶν ἐπιβουλήν.

[2] Such phrases are common in the Liturgies. A close parallel is found in the *Embolismus* of the *Liturgia Coptitarum S. Cyrilli* (Swainson p. 63), libera nos a malo: actiones diabolicas a nobis remove: insidias per consilia improborum hominum omnes inutiles effice. Similar petitions will be found in Swainson pp. 21, 47 (Satanam...deprime sub pedibus nostris velociter: scandala et eorum autores compesce), 363.

[3] The construction of ῥύσασθαι with a simple genitive is characteristic of this Liturgy. It occurs in the comment of Gregory of Nyssa on this clause (p. 174) and in words of Chrys. quoted above p. 121. Comp. λύτρωσαι αὐτοὺς τῆς παλαιᾶς πλάνης (Swainson p. 180), τὸν...λαὸν ἐλευθερώσας ἀκαθαρσίας (id. p. 184). I have noticed it also in the newly recovered Greek text of the Apology of Aristides c. xii., εὐπόρησε ῥύσασθαι ἑαυτὸν τοῦ θανάτου.

ἡμᾶς ἀπὸ τοῦ πονηροῦ. πονηρὸς δὲ ὁ ἀντικείμενος δαίμων, ἀφ' οὗ ῥυσθῆναι εὐχόμεθα. Cyril is here expounding the Lord's Prayer in its place in the Liturgy between the Great Intercession for the Living and the Dead (§ 8 ff., *εἶτα μετὰ ταῦτα τὴν εὐχὴν λέγομεν ἐκείνην, ἣν ὁ σωτὴρ παρέδωκε τοῖς οἰκείοις αὐτοῦ μαθηταῖς* § 11) and the call of the Bishop (or Priest, *ὁ ἱερεύς*), *τὰ ἅγια τοῖς ἁγίοις.* Further, he is explaining it in the regular course of catechetical instruction. Thus his evidence is of special interest and importance. In the first place catechetical instruction commonly followed traditional lines of thought and of exegesis. In the second place an exposition of the Lord's Prayer as used in the Liturgy could hardly be at variance with the general tone of the actual Liturgy itself. We are therefore enabled to judge what was the teaching of the Liturgy in use at Jerusalem in the middle of the fourth century on the relation of the faithful to the temptations of the devil; for it is to the faithful that this petition of the Lord's Prayer when used just before the actual Communion must refer. With this evidence of Cyril we must connect on the one hand the 'Embolismus' in the Liturgy of St James (p. 153), which seems in some form to have been in use at a later time in Palestine (Hammond p. xliii), and on the other hand the evidence derived from the 'Clementine' Liturgy. The coincidence of two distinct lines of liturgical evidence, the 'Clementine' Liturgy and the exposition of Cyril, seems to afford a fair indication what was the tendency of thought in a very early archetypal form of Liturgy, and to enable us to discern what interpretation the devotional instinct of the early generations of Christians gave to the words *ἀπὸ τοῦ πονηροῦ*[1].

This is a convenient point at which to break off this catena of early expositions of and references to the last petition of the Lord's Prayer. To follow the stream further would necessitate the discussion of Augustine's position as an exegete; and would thus introduce us into a fresh region of Church History, that of later 'Latin Christianity.' We have examined thirteen witnesses. Some of these, Clement, Hermas, the Clementine Homilies, Tertullian, Cyprian, Origen, Dionysius and Peter of Alexandria, the 'Clemen-

[1] On further evidence to be derived from Liturgies see note B, on p. 151.

tine' Liturgy, Cyril of Jerusalem, have indeed given evidence before, but have been dismissed before the whole truth had been elicited from them. The rest, viz. the *Didaché*, the Ancient Homily, the Letter of the Churches of Vienne and Lyons, have, so far as I know, spoken now for the first time[1].

Their evidence may be thus summarised. One witness, that is the *Didaché*, is doubtful, if not adverse to the view maintained in this essay; some explanation however of the adverse part of this evidence can be given. The evidence of one witness, who has been brought forward on the other side, that is Clement, is now seen to be irrelevant. One witness, viz. Hermas, is not consistent, but perhaps on the whole favours the view here taken. The remaining ten give clear and ample testimony to the interpretation which we have already arrived at from a study of the New Testament. They represent different parts of Christendom. 'The Ancient Homily,' as it would appear, speaks from Corinth (see Bp Lightfoot *Clement* ii. p. 197 ff.). The Letter of the Churches of Southern Gaul shews us the mind of these Churches, which were offshoots from, and in close correspondence with, the Apostolic Churches of Asia Minor. The 'Clementine Homilies' give us the traditional view held by Jewish Christians, those probably of the East (Dr Salmon in *D. C. B.* i. p. 577). Tertullian and Cyprian speak from Carthage; Origen from Alexandria and afterwards from Palestine. Origen's view is repeated by his pupil Dionysius, and by Peter, both Bishops of his early home. The last two witnesses, the 'Clementine' Liturgy, with whatever Church it is to be connected, and Cyril, who takes us back to the Mother Church of Christendom, combine to represent to us a very early devotional tradition. It is hardly too much to say that the unanimity of these witnesses, combined with the variety of their character and origin, is conclusive as to the mind of the Church of the first three centuries.

[1] Unless I may except a short note (p. 124) in my essay on 'Chrysostom' (1887).

A. *Note on the 'Songs' in St Luke's Gospel in relation to ancient Jewish Prayers* (see p. 128 n.).

A comparison of the *Benedictus* with Clement's Epistle (see above, p. 128 n.) suggests a larger problem of great interest, closely connected with the subject of the relation of the Church to the Synagogue discussed in the Introduction. Bp Lightfoot (*Clement* i. p. 392 ff.) has shewn the affinities between the Epistle of Clement and the 'Eighteen Benedictions.' The further problem at once confronts us—Is there any connexion between the 'Songs' of St Luke's Gospel (for the whole series must be considered together) and ancient Jewish Prayers?

For the purpose of comparison I take those parts of Jewish Prayers which appear to have been in most frequent use from very early times, viz., the Introductory and Concluding Benedictions of the Shema, the Eighteen Benedictions, the Kadish and the Kedusha (see Dr Ginsburg's art. *Synagogue* in Kitto-Alexander *Cyclop. of Bibl. Lit.*). Passages the text of which seems doubtful I have marked with an asterisk.

(1) The Magnificat.	The Eighteen Benedictions.
Lc. i. 49 *ἐποίησέν μοι μεγάλα ὁ δυνατός.* Comp. *v.* 51, *ἐποίησεν κράτος.*	2 Thou art mighty (גבור) for ever, O Lord....O Thou of mighty acts (בעל גבורות).
καὶ ἅγιον τὸ ὄνομα αὐτοῦ.	3 Thou art holy, and Thy name is holy.
51 f. *διεσκόρπισεν ὑπερηφάνους διανοίᾳ καρδίας αὐτῶν· καθεῖλεν δυνάστας ἀπὸ θρόνων καὶ ὕψωσεν ταπεινούς, πεινῶντας ἐνέπλησεν ἀγαθῶν καὶ πλουτοῦντας ἐξαπέστειλεν κενούς.*	*12 Let all proud men perish in a moment....Bow them down speedily in our days. Blessed art Thou, O Lord, that breakest the enemies in pieces, and bowest down the proud. 13 Upon the righteous and upon the pious...let Thy compassions, we pray Thee, be moved. 16 Send us not away, our King, empty from Thy presence.
54 *ἀντελάβετο Ἰσραὴλ παιδὸς αὐτοῦ, μνησθῆναι ἐλέους, καθὼς ἐλάλησεν πρὸς τοὺς πατέρας ἡμῶν, τῷ Ἀβραὰμ καὶ τῷ σπέρματι αὐτοῦ εἰς τὸν αἰῶνα.*	1 That bestowest gracious benefits (חסדים)...and rememberest the piety of the fathers (חסדי אבות)...O Lord the Shield of Abraham. 2 Fulfilling His truth to them that sleep in the dust.

(2) The Benedictus.

Lc. i. 68 εὐλογητὸς Κύριος ὁ Θεὸς τοῦ Ἰσραήλ, ὅτι ἐπεσκέψατο καὶ ἐποίησεν λύτρωσιν τῷ λαῷ αὐτοῦ.	1 Blessed art Thou, O Lord, our God and the God of our fathers, the God of Abraham, the God of Isaac, the God of Jacob...Even He that bringeth a Redeemer unto their sons' sons for His Name's sake in love. 2 Setting at liberty them that are in bonds. *7 Redeem us with a perfect redemption... Thou, O God, art a strong Redeemer. Blessed art Thou, O Lord, the Redeemer of Israel. 10 Sound a great trumpet for our freedom ; and lift up a banner to gather our captives... He that gathereth the outcasts of His people Israel.
69 καὶ ἤγειρεν κέρας σωτηρίας ἡμῖν ἐν οἴκῳ Δαυεὶδ παιδὸς αὐτοῦ.	14 Establish in the midst of her [Jerusalem] speedily the throne of David. 15 Cause the shoot of David Thy servant to spring forth ; and let his horn be exalted in Thy salvation. Blessed art Thou, O Lord, that causest the horn of salvation to spring forth.
71 σωτηρίαν ἐξ ἐχθρῶν ἡμῶν καὶ ἐκ χειρὸς πάντων τῶν μισούντων ἡμᾶς...... 74 τοῦ δοῦναι ἡμῖν ἀφόβως ἐκ χειρὸς ἐχθρῶν ῥυσθέντας...	See the passages from the 12th Benediction quoted above as parallel to Lc. i. 51 f.
72 f. ποιῆσαι ἔλεος μετὰ τῶν πατέρων ἡμῶν καὶ μνησθῆναι διαθήκης ἁγίας αὐτοῦ, ὅρκον ὃν ὤμοσεν πρὸς Ἀβραὰμ τὸν πατέρα ἡμῶν.	See the passages quoted above as parallel to Lc. i. 54.
75 λατρεύειν αὐτῷ ἐν ὁσιότητι καὶ δικαιοσύνῃ ἐνώπιον αὐτοῦ πάσαις ταῖς ἡμέραις ἡμῶν.	13 Upon the righteous and upon the pious.... 5 Turn us again, O Father, to Thy law ; and make us draw near, our King, to Thy service (לעבודתך); and
ἐν ἀφέσει ἁμαρτιῶν αὐτῶν (v. 77).	bring us back with a perfect repentance to Thy presence. 17 May the service (עבודת) of Thy people Israel be pleasing to Thee perpetually[1].

[1] This Benediction is probably subsequent to the destruction of the Temple. But it may incorporate an earlier formula.

77 τοῦ δοῦναι γνῶσιν σωτηρίας τῷ λαῷ αὐτοῦ.

4 Thou graciously givest to man knowledge, and teachest man understanding. So graciously give unto us knowledge and understanding and wisdom.

ἐν ἀφέσει ἁμαρτιῶν αὐτῶν.

6 Pardon us, our Father, for we have sinned. Forgive us, our King, for we have transgressed.

78 διὰ σπλάγχνα ἐλέους Θεοῦ ἡμῶν.

13 Upon us let Thy compassions (רחמיך) be moved, O Lord our God.

*19 Grant...grace and mercy, righteousness and compassion unto us.

79 ἐπιφᾶναι τοῖς ἐν σκότει καὶ σκιᾷ θανάτου καθημένοις, τοῦ κατευθῦναι τοὺς πόδας ἡμῶν εἰς ὁδὸν εἰρήνης.

*19 For in the light of Thy countenance Thou hast given to us, O Lord our God, the Law and life,...blessing and peace. May it be good in Thine eyes to bless Thy people Israel with abundant strength and peace.

The Benediction at the beginning of the Shema: Blessed art Thou...who createst light...who makest peace... He in mercy causeth the light to shine upon the earth and the inhabitants thereof.

(3) The Gloria in Excelsis.

Lc. ii. 14 δόξα ἐν ὑψίστοις Θεῷ καὶ ἐπὶ γῆς εἰρήνη ἐν ἀνθρώποις εὐδοκίας.

The Kadish: May He who makes peace in His high places (במרומיו) confer peace upon us and upon all Israel.

Comp. Lc. xix. 38 ἐν οὐρανῷ εἰρήνη καὶ δόξα ἐν ὑψίστοις.

The Kedusha: We will sanctify Thy name in this world as they [the Angels] sanctify it in the high heavens (בשמי מרום); as it is written by the prophet (Is. vi.)....Blessed be the glory of the Lord from His place.

(4) The Nunc dimittis.

Lc. ii. 29 νῦν ἀπολύεις τὸν δοῦλόν σου... ἐν εἰρήνῃ.

2 Loosing them that are in bonds.

*9 May its (the year's) close be... peace.

31 ὅτι εἶδον οἱ ὀφθαλμοί μου τὸ σωτήριόν σου.

17 May our eyes behold when Thou returnest with compassion to Zion.

The great root-thoughts—salvation, mercy, deliverance, benediction—are, it will be seen, common to the Jewish Prayers and the 'Evangelical Songs.' The Prayers and the 'Songs' are of course both ultimately based on the Old Testament; and in this and other aspects the parallels which I have pointed out above may be compared with those which have been found between the Lord's Prayer and Jewish formulas. The suggestion which seems implied in these resemblances, viz., that the utterances of the Virgin Mary, Zacharias, and Simeon, at supreme crises of their lives were largely based on familiar forms of devotion, is psychologically natural. They spoke as 'filled with the Holy Ghost' (Lc. i. 67); for they gave a new meaning to current thoughts and expressions. The Angelic Song took a form which would not be wholly unfamiliar to pious Israelites.

The 'Songs' however come to us in a literary form and in a Greek translation. The question then arises, May not the Greek version of Jewish Prayers used in the Hellenistic Synagogues underlie the 'Songs' as they are given to us in St Luke's Gospel? There is one piece of evidence upon which I wish briefly to touch, viz., 'the Psalms of Solomon.' Professor Ryle and Mr James in their recent edition of these Psalms have in their Introduction (p. xci f.) collected a considerable number of instances of the "similarity in phraseology between our Psalms [i.e. the Psalms of Solomon] and the 'Songs' in Luke i. ii." To these instances add Ps. viii. 31 *εἶδον οἱ ὀφθαλμοὶ αὐτῶν* (? *ἡμῶν*) compared with Lc. ii. 30, Ps. xi. 2 *ἠλέησεν ὁ Θεὸς Ἰσραὴλ ἐν τῇ ἐπισκοπῇ αὐτῶν* compared with Lc. i. 68. But the Editors do not offer any explanation of the phenomenon which they notice. May not the explanation be found in a common source whence the phrases in these Psalms and in the Songs of the N. T. are derived, viz., the Greek Jewish Prayers of the Hellenistic Synagogues? As Prof. Ryle and Mr James have not, so far as I have noticed, touched on the subject, I venture to add a few notes and references in regard to the relation of 'the Psalms of Solomon' to ancient Jewish Prayers. (1) The two Editors draw attention (p. li) to the references in the Psalms to the doctrine of retribution and to that of the resurrection. The second Benediction ('Thou causest the dead to live... quickening the dead in Thy plenteous compassion. Blessed art Thou, O Lord, that bringest the dead to life') should be compared; it, like the Psalms of Solomon, was probably directed against Sadducean doctrine. (2) Compare Ps. Sol. ii. 35 ff., iv. 28 f., vii. 4 ff., xii. 8, xiii. 10 f. with Benedictions 12, 13; Ps. ix. 12 f. with Benediction 5; Ps. xvii. 23 with Benedictions 14, 15. (3) The close similarity of thought between the Psalms and the Benedictions will be shewn by a study of the following passages of the Psalms, ii. 41 (*εὐλογητὸς κύριος εἰς τὸν αἰῶνα ἐνώπιον τῶν δούλων αὐτοῦ*, words which close the Psalm), v. 16, 17, 21, 22, vi. 9 (*εὐλογητὸς κύριος ὁ ποιῶν ἔλεον τοῖς ἀγαπῶσιν αὐτὸν ἐν ἀληθείᾳ*, words which close the Psalm), viii. 37 f., ix. 20, x. 4 ff., xi. 9, xvii. 25 f., xviii. 1 ff. (4) I have suggested (see above p. 18) that the phrases *τοῖς ἀγαπῶσιν* (*αὐτόν*), *τοῖς ὑπομένουσιν* (*αὐτόν*) are derived from Greek Jewish Prayers: compare Ps. Sol. iv. 29 (*γένοιτο, κύριε, τὸ ἔλεός σου ἐπὶ πάντας τοὺς ἀγαπῶντάς σε*), vi. 9 (quoted just above), x. 4 (*τὸ ἔλεος κυρίου ἐπὶ τοὺς ἀγαπῶντας αὐτὸν ἐν ἀληθείᾳ*), xiv. 1 (*πιστὸς κύριος τοῖς ἀγαπῶσιν αὐτὸν ἀληθείᾳ, τοῖς ὑπομένουσι παιδείαν αὐτοῦ*). I have also pointed out (see above p. 18) how frequent in early Christian liturgical fragments is the petition for the gathering together of the scattered, a petition which seems based upon the 10th Benediction: compare Ps. Sol. viii. 34 (*συνάγαγε τὴν διασπορὰν Ἰσραὴλ μετ' ἐλέου καὶ χρηστότητος*), xi. 3[1]. It will be remembered that the starting point of this investigation was the fact of a certain resemblance between a passage of Clement's Epistle (which certainly is closely connected with Jewish Prayers) and the Benedictus (see above p. 128 n.).

To sift the matter with real thoroughness would require among other things an attempt to attain to a critical text of the Jewish Prayers, a careful examination of the Hebrew of these Prayers and of the passages of the O. T. in the original Hebrew and in the LXX. on which the Jewish formulas are ultimately based. Such a work lies outside the scope of a note like the present. I venture however to hope that I have shewn that there is a problem connected with the 'Songs' in St Luke's Gospel which invites thorough treatment.

B. *Note on the bearing of some of the Offices and Liturgies on the interpretation of* ἀπὸ τοῦ πονηροῦ (see p. 145).

While I fully recognise that only a thorough liturgical scholar can appraise accurately the value of the evidence of the Liturgies on such a matter as that under discussion, I think that a collection of passages bearing on the point may not be without interest and importance.

(1) Baptismal and kindred offices. (*a*) In a Greek form for making a catechumen (Assemani *Cod. Liturg.* i. p. 110) there occurs the petition, *σὺ ἐξείλου τὴν ψυχὴν τοῦ δούλου σου ἐκ τοῦ πονηροῦ...μὴ συγχωρήσῃς πνεύματί τινι πονηρῷ χώραν ἐν αὐτῷ ἔχειν*[2]. (*b*) In a Greek 'Confirmation' office (Assemani *Cod. Liturg.* iii. p. 57) we find the prayer *ῥῦσαι ἀπὸ τοῦ πονηροῦ καὶ πάντων τῶν ἐπιτηδευμάτων αὐτοῦ*. The term 'the evil one' occurs in the Syrian Baptismal rite given in the Offices of the Patriarch Severus (see above p. 37), 'Gratias agimus tibi hac de causa quod dignos effeceris servos tuos ut ad sanctum baptisma accederent et abrenunciarent malo (ܒܝܫܐ).' Comp. Cyril, Migne *P. G.* 33 p. 1069 (*ἀποτάσσομαί σοι, Σατανᾶ, σοὶ τῷ πονηρῷ καὶ ὠμοτάτῳ τυράννῳ*), Jerome *Com. in Mat.* xxv. 26 (renuntio tibi, diabole, et pompae tuae et vitiis tuis et mundo tuo, qui in maligno positus est), though in both these passages the term in question may be an addition of the writer.

[1] In the *Test. xii Patriarcharum* the phrase *σπλάγχνα ἐλέους* (Lc. i. 78) occurs in *Zab.* 7, 8. With Lc. ii. 32 compare *Benj.* 11 (*γνῶσιν καινὴν φωτίζων πάντα τὰ ἔθνη, φῶς γνώσεως ἐπεμβαίνων τῷ Ἰσραὴλ ἐν σωτηρίᾳ*).

[2] Cyril of Jerus. (Migne *P.G.* 33 p. 1080) *τὸ ἐπιορκιστὸν τοῦτο ἔλαιον...δύναμιν τηλικαύτην λαμβάνει, ὥστε...πάσας ἀοράτους τοῦ πονηροῦ ἐκδιώκειν τὰς δυνάμεις.*

(2) The Liturgies proper. It will be best to collect separately three groups of passages, viz. (*a*) passages in which the *neuter* interpretation is definitely assumed; (*b*) phrases which bear some resemblance to the last petition of the Prayer, and which may be in some cases indirect references to it; (*c*) passages which clearly support the *masculine* interpretation. The references given are to Dr Swainson's *Greek Liturgies* (unless it is otherwise stated), as that is the nearest approach to a critical edition.

(*a*) *Neuter interpretation.* (i) The *Coptic Liturgy*, *Anaphora of St Basil* (Hammond p. 223), ne nos inducas in temptationem, neque permittas ullam iniquitatem in nos dominari, imo potius libera nos ab actionibus inutilibus, earumque cogitationibus, earum motibus, aspectibus earum, illecebris earum; temptationemque extingue et repelle a nobis. (ii) The Roman and Ambrosian rites (Hammond p. 344), the Gregorian and Gelasian Canon (Hammond p. 372 f.), Libera nos, quaesumus, Domine, ab omnibus malis praeteritis, praesentibus, et futuris. The Lord's Prayer had preceded. (iii) Mozarabic rite (Hammond p. 345): after the Lord's Prayer the Presbyter says, Liberati a malo, confirmati semper in bono. (iv) The Gallican rite has a varying formula succeeding the Lord's Prayer. Hammond (p. 345) gives that for the Nativity, Libera nos, omnipotens Deus, ab omni malo, et custodi nos in omni opere bono.

(*b*) *Possible references and paraphrases.* There are many petitions in the Deacon's Litany and elsewhere in the several Liturgies which seek for *deliverance from* various evils, e.g. *Lit. of St James* p. 230 f., ὑπὲρ τοῦ ῥυσθῆναι ἡμᾶς ἀπὸ πάσης θλίψεως, ὀργῆς, κινδύνου καὶ ἀνάγκης, αἰχμαλωσίας, πικροῦ θανάτου, καὶ τῶν ἀνομιῶν ἡμῶν. Similar prayers will be found on pp. 125, 166, 224, 234, 250, 280. Not unfrequently petitions begin with the words ῥῦσαι ἡμᾶς, which yet can hardly be thought to be expansions of the clause of the Lord's Prayer. Thus *Lit. of the Presanctified* p. 178 ἀλλὰ ῥῦσαι ἡμᾶς ἐκ πάντων τῶν θηρευόντων τὰς ψυχὰς ἡμῶν, *Lit. of St James* p. 331 ῥῦσαι ἡμᾶς ἀπὸ τῆς φοβερᾶς καὶ ἀνεξιχνιάστου καὶ φρικτῆς ἡμέρας τῆς κρίσεως. Again, there are other petitions of which the following may be considered a type: ῥῦσαι ἡμᾶς ἀπὸ παντὸς πειρασμοῦ διαβολικοῦ τε καὶ ἀνθρωπίνου (*Lit. of St James* p. 224 f.), πάντα δὲ φθόνον, πάντα πειρασμόν, πᾶσαν σατανικὴν ἐνέργειαν, καὶ ἀνθρώπων πονηρῶν ἐπιβουλήν, ἀποδίωξον ἀφ' ἡμῶν (*Lit. of Alexandria* p. 4). These and such like petitions together with what seems to be, if my suggestion (p. 121 f.) be true, a Jewish liturgical phrase, viz. ἀπὸ παντὸς πονηροῦ (πράγματος), must be taken into account in considering those passages which seem to make for a neuter interpretation. They would always create a tendency towards expanding the simple expression of the masculine interpretation and so diluting or eliminating it. In this connexion the following series of passages is very significant: (i) the Scriptural source Rom. xvi. 20 (ὁ δὲ θεὸς τῆς εἰρήνης συντρίψει τὸν Σατανᾶν ὑπὸ τοὺς πόδας ὑμῶν ἐν τάχει): the meaning here cannot be questioned: (ii) Rom. *l. c.* is quoted (with necessary adaptations) in the 'Clementine' Liturgy (Hammond p. 6): (iii) *Lit. of Alexandria* p. 46 f., τὸν Σατανᾶν καὶ πᾶσαν αὐτοῦ τὴν ἐνέργειαν καὶ πονηρὰν δύναμιν σύντριψον ὑπὸ τοὺς πόδας ἡμῶν. (iv) *Lit. Copt. S. Basilii* p. 21, universos eorum hostes visibiles et invisibiles contere et deprime sub vestigiis eorum velociter: (v) *Canon Universalis Aethiopum* p. 21, omnes hostes et adversarios eorum subjice et contere sub pedibus eorum velociter. Thus the primary reference to Satan, which in this case is certain, is lost in process of liturgical development.

(*c*) *Masculine interpretation.* The following passages are clear: (i) *Lit. of Alexandria* p. 6 (*Cod. Rossanensis*), ἀλλὰ ῥῦσαι ἡμᾶς ἀπὸ τοῦ πονηροῦ καὶ ἐκ τῶν ἔργων αὐτοῦ. (ii) *ib.* p. 62, ἀλλὰ ῥῦσαι ἡμᾶς ἀπὸ τοῦ πονηροῦ...σὺ γὰρ ἔδωκας ἡμῖν ἐξουσίαν πατεῖν ἐπάνω ὄφεων καὶ σκορπίων καὶ ἐπὶ πᾶσαν τὴν δύναμιν τοῦ ἔχθρου. (iii) *Lit. of St James* p. 306 ff. (all four MSS. given by Dr Swainson give substantially the same reading), ἀλλὰ ῥῦσαι ἡμᾶς ἀπὸ τοῦ πονηροῦ, καὶ ἐκ τῶν ἔργων αὐτοῦ, καὶ πάσης ἐπηρείας καὶ μεθοδείας αὐτοῦ, καὶ τέχνης καὶ ἀπάτης αὐτοῦ. The Syriac (Hammond p. 78) has a much simpler Embolismus. (iv) *The Coptic Liturgies.* (*a*) *Lit. Copt. S. Basilii* p. 5, omnem invidiam, omnem temptationem, omnem operationem Satanae et consilium hominum improborum, impetumque hostium tam occultorum quam manifestorum depelle a nobis.... Tu enim ipse es, qui dedisti nobis potestatem calcandi serpentes et scorpiones, omnemque virtutem inimici. Et ne nos inducas in temptationem, sed libera nos a malo[1]. (*b*) *Lit. Copt. S. Cyrilli* p. 63, sed libera nos a malo: actiones diabolicas a nobis remove: insidias per consilia improborum hominum omnes inutiles effice. (*c*) *ib.* p. 73, libera eos ab operibus malis diaboli, et contere omnia opera eius sub pedibus illorum velociter. (v) *The Syrian Liturgy of SS. Adaeus and Maris* (Hammond p. 280), sed libera et salva nos a malo et ab exercitibus eius.

To arrive at an approximately correct estimate of the value of this evidence the following points must be borne in mind: (i) The evidence for the neuter interpretation is found almost exclusively in Latin Liturgies, which either in their original formation or in their subsequent development would not be outside the influence of St Augustine's teaching. (ii) The masculine interpretation is found in passages, notably in the different forms of the Embolismus, where the reference to the Lord's Prayer is direct and certain. (iii) The variety of the witnesses is a noteworthy fact. The evidence comes to us from the Church of Alexandria, probably in the Greek Liturgy of St James from the Patriarchate of Antioch, from the Coptic Church of Egypt,

[1] With this it is very instructive to compare the parallel passage in the Ethiopic Canon (p. 5), omnem invidiam, omnem dolum, omnemque operationem Satanae, omnem machinationem hominum improborum, *insultationemque inimici secretam et manifestam* procul fac...quia tu es qui dedisti nobis potestatem calcandi serpentes et scorpiones, omnemque virtutem inimici. Et ne nos inducas, Domine, in temptationem, sed libera et eripe nos ab *omni* malo. The reference here to Satan's enmity in the introduction to the petition is plainer than in the Coptic Lit. quoted above in the text; in the actual petition however the reference is lost in a paraphrase.

from the Church of Eastern Syria in the Liturgy of SS. Adaeus and Maris. Again, the passages quoted above from a Baptismal and a 'Confirmation' Office are at one with those cited from the Liturgies. (iv) These different pieces of evidence, the several dates of which I have not attempted to ascertain, must be taken in connexion with the liturgical evidence derived from the 'Clementine' Liturgy and from Cyril of Jerusalem. These two latter authorities, the respective dates of which are within certain limits fixed, and whose agreement, as we have seen, points to still more ancient liturgical usage, shew clearly that in their interpretation of the last clause of the Lord's Prayer the later Liturgies are not introducing an innovation.

(iv). Evidence derived from the Early Versions.

(*a*) The Syriac Versions.

The importance of these Versions has been insisted on more than once in this Essay (see p. 39 n.), on the ground that they represent approximately the original Aramaic of our Lord's utterances.

The Old Syriac, inserting the petition for deliverance in St Luke, has in both Gospels the following rendering:

ܐܠܐ ܦܨܢ ܡܢ ܒܝܫܐ

the-evil (-one) from deliver-us but

The Syriac Vulgate has the same translation in St Matthew, and it is again repeated (except in regard to the translation of 'us') in the Jerusalem and the Philoxenian Versions. In St Luke the Vulgate Syriac introduces another verb.

The main points in regard to the evidence of these Versions may be briefly stated thus:

1. In the two passages in the New Testament where in the Greek the neuter interpretation is certain, viz. Luke vi. 45 (*προφέρει τὸ πονηρόν*) and Rom. xii. 9 (*ἀποστυγοῦντες τὸ πονηρόν*), the Vulgate has the definite feminine (ܒܝܫܬܐ), the number of course depending on the pointing. The former passage is wanting in the Curetonian fragments of the Gospels.

2. In the following passages, where the masculine is grammatically certain, viz. Matt. xiii. 19, 1 Cor. v. 13, 1 John ii. 13, 14, v. 18, the Vulgate Syriac has ܒܝܫܐ. The Curetonian fragments shew that in the first of these passages, which is the most

important, the Vulgate is but repeating the rendering of the Old Syriac. These passages indicate that the simple word (without the addition of ܓܒܪܐ as in Luke vi. 45) was felt to be a clear and sufficient translation of the phrase 'the evil man' or, when that required to be represented, 'the evil-one.'

3. In two passages the word ܒܝܫܐ is gratuitously introduced where it is not required by the Greek and where the interpretation is certain.

In St Matthew xiii. 38, 39 (*τὰ δὲ ζιζάνιά εἰσιν οἱ υἱοὶ τοῦ πονηροῦ, ὁ δὲ ἐχθρὸς ὁ σπείρας αὐτά ἐστιν ὁ διάβολος*). The Old Syriac has ܒܝܫܐ not only in the first clause but, as the equivalent of *ὁ διάβολος*, in the second also

In Acts x. 38 (*τοὺς καταδυναστευομένους ὑπὸ τοῦ διαβόλου*) the Vulgate Syriac represents *τοῦ διαβόλου* in the same way.

These two passages were pointed out by Bishop Lightfoot. Canon Cook however in his reply passed them over in silence. They are manifestly of crucial importance. For in the first place this rendering of Matt. xiii. 39 clears up, as far as the Syriac is concerned, the meaning of the ambiguous word in *v.* 38, and with it, it can hardly be questioned, that of the other passages in St Matthew commonly considered doubtful. The Version which (unless indeed there was some variation of reading in the Greek, other evidence for which has disappeared) introduced the word as a name for Satan in xiii. 39 could hardly have intended to express a different idea by the same word in vi. 13. And in the second place the two passages together shew that ܒܝܫܐ was current as a recognised name for Satan among Syrian Christians from the second century and onwards, and thus form a link between the acknowledged usage of later Syriac writers (see Payne Smith *Syr. Thes.*) and that of our Lord's time which is the 'unknown quantity' in the problem.

4. The facts reviewed above seem fairly decisive as to the gender of ܒܝܫܐ in those passages where the meaning of the Greek must remain uncertain to the scholar who confines his studies to accidence, viz. Matt. v. 37, 39, xiii. 38, John xvii. 15, 2 Thess. iii. 3, Eph. vi. 16, 1 John iii. 12, v. 19. The passages in St Matthew here referred to are happily included in what remains to us of the Old Syriac Version.

To sum up, while in forming a judgment we must make allowance both for our tendency to Western over-refinement and rigidity in interpreting Semitic modes of thought and expression and also for the fact that Syriac usage in regard to the way of expressing the neuter fluctuated, yet it does not seem too much to say that the evidence of the Syriac Versions certainly favours the masculine interpretation of ἀπὸ τοῦ πονηροῦ.

(*b*) The Latin Versions.

The materials accessible at the present time to the student of the Latin Versions are not sufficient to insure absolute completeness in results. Still in the investigation which follows I hope that the evidence collected will justify an opinion as to the bearing of the Latin Versions on the point of interpretation under discussion which will not hereafter require serious modification.

(1) The Old Testament.

The group of passages in Deuteronomy xiii. 5, xvii. 7, 12, xix. 19, xxi. 21, xxii. 21, 22, 24, xxiv. 7 is worth study in the Latin Versions. The type of rendering given in the LXX. is ἐξαρεῖς τὸν πονηρὸν ἐξ ὑμῶν αὐτῶν. The Vatican MS. has τὸν πονηρόν in each passage. The variant τὸ πονηρόν however would be liable to arise in all the passages as it has done in xiii. 5, xix. 19 (see Tischendorf). It is of some importance to notice that St Paul (1 Cor. v. 13) in a general reference to these passages has τὸν πονηρόν, and that Aquila has τὸν πονηρόν in xxiv. 7 (see Field *Hexapla*), the only passage of the group of which any rendering of the other Greek Versions has been preserved. We may therefore conclude that, though the neuter reading existed, the reading generally current was τὸν πονηρόν.

Putting aside the Latin rendering of the verb as unimportant for our present purpose[1], we note four renderings of the noun in the Latin Versions.

(i) *Malum* is the commonest rendering. So Tert. *adv. Marc.*

[1] The verb used is the future or imperative of *tollere* or *auferre*. In xxii. 22 however the reading in Ziegler's *Fragmenta* is *eradicabis*. Jerome *adv. Helvid.* c. 4 has *eradicabitis*. At first sight this word seems to imply the neuter interpretation. But usage does not confirm this impression. Thus the Speculum (ed. Weihrich, *Corp. Scrip. Eccl. Lat.* xii. p. 537) reads in Deut. xviii. 12, eradicabit eos a te (Vulgate, delebit eos).

v. 14 (comp. *adv. Hermog.* 11), Lucifer *de Sancto Athan.* i. (ed. Hartel p. 75) quoting Deut. xvii. 12, and the Speculum (ed. Weihrich p. 460) quoting xvii. 12. This rendering is consistently followed by Jerome in the Vulgate. Tertullian (*loc. cit.*), it should be noticed, takes malum as neuter; for arguing against Marcion's dualism he asks, Aliud est enim apud creatorem Auferte malum de vobis, et Declina a malo et fac bonum?

(ii) *Malignum* is given as the rendering in xvii. 7 by Lucifer (ed. Hartel p. 75), in xxii. 21 by Augustine *Quaest. in Deut.* (Migne *P. L.* 34 p. 762), in xxii. 21, 24 by the *Fragmenta Monacensia* (Ziegler *Bruchstücke einer Vorhieronymianischen Übersetzung des Pentateuch,* München, 1883), in xxiv. 7 by Augustine (Migne *P. L.* 34 p. 764). Augustine (see below p. 164) takes malignum as masculine.

(iii) *Nequam* is found in xxii. 22 as given in the *Fragmenta Monacensia.*

(iv) *Iniquum* is found in Lucifer (ed. Hartel p. 77) who, it will be noticed, gives three renderings of τὸν πονηρόν (τὸ πονηρόν) in as many pages. The whole quotation runs thus: Testificatus est iniqua ..facite ei quemadmodum nequiter egit facere adversus fratrem suum, et auferes iniquum ex vobis ipsis (Deut. xix. 18 f.). It seems clear that iniquum is here masculine.

This group of passages is of special interest as giving all the renderings of ὁ πονηρός which are found in the New Testament.

In Job xxi. 30 where the Vulgate has εἰς ἡμέραν ἀπωλείας κουφίζεται ὁ πονηρός, the Old Latin as given in Sabatier's representation of *Cod. Majoris Monasterii* (see Bp Westcott art. *Vulgate, Dict. of the Bible* iii. p. 1692) and the Vulgate (*Cod. Amiatinus*) both read, In diem perditionis servatur malus. In such a context it would be very natural to take malus as referring to Satan. Thus in the interlinear Commentary on Job printed with Jerome's works (Migne *P. L.* 23 p. 1437), assigned by some to his friend Philip (see *D. C. Biog.* iv. p. 357), there is the gloss, antiqui hostis vel impii in hoc mundo. Again, Gregory the Great *Expositio in beatum Iob seu Moralium Libri* (Migne *P. L.* 75 p. 1117) writes thus on *v.* 31: Beatus Iob dum de omnium malorum corpore loqueretur, subito ad omnium iniquorum caput verba convertit: vidit enim quod in fine mundi Satan hominem ingrediens, &c., where the reference at least in part is to *v.* 30. If then we could be sure that this part of the Old Latin rendering of the Old Testament was pre-Christian (see Bp Westcott art. *Vulgate, D. B.* iii. p. 1691), we should have grounds for arguing that the passage supplied an important precedent for the translation of ὁ πονηρός in the New Testament. In any case we see the associations connected with the term malus in the Latin Bible.

(2) New Testament.

In the Gospels the evidence as to the Old Latin is fairly abundant. The greatest assistance, especially in regard to St Matthew, is found in the first volume of Bishop Wordsworth's edition of the Vulgate. To this volume (p. xxxiii) and to Dr Hort's *Introduction* (p. 81) I must refer for the classification which is adopted in the following table of the MSS. to which I refer.

(1) 'African text': (i) *Cod. Palatinus* = *e* does not contain the earlier chapters of St Matthew; it begins at xii. 49. The portion containing xiii. 19 is detached and is given in T. K. Abbott's edition of Cod. Z. (ii) *Cod. Bobiensis* = *k* contains parts of St Matthew and St Mark.

(2) 'European text': (i) *Cod. Vercellensis* = *a*, according to Bp Wordsworth, has a 'European' text in St Matthew, a 'mixed' text in the other Gospels. (ii) *Cod. Veronensis* = *b*. (iii) *Cod. Claromontanus* = *h*. (iv) *Cod. Monacensis* = *q* does not contain Matt. v. 25—vi. 4.

(3) 'Italian text': *Cod. Brixianus* = *f*.

(4) 'Mixed text': (i) *Cod. Vercellensis* = *a* (see above). (ii) *Cod. Colbertinus* = *c*. (iii) *Cod. Corbeiensis* 1 = ff_1. (iv) *Cod. Corbeiensis* 2 = ff_2. (v) *Cod. Sangermanensis* = g_1. (vi) *Cod. Bezae* (Lat. vers.) = *d*.

(5) 'Vulgate': (i) *Cod. Amiatinus* = A. (ii) *Cod. Dublinensis* ('Book of Armagh') = D. (iii) *Cod. Egertonensis* = E. (iv) *Cod. Lichfeldensis* = L. (v) *Cod. Kenanensis* ('Book of Kells') = Q. (vi) *Cod. Rushworthianus* ('Gospels of Mac Regol') = R.

Matt. v. 37.

(1) (2) (3) (5) a malo; so Tert. *de Praescr. Haer.* 26, *de Carne Christi* 23, *adv. Prax.* 9.

(4) a malo.

de malo *d*. So Hilary *in loco* (Migne *P. L.* 9 p. 940).

Matt. v. 39.

(1) non resistere adversus nequam nequam (*sic*) *k*.

(2) (3) non resistere malo.

(4) non resistere malo.

malum g_1.

(5) non resistere malo.

a malo EQ.

Aug. *de Serm. Dom.* iii. (Migne *P. L.* 34 p. 1258) has: non resistere adversus malum.

Matt. vi. 13.

(1) (2) (3) (4) (5) libera nos a malo.

Tertullian *de Orat.* viii. devehe (*v.l.* evehe) nos a malo; *de Fuga* ii. erue nos a maligno. As the phrase 'a maligno' does not, so far as I know, occur in any other authority for the O. L. text, it is probable that Tertullian here gives an original rendering, as he not unfrequently does (Dr Hort *Introduction* p. 78). 'Erue' however is found in Lc. xi. 4 in *f*.

Matt. xii. 35.

(1) nequam homo de nequa thesauro emittit nequam *k*. So Cyprian *Ep.* 55 (58).

(2) (3) (4) (5) malus homo de malo thesauro profert mala (mala profert *h*).

Matt. xiii. 19.

(1) malus *e*. nequam *k*.

(2) malus *a b q*. malignus *h*.

(3) malus *f*.

(4) malus *c* ff_1 ff_2 g_1. malignus *d* g_2[1].

(5) malus *plerique*. malignus DLQR.

Matt. xiii. 38.

(1) fili maligni *e*. f. mali *k*.

[1] A second MS. taking its name from the Abbey of St Germain, sometimes cited by Sabatier.

(2) f. nequitiae *a*. f. maligni *h q*. f. iniqui *b* (so Augustine in the *Speculum*, Mai *Patr. Nova Biblio.* i. Pars ii. p. 112).

(3) f. maligni *f*.

(4) f. nequam *ff*$_1$. f. nequitiae *c ff*$_2$ *g*$_1$. f. maligni *d*.

(5) f. nequam *plerique*. diabuli nequam Q.

Compare Iren. iv. 66, 67. Rursus in zizaniis ait: zizania sunt filii maligni...juste scriptura eos qui in abscessione perseverant semper filios diaboli, et angelos dixit maligni. The passage is of importance as shewing (*a*) the interpretation which Irenaeus gave to the τοῦ πονηροῦ, and (*b*) that the translator deliberately adopted the form 'filii maligni' when the context of his author required that 'maligni' should be the genitive masculine.

Luke vi. 45.

(1) malus homo de malo thensauro cordis sui malum proferet *e*. vacat *k*.

(2) malus (homo *q*) de malo thensauro (cordis sui *q*) proferet (profert *q*) mala *b q*.

(3) malus homo de malo thensauro cordis sui profert malum *f*.

(4) nequam de malo profert malum *a*. malus homo de malo (thesauro cordis sui *c*) profert malum *c ff*$_2$. malus de malo froferet (*sic*) malum *d*.

(5) malus homo de malo profert malum.

Luke xi. 4.

(1) vacant *e k*.

(2) Cod. Vindobonensis (see Bp Wordsworth *Vulgate* p. xxxii) has: eripe nos a malo.

(3) erue nos a malo *f* (cf. Tert. *de Fuga* ii). All other authorities appear to have: libera nos a malo.

John xvii. 15.

(1) ut serves eos a malo *e*.

(2) ut serves eos a malo *b*.
ut conserves illos a maligno *q*.

(3) ut conserves eos a maligno *f*.

(4) ut serves eos a malo *c ff*$_2$.
ut serves eos de iniquo *d*.

(5) ut serves eos ex malo.

When we turn from the Gospels to the Epistles we become

conscious of the lack of evidence as to the Old Latin texts. 'The delusive habit of quoting as Old Latin the Latin texts of bilingual MSS,' Dr Hort remarks (*Introduction* p. 82), 'has obscured the real poverty of evidence.' It will be sufficient for my present purpose to record the rendering of the Vulgate (*Cod. Amiatinus*), and to note some of the more important variations as they appear in Patristic quotations. The greatest help is derived here as elsewhere from the monumental work of Sabatier. Unfortunately none of the passages in the Pauline Epistles, to which I have occasion to refer, are found in the Freisingen Fragments (Ziegler, *Itala-fragmenta*, Marburg, 1876), which appear to give an 'Italian text' (Dr Hort, *Introduction, Notes on Select Readings* p. 5).

Rom. xii. 9 odientes malum. Tert. *adv. Marc.* v. 14 odio habentes malum.

1 Cor. v. 13 auferte malum ex vobis ipsis. Compare the group of passages from Deuteronomy (see above, p. 156 f.). Compare Tert. *adv. Hermog.* 11 frustra laboramus de auferendo malo ex nobis ipsis. That Tertullian took 'malum' as masculine is clear from *de Pudic.* 13 incesto...quem scilicet auferri jussisset de medio ipsorum. The same interpretation is presupposed by the words in *de Aleatoribus* 4 Apostolus iterum dixit: eximite malos e medio vestro.

Gal. i. 4 ut eriperet nos de praesenti saeculo nequam. Jerome *in loco* has de...malo. Augustine *in loco* and in *de Pecc. Mer.* (Migne *P.L.* 44, p. 135) has de...maligno.

Eph. vi. 12—16 contra spiritualia nequitiae (*v.* 12)...in die malo (*v.* 13)...omnia tela nequissimi ignea (*v.* 16).

In *v.* 12 spiritualia nequitiae is as old as Cyprian, *Test.* iii. 117, and Tert., e.g. *adv. Marc.* v. 18. But there are the following variations (i) hostes spirituales nequitiae (Tert. *adv. Marc.* iii. 14), (ii) spiritualia malitiae (Tert. *adv. Marc.* iv. 24, *de Jejun.* 17). Compare: malitia spiritualis (*Apol.* 22). (iii) spiritus nequitiae, Cypr. *Ep.* 55 (58). (iv) spirituales nequitias, so Hilary often, see e.g. *in Ps.* lv. (Migne *P.L.* 9, p. 390). (v) nequitiam spiritualium (Ambrose *de Parad.* xii., Migne *P.L.* 14, p. 302).

In *v.* 13 Cyprian [*Test.* iii. 117, *Ep.* 55 (58)] has: in die nequissimo; Vigilius Thapsensis *de Trinitate* xii. (Migne *P.L.* 62, p. 320) in die maligno.

In *v.* 16 (i) Cyprian has: omnia candentia iacula nequissimi (*Test.* iii. 117); (ii) Ambrose (*de Sp. Sancto* iii. 7, Migne *P. L.* 16, p. 786) omnia tela maligni ignita; Leo (*Serm.* 39, Migne *P. L.* 54, p. 266) omnia tela maligni ignea; (iii) Zeno of Verona (*Tract.* 43, Migne *P. L.* 11, p. 496) omnes sagittas illius mali. (iv) The following glosses should be noticed. Tertullian has: omnia diaboli ignita tela (*adv. Marc.* iii. 14), tela diaboli (*de Fuga* 9). Hilary in an indirect reference has: ignita diaboli tela (*in Ps.* cxlii., Migne *P. L.* 9, p. 838).

2 Thess. iii. 3 qui confirmavit vos et custodiet a malo (*v.* 2 ut liberemur ab importunis et malis hominibus).

2 Tim. iv. 18 liberabit me Dominus ab omni opere malo.

1 John ii. 13 f. vicistis malignum. Ambrose *Enarr. in Ps.* xxxvi. § 52 (Migne *P. L.* 14, p. 992) has: vicistis malum.

iii. 12 ex maligno erat...operà eius maligna erant.

v. 18 f. malignus non tangit eum...mundus totus in maligno positus est.

The readings in 1 Jn. iii. 12, v. 18 f. given above are those of the Freisingen Fragments (Ziegler, *Itala-fragmenta*) which in this Epistle probably represent an 'Italian' text (Dr Hort, *Notes on Select Readings* p. 5). These fragments unfortunately do not include ii. 13 f.

It remains to review the evidence of the Latin Versions, so far as it has been here collected.

(1) Passages where the neuter is grammatically certain: malum is used in Lc. vi. 45, Rom. xii. 9, compare Tertullian's comment on the passages from Deuteronomy (see above, p. 157); nequam is used in Matt. xii. 35 (1).

(2) Passages where the masculine is for some reason certain: malus is used in Job xxi. 30, Matt. xiii. 19, Lc. vi. 45 (2) (4) *d*, 1 Cor. v. 13, 1 John ii. 13 f. (Ambrose); malignus in Deut. xxiv. 7 (Augustine), Matt. xiii. 19, 38 (translator of Irenaeus), 1 John ii. 13 f., iii. 12, v. 18 f.; nequam in Matt. xiii. 19 (1), Lc. vi. 45 (4).

(3) In one or two cases where the gender is grammatically uncertain, a gloss is inserted in the text which witnesses to the hold obtained by the masculine interpretation. Such glosses are

diabuli nequam in Matt. xiii. 38 (5), the insertion of the word diaboli in Eph. vi. 16 (see above). Against these must be weighed the filii nequitiae in Matt. xiii. 38, which, it should be noticed, occurs in representatives of two groups of MSS.

(4) Three words, iniquus, nequam, malignus, are used in some authorities in passages where malus is also found. (*a*) iniquus is so found in Deut. (see above, p. 157), Matt. xiii. 38 (2), John xvii. 15 (4). The rare use of the word in this series of passages, in none of which is the masculine interpretation grammatically certain, has little or no interpretative value. (*b*) nequam is so found in Deut. (see above, p. 157), Matt. v. 39 (1), xii. 35 (1)*, xiii. 19 (1)*, xiii. 38 (4) (5), Lc. vi. 45 (4)*, Matt. xii. 35 (de nequa thes.), Gal. i. 4. In the last two places the word is applied to a thing, expressed by a noun; in the passages marked with an asterisk it is certainly masculine. The word is somewhat more naturally used of a person; note the gloss of Q in Matt. xiii. 38 and the use of the superlative, which can hardly be used of abstract evil, in Eph. vi. 16. Hence the occurrence of the word as an alternative rendering in Matt. v. 39, xiii. 38 slightly inclines towards the masculine interpretation of the doubtful phrase in these verses. (*c*) malignus is the most important alternative translation of πονηρός. It is found in (i) Matt. xiii. 19 (2) (4) (5), xiii. 38 (translator of Iren.), 1 John ii. 13, v. 18 where the masculine is certain; (ii) Gal. i. 4, Eph. vi. 13 (Vigilius), where it qualifies a noun denoting a thing; (iii) Matt. vi. 13 (Tert.), xiii. 38 (1) (2) (3) (4), John xvii. 15 (2) (3), 1 John iii. 12, v. 19, Eph. vi. 16 (Ambr., Leo), where the gender is grammatically doubtful, though in the last passage the masculine is generally admitted for exegetical reasons to be certain. In 1 John iii. 12, v. 18 the gender is masculine, but here there is no evidence that malus was used as a translation. As to these passages, in the *first* place we notice that the use of malignus to represent πονηρός is not confined to any one class of authorities but occurs in each in turn. *Secondly* we ask the question why the word so often takes the place of malus as an equivalent of πονηρός. An answer to this question will be found (*a*) in a brief study of the use of the word malignus in the Latin Bible; (*b*) in two passages from Augustine.

When we turn to the Vulgate as given in the Cod. Amiatinus

we find the word used (i) of persons: Job v. 12, viii. 20, Ps. v. 6 (non habitabit juxta te malignus), ix. 15 (brachium peccatoris et maligni), xiv. 4 (ad nihilum deductus est in conspectu eius malignus), c. 4 (declinantem a me malignum non cognoscebam), cxviii. 115 (declinate a me maligni), Lc. viii. 2 (curatae ab spiritibus malignis); (ii) of things: Ps. cxliii. 10 (de gladio maligno), Baruch i. 22 (cordis nostri maligni), Jas. iv. 16 (omnis exultatio talis maligna est), 2 John 11 (communicat operibus illius malignis), 3 John 10 (verbis malignis garriens in nos). To this last group of passages the following given by Rönsch *Itala u. Vulgata* p. 333 should be added: Prov. xx. 8 non adversabitur ei quidquam malignum *Cod.* i. 1. 18 (dissipat omne malum *Vulg.*), Jer. xxiii. 22 a malignis cogitationibus *Wirceb.* (a cogitationibus suis pessimis *Vulg.*), Jon. iii. 8, 10 de via sua maligna (mala *Vulg.*)...a viis suis malignis (via mala *Vulg.*) *Weing.* Mic. ii. 3 quoniam tempus malignum est *Fuld.* (pessimum est *Vulg.*). A review of these passages shews that Biblical usage agrees with *a priori* probability, and that malignus (=maligenus), the opposite of benignus, is naturally and properly used of persons; in the Psalms the word 'malignus,' like the word 'sinner,' has almost a technical sense. If the word is applied to things, it is almost exclusively when personal qualities are transferred to them.

The two following passages from Augustine shew that this characteristic sense of malignus was explicitly recognised by Latin writers: (*a*) *Quaest. in Deut.* 39 (Migne *P. L.* 34, p. 764), after quoting 1 Cor. v. 13 (auferte malum) he continues: nam Graecus habet τὸν πονηρόν, quod etiam hic scriptum est. Hoc autem potius *malignum* solet interpretari quam *malum*, nec ait τὸ πονηρόν, id est, hoc malignum, sed τὸν πονηρόν, quod est, hunc malignum...Quamvis aliter illud apostolicum possit intelligi ut unusquisque *malum vel malignum* [note the order in which the alternatives are placed] ex se ipso sit jussus auferre. Qui sensus acceptabilior esset, si *hoc malum vel hoc malignum*, non autem *hunc malignum* in Graeco inveniretur. Nunc autem credibilius est de homine dictum quam de vitio. Quamquam possit eleganter intelligi etiam homo auferre a se malum hominem (Eph. iv. 22 veterem hominem). (*b*) Aug. *in Gal.* i. 4 (Migne *P.L.* 35, p. 2108), seculum praesens malignum propter malignos homines, qui in eo sunt, intelligendum est, sicut dicimus et malignam domum propter malignos inhabitantes in ea.

Thus, in passages where malus is found in the oblique cases, the occurrence of the corresponding case of malignus in other Latin authorities becomes a strong argument for the masculine interpretation. In Matt. v. 37, 39, Lc. vi. 45 (malum), where an oblique case of malus occurs without malignum as an alternative rendering, the neuter is the certain or the almost universally accepted interpretation. In 2 Thess. iii. 3 the *a malo* was probably looked upon as a quotation from the Lord's Prayer, though it should be remembered that with our present slight evidence for the Latin texts of the Pauline Epistles we are unable to assert that no other rendering was current. Thus we are brought to Matt. vi. 13, Lc. xi. 4. Here three points are to be noticed: (i) the rendering *a malo* was, we may believe, early fixed by devotional usage. It was the obvious translation of the Greek word and seems to be a precise example of the 'simplicitas interpretationis' of which Tertullian speaks (*adv. Prax.* 5, comp. *de Monogam.* 11). (ii) Tertullian, who discusses the petition in *de Oratione* and in *de Fuga* (see above, p. 134 f.), while in both Tracts he adopts the masculine interpretation, in the second of them, which is of later date than the former, characteristically gives the revised rendering *a maligno*. His attempt to introduce this new rendering brings into prominence the interpretation which he had already given of *a malo*; his failure indicates how strong was the hold which the old translation had on Christian men. (iii) The translation *a malo* must be viewed in the light of those passages of the New Testament in which the word is certainly masculine, and of those in which the use of an oblique case of malignus in some authorities supports the masculine interpretation of the corresponding case of malus.

To sum up, the evidence of the Latin Versions taken as a whole, and the decisive evidence of Tertullian and of Cyprian, whose interpretation is repeated by several Latin writers (see above, pp. 67 f., 137 n.) on whom probably the spell of Augustine's influence had not rested, are the two sides of an arch which, meeting together and mutually strengthening each other, firmly support the conclusion that the early Latin-speaking Christians held the last petition of the Lord's Prayer to refer to Satan[1].

It remains to bring together in a brief statement the main results of this lengthy discussion of different classes of evidence. The record of our Lord's life and teaching in the Gospels gives what I cannot but think is a conclusive confirmation of the view that Christ taught His followers in the closing petition of the Prayer to ask for deliverance from Satan in his manifold enmity against man. The Apostolic teaching of the Epistles of the New Testament, the witness of writers of the early Church, several of whom happen to be typical writers, the choice of words in certain passages in two of the earliest versions of the New Testament, supply evidence which powerfully supports the verdict based on the testimony of the Gospels. Two passages, however, one from a Pauline Epistle (2 Tim. iv. 17 f.), the other from what is perhaps the earliest Christian document outside the New Testament (see above, pp. 119 ff., 126 f.), may be considered as ambiguous or even as adverse. The utmost however which can be said seems to be that these two passages indicate that the neuter interpretation, which

[1] I have not the knowledge requisite for the discussion of the Egyptian Versions. On two points however I may briefly touch. (i) Canon Cook (*A Second Letter* p. 44), so far as I can judge, makes good his contention, that the Memphitic version has in 1 Jn. v. 19 'lieth in evil (wickedness).' Dionysius of Alexandria, as we have already seen (p. 140), gives the neuter interpretation of that passage. Should we not connect the interpretation given in the Memphitic version with that of Dionysius? In the same way the difficulties which Dionysius felt as to the Apocalypse may reflect the position which the Memphitic and Thebaic versions took as regards this Book (Bp Lightfoot in Scrivener's *Introduction* p. 398, ed. 3). Anyhow the example of Dionysius shews that it is possible to affirm the neuter interpretation of 1 Jn. v. 19 and the masculine interpretation of Matt. vi. 13. The interpretation of the former passage in the Memphitic does not raise any presumption as to its interpretation of the latter. (ii) Canon Cook, claiming the Memphitic Version as a witness on his side, admits that there is some probability that the Thebaic Version is against him. He seeks however to break the force of this adverse evidence by the suggestion that the masculine rendering is due to the influence of Origen. The answer to this suggestion is two-fold. On the one hand it has been clearly shewn that the masculine interpretation is not the invention of Origen. On the other hand, in the one clause of the Prayer of which the genius of Origen did, as it seems, give currency to a new interpretation, both the Thebaic and Memphitic Versions embody an earlier and simpler interpretation ('coming bread,' 'bread of tomorrow').

clearly is grammatically possible, was not absolutely unknown in early times. With these two exceptions the tenour of early evidence is one. In particular the consideration of the liturgical evidence, where many lines converge towards one point, leaves no doubt as to the way in which the last petition of the Prayer was interpreted in early times or rather, as I think the whole body of evidence clearly shews, continuously from the first, by the devotional instinct of the Christian Church.

VIII.

[Ὅτι σοῦ ἐστιν ἡ βασιλεία καὶ ἡ δύναμις καὶ ἡ δόξα εἰς τοὺς αἰῶνας. Ἀμήν (St Matthew).]

THAT the true text of St Matthew's Gospel has no doxology at the close of the Lord's Prayer cannot be considered doubtful. The authorities which add a doxology differ as to the exact form. The theory, which finds an explanation of some of the problems connected with the Lord's Prayer in an adaptation or expansion of the Prayer for liturgical use, has in regard to the doxology its most obvious application. Nowhere except in the petition for 'daily bread' has early liturgical usage made so deep and lasting a mark on the Lord's Prayer as in the addition of the doxology.

A brief statement of some of the facts about the use of doxologies in the early Church may be useful. The complete discussion of the subject would require thorough knowledge of the liturgical forms of Jews and Christians alike.

In 1 Chron. xxix. 10 f. we have a point where liturgical streams which afterwards flowed widely apart are united. The passage runs thus in the LXX.: *εὐλογητὸς εἶ, Κύριε ὁ θεὸς Ἰσραήλ, ὁ πατὴρ ἡμῶν ἀπὸ τοῦ αἰῶνος καὶ ἕως τοῦ αἰῶνος. σύ* (so Cod. B; Cod. A *σοί*: Hebr. לְךָ), *Κύριε, ἡ μεγαλωσύνη καὶ ἡ δύναμις καὶ τὸ καύχημα καὶ ἡ νίκη καὶ ἡ ἰσχύς.*

Here side by side are two types of doxologies. The *first* doxology begins with the word 'Blessed.' Such a form occurs frequently in the Old Testament, especially in the Psalms. It is the essentially Hebraistic type. It is found in the New Testament (Lc. i. 68, 2 Cor. i. 3, xi. 31, Rom. i. 25, ix. 5, Eph. i. 3, 1 Pet. i. 3), and instances of its use in the worship of the Temple are given in Lightfoot's *Horae Hebraicae* on Matt. vi. 13. It is very common in Jewish Prayer Books. Its absence, so far as I know, in the liturgical portions of early Christian literature[1] suggests that it had not so prominent a place in the formulas of the Hellenistic as in those of the Hebrew Synagogues.

The *second* doxology is of the kind familiar to us in connexion with the Lord's Prayer. Such passages in the Old Testament as Ps. xxviii. 1, xcv. 7, ciii. 31, 1 Chron. xvi. 27 should be compared. This type of doxology is very common in the New Testament. Bp Westcott (*Hebrews* p. 464 f.) has collected the passages and has brought out many points of interest in regard to them. Outside the Apostolic writings, it is very frequently found, its exact form varying, in the liturgical portions of the *Didaché*, of Clement's Epistle, of the Martyrdom of Polycarp. The phenomena are all explained if we suppose that this liturgical usage passed over from the Synagogues of the Hellenistic Jews into those of the Christian 'Brethren.' The evidence for this will, at least in part, appear in the following discussion.

In this form of doxology there are normally four elements: (i) The reference to God—*σοί, σοῦ, αὐτῷ, ᾧ*. (ii) The verb, which is always, I believe, in the indicative, *ἐστίν*, e.g. *Didaché* viii. 2, Clem. 58. The verb however is commonly omitted, always so in the simplest forms. (iii) That which is ascribed to God, 'glory,' 'power.' (iv) The description of eternity.

Thus the simplest form is:

(i) *σοί* (*ᾧ*)

[(ii) *ἐστίν*]

(iii) *ἡ δόξα*

(iv) *εἰς τοὺς αἰῶνας* (*τῶν αἰώνων*) (*ἀμήν*).

This form is found in Gal. i. 5, *Rom. xi. 36, 2 Tim. iv. 18, Hebr. xiii. 21, *Did.* ix. *2, *3, x. *2, *4, Ep. Clem. 38, 43, 45, 50, 'the Ancient Homily' 20 (where the simple formula *αὐτῷ*...sums up an elaborate preface *τῷ μόνῳ θεῷ ἀοράτῳ κ.τ.λ.*), *Clem. Hom. (ed.

[1] Ign. *Eph.* 1 can hardly be considered an exception. It is however found in the Liturgies, e.g. 'Clementine' Liturgy (Hammond p. 16) *ἅγιος...τῆς δόξης αὐτοῦ· εὐλογητὸς εἰς τοὺς αἰῶνας· ἀμήν.* *Lit. of St James* (Hammond p. 26, Swainson p. 218) *μεθ' οὗ εὐλογητὸς εἶ καὶ δεδοξασμένος σὺν τῷ παναγίῳ καὶ ἀγαθῷ καὶ ζωοποιῷ σου πνεύματι, νῦν καὶ ἀεὶ καὶ εἰς τοὺς αἰῶνας. ἀμήν.* So in *Lit. St Chrys.* (Hammond p. 119, Swainson p. 136). Thus the ancient form was elaborated and Christianised.

Dressel p. 9). The passages marked with an asterisk have the simpler εἰς τοὺς αἰῶνας. In all the passages except those in the *Didaché* ἀμήν is added[1]. This last point is of itself sufficient to mark the formula as liturgical.

Each of the elements in this normal form admits of variation and elaboration. The variations in (iv) are not of great importance. In the *Didaché* the severely simple εἰς τοὺς αἰῶνας is throughout adhered to. In Clement 64 we find καὶ νῦν καὶ εἰς πάντας τοὺς αἰῶνας τῶν αἰώνων, in *Mart. Polyc.* 21 ἀπὸ γενεᾶς εἰς γενεάν (cf. 14). Still more elaborate forms occur in Eph. iii. 21, Jude 25, 2 Pet. iii. 18.

The elaboration of (iii) gives rise to very various forms. When δόξα stands alone it always has the article. When another word is added, usage varies, but the variations can be left out of account. In 1 Tim. vi. 16, 1 Pet. iv. 11 (comp. v. 11), Apoc. i. 6 (τὸ) κράτος, in the *Didaché* (viii. 2, ix. 4, x. 5) ἡ δύναμις is added. Longer forms are found in Jude 25 (δόξα μεγαλωσύνη κράτος καὶ ἐξουσία), Apoc. v. 13, vii. 12 (ἡ εὐλογία καὶ ἡ δόξα καὶ ἡ σοφία καὶ ἡ εὐχαριστία καὶ ἡ τιμὴ καὶ ἡ δύναμις καὶ ἡ ἰσχύς), Clem. 64 (δόξα καὶ μεγαλωσύνη, κράτος, τιμή, comp. 61, 65, Mart. Polyc. 20, 21).

There is no variation in regard to (ii), unless the ἐγένετο of Apoc. xii. 10 should be noticed in this connexion, until we turn to the Liturgies. Thus, to take a single example which will also illustrate the elaboration of later doxologies, in the Liturgy of St James (Hammond p. 48, Swainson p. 324 f.) we find the following form: σοὶ γὰρ πρέπει καὶ ἐποφείλεται παρὰ πάντων ἡμῶν πᾶσα δοξολογία, τιμή, προσκύνησις, καὶ εὐχαριστία, τῷ πατρὶ καὶ τῷ υἱῷ καὶ τῷ ἁγίῳ πνεύματι, νῦν καὶ ἀεί, καὶ εἰς τοὺς αἰῶνας τῶν αἰώνων.

The variations in (i) have a special importance, for through them the ancient form, inherited, as I suppose, from the Jewish Synagogue, became Christianised. This new stamp was given to the doxology in one of three ways. (*a*) Sometimes the divine glory is ascribed to the Son. This is the case in 2 Tim. iv. 18, 2 Pet. iii. 18, Apoc. i. 6, *Mart. Polyc.* 21. 1, 4, and perhaps in Clem.

[1] But when the doxology of *Did.* ix. 3 reappears in *Constit. Ap.* vii. 25 and in Athan. *de Virgin.* 13, the ἀμήν is added.

20, 50. (*b*) Sometimes Christ is represented as the mediator (δι' οὗ), as in Rom. xvi. 27[1], Jude 25, *Didaché* ix. 4, Clem. 58, 61, 64, 65, *Mart. Polyc.* 14 (the Martyr's prayer), 20. (*c*) Sometimes the Three Persons of the Trinity are named. I do not think that this form occurs earlier than the prayer of Polycarp before his martyrdom, δι' οὗ σοι σὺν αὐτῷ καὶ πνεύματι ἁγίῳ ἡ δόξα (14); so 22, 3 (ᾧ ἡ δόξα σὺν πατρὶ καὶ ἁγίῳ πνεύματι).

In the controversies of the fourth century about the doctrine of the Son and of the Holy Spirit, the varying forms of doxology, which fall under the last head, were degraded into the watchwords of theological strife. For this stage of their history it must be sufficient to refer to the *locus classicus* in Hooker's *Ecclesiastical Polity* v. 42. 7 ff.[2]

The earliest doxologies, to pass to a subordinate matter, appear to begin with a personal pronoun (σοί, σοῦ), or with the relative (ᾧ). The insertion of ὅτι (ὅτι σοῦ ἐστιν κ.τ.λ.) is as old as the *Didaché*, where it is used to introduce the doxology at the close of two Eucharistic formulas (ix. 4, x. 5), and also at the end of the Lord's Prayer (viii. 2). Though the form of the doxology at the end of the Lord's Prayer varied, yet (so far as I have observed) it always commences with ὅτι[3]. It may be added that, when the doxology came into use as a formula complete in itself, or, especially in the Western Church, as the constant ending of the Psalms recited in worship (Bingham *Antiquities* Bk. XIV. ch. ii.), the first element of the normal form was eliminated altogether. This adaptation is probably to be traced back through the *Gloria in Excelsis* (*Apost. Constit.* vii. 47) to the Angelic Hymn (Lc. ii. 14 δόξα ἐν ὑψίστοις θεῷ κ.τ.λ.). The grace after meat in Athan. *de Virgin.* 14, a tract which preserves very ancient forms, contains perhaps the oldest instance of this usage. It is as follows: ἐλεήμων καὶ οἰκτίρμων ὁ κύριος, τροφὴν ἔδωκε τοῖς

[1] Comp. the very remarkable form in Eph. iii. 21 (αὐτῷ ἡ δόξα ἐν τῇ ἐκκλησίᾳ καὶ ἐν Χριστῷ Ἰησοῦ).

[2] The familiar words of the 'Constantinopolitan' Creed (τὸ σὺν πατρὶ καὶ υἱῷ... συνδοξαζόμενον) are of course a relic of this strife.

[3] Thus the doxology was taken in close connexion with the petition for deliverance from Satan. Thus Chrysostom *in loco*: οὐκοῦν εἰ αὐτοῦ ἐστιν ἡ βασιλεία, οὐδένα δεδοικέναι χρή, ἅτε οὐδενὸς ὄντος τοῦ ἀνθισταμένου, καὶ πρὸς αὐτὸν τὴν ἀρχὴν διανεμομένου.

φοβουμένοις αὐτόν· δόξα πατρὶ καὶ υἱῷ καὶ ἁγίῳ πνεύματι καὶ νῦν καὶ ἀεὶ καὶ εἰς τοὺς αἰῶνας.

From the form of the doxologies we turn to the position which they occupy in early Christian writings. If we put aside the Apostolic Epistles, it is true to say that they are found with but few exceptions in a liturgical context. This becomes clear as to the prayer of Polycarp when the words which precede the doxology are quoted, 'For this cause, yea and for all things, I praise Thee, I bless Thee, I glorify Thee, through the eternal and heavenly High Priest, Thy beloved Son, through Whom to Thee with Him and the Holy Spirit be glory both now [and ever] and for the ages to come. Amen.' Here Bp Lightfoot draws attention to the close parallel between these words and the *Gloria in Excelsis* as given in *Apost. Constit.* vii. 47, and notes the liturgical complexion of the words which follow, *ἀναπέμψαντος δὲ αὐτοῦ τὸ ἀμήν* (comp. e.g. Justin Martyr *Apol.* i. 65, 67). Polycarp in fact is represented as using when he came to die a form of prayer closely akin to that which he had often used as *ὁ προεστώς*, to quote Justin's phrase, in the congregation.

What Polycarp did in the hour of his fiery triumph, Clement does all through his letter. In the prayer at the close of the Epistle, in which two of the doxologies referred to above are found, 'his language,' says Bishop Lightfoot, 'naturally runs into those antithetical forms and measured cadences which his ministrations in the Church had rendered habitual with him.' But this is not all. 'The litany at the close is only the climax of the epistle, which may be regarded as one long psalm of praise and thanksgiving on the glories of nature and of grace' (Bp Lightfoot *Clement* i. p. 386)[1].

Even more instructive is the study of the doxologies in the *Didaché*. Here there are three forms of doxology. (*a*) The simple form *σοὶ ἡ δόξα εἰς τοὺς αἰῶνας*. This occurs in the thanksgiving over the cup (ix. 2), over the bread (*τὸ κλάσμα*) (ix. 3), twice (x.

[1] Two points in detail may be noticed, (*a*) three doxologies occur in close connexion with the mention of the divine Name (43, 45, 64); (*b*) the parallel between *οὗτος...ἐλλόγιμος ἔσται εἰς τὸν ἀριθμὸν τῶν σωζομένων διὰ Ἰ. Χρ., δι' οὗ κ.τ.λ.* (58, see Bp Lightfoot's note) and *Mart. Polyc.* 14 (*τοῦ λαβεῖν με μέρος ἐν ἀριθμῷ τῶν μαρτύρων*).

2, 4) in the Eucharistic formula after Communion (*μετὰ τὸ ἐμπλησθῆναι*). The substantial identity of this form with that found in the Apostolic Epistles and in Clement has already been pointed out (p. 169). (*b*) The longest form in the *Didaché* (*σοῦ ἐστιν ἡ δόξα καὶ ἡ δύναμις διὰ Ἰησοῦ Χριστοῦ εἰς τοὺς αἰῶνας*) occurs at the close of the remarkable prayer that the Church may be made one as the bread is one (ix. 4). (*c*) The intermediate form (*σοῦ ἐστιν ἡ δύναμις καὶ ἡ δόξα εἰς τοὺς αἰῶνας*) closes the second prayer for the gathering together of the Church[1] (x. 5) and also the Lord's Prayer (viii. 2).

Regarding these passages together, we learn that the liturgical usage of the Christian Church, inherited no doubt from the Hellenistic Synagogues, was to close a prayer with a doxology. The passages in the *Didaché* and in the Martyrdom of Polycarp are obvious examples of this custom. A doxology ends the great prayer in Clement's Epistle (59—61) and the prayer in c. 64. Hence the addition of a doxology to the Lord's Prayer was the simple following out of the prevailing use.

This conclusion is fully corroborated by the evidence supplied by the *Didaché*. Here the same doxology which closes the post-communion form of thanksgiving and intercession (x. 5) closes also the Lord's Prayer (viii. 2). No testimony could be clearer or more to the point than this. It might further be suggested that the frequent connexion of a doxology with liturgical forms belonging to the Eucharistic Service of Holy Communion (*Didaché*, Clement, Prayer of Polycarp) points to the purpose of the addition of the doxology to the Lord's Prayer, viz. the adaptation of the Prayer for use in that service[2].

[1] The formula in c. x. may be said to contain in an embryo form what appeared in later liturgies as (*a*) the Great Intercession (e.g. Hammond p. 18); (*b*) the expansion of the Lord's Prayer (Preface, Embolismus; e.g. Hammond p. 47 f.); (*c*) the formula *τὰ ἅγια τοῖς ἁγίοις* (*εἴ τις ἅγιός ἐστιν, ἐρχέσθω Did.*; Hammond p. 21, where as in *Did.* the words *ὡσαννὰ τῷ υἱῷ Δαβίδ* have a place in the context).

[2] It should be noted however that in the Liturgy to which Cyril of Jerusalem witnesses (*Catech.* xxiii. 18) the Prayer closed with *ἀμήν* without a doxology. It is remarkable that in two passages where St Paul seems to be referring to the last petition of the Lord's Prayer (Gal. i. 4 f., 2 Tim. iv. 18 ff., see above, pp. 115, 119) he passes into a doxology, using the same form in both places. The immediate occasion of the thanksgiving no doubt is the thought of deliverance, general (Gal. i. 4) and

One point remains to be considered, the variation in the form of the doxology which is attached to the Lord's Prayer in different authorities. The fact that such diversities exist of itself confirms the conclusion at which we have arrived. A consideration of some of these variations still further strengthens the position. We will confine our attention to the third element (iii) in the doxology, which is indeed its kernel.

The Old Latin Cod. Bobiensis (k) has: quoniam est tibi virtus in saecula saeculorum. If virtus here represents *ἡ δύναμις*, this form in which the simple *ἡ δύναμις* takes the place of the simple *ἡ δόξα* is, so far as I know, unique. The simple *τὸ κράτος* (*Vulg.* imperium) is found in 1 Pet. v. 11.

The Thebaic Version has: quoniam tuum est robur et potentia in aevum aevi. Here also, if the Greek text represented is *ἡ δύναμις καὶ ἡ ἰσχύς* (Dr Hort, *Introduction*, *Notes on Select Readings* p. 8), we have a unique form. *ἡ ἰσχύς* however has a place in 1 Chron. xxix. 11; combined with a preceding *ἡ δύναμις* it ends the long series in Apoc. vii. 12. This may be considered sufficient evidence for the supposition that this form was current in the worship of the Hellenistic Synagogues. Gregory of Nyssa (Migne *P. G.* 44, p. 1193) ends his exposition of the Lord's Prayer thus, *ἀπὸ τοῦ πονηροῦ τοῦ ἐν τῷ κόσμῳ τούτῳ τὴν ἰσχὺν κεκτημένου, οὗ ῥυσθείημεν χάριτι τοῦ χριστοῦ, ὅτι αὐτῷ ἡ δύναμις καὶ ἡ δόξα ἅμα τῷ πατρὶ καὶ τῷ ἁγίῳ πνεύματι νῦν καὶ ἀεὶ καὶ εἰς τοὺς αἰῶνας τῶν αἰώνων· ἀμήν.* The passage is a good illustration of the combination of elaboration and conservatism which is an important element in liturgical history. The kernel of the doxology (*ἡ δύναμις καὶ ἡ δόξα*) is identical with that of the doxology which ends the Lord's Prayer in the *Didaché* (viii. 2, x. 5).

The Old Syriac, which presupposes a Greek text *ἡ βασιλεία καὶ ἡ δόξα*, is, so far as I know, the earliest form in which 'the kingdom' has a place. It would appear probable in view of such passages as Ps. cxliv. 11 (*δόξαν τῆς βασιλείας σου ἐροῦσιν*), 12 that this doxology is an independent form. However this may be, it is remarkable that *ἡ βασιλεία* does not occur in the doxologies

personal (2 Tim. iv. 18). But if the doxology was already in use at the end of the Lord's Prayer (cf. 1 Cor. xiv. 16), devotional habit may have prompted the addition.

with which we have at present dealt. The nearest approach to it is in the doxology with which Clement ends his letter, *δόξα, τιμή, κράτος καὶ μεγαλωσύνη, θρόνος αἰώνιος*[1] (so *Mart. Polyc.* 21). The extraordinary richness in this respect of the Apocalypse supplies a *doxological form* containing the word, *ἄρτι ἐγένετο ἡ σωτηρία καὶ ἡ δύναμις καὶ ἡ βασιλεία τοῦ θεοῦ ἡμῶν καὶ ἡ ἐξουσία τοῦ χριστοῦ αὐτοῦ* (xii. 10, comp. xi. 15, 17). This passage, taken in connexion with the fact that the Hebrew of 1 Chron. xxix. 11 is לך יהוה הממלכה, which is represented in some forms of the LXX. by *σοί, Κύριε, ἡ βασιλεία* (see Field *Hexapla, in loco*), tends to shew that a form of doxology with a reference to 'the kingdom' may have been current among the Jews[2]; the combination of authorities—the Hebrew text of the Old Testament, the Apocalypse, the Old Syriac—suggests that the form was Hebrew rather than Hellenistic.

The doxology, which closes the Lord's Prayer in the familiar English use[3], and which may be a conflation of the form just noticed (*ἡ βασιλεία καὶ ἡ δόξα*) and the form witnessed to by the *Didaché* (*ἡ δύναμις καὶ ἡ δόξα*), is first, I believe, found in the *Apost. Constit.* iii. 18, vii. 24[4]. It occurs in Chrysostom's Commentary on St Matthew (vii. 253 D), at the close of the Embolismus in the Liturgy of St James (Hammond p. 48, Swainson p. 309) and in other Liturgies, e.g. in the Anaphora of St Basil (Hammond p. 126, Swainson p. 167), though in the Liturgies a reference to the Holy Trinity and a more elaborate description of eternity are added. The fact that it gained a place in the 'Syrian' text explains its almost undisputed supremacy in later times.

If the further question is asked why copyists and translators and commentators add a doxology to the longer form of the Prayer found in St Matthew's Gospel, the answer is not far to seek, and it

[1] Ps. xliv. 7 *ὁ θρόνος σου, ὁ θεός, εἰς αἰῶνα αἰῶνος.* Comp. Hebrews i. 8 f.

[2] Comp. Dan. vii. 14 *καὶ αὐτῷ ἐδόθη ἡ ἀρχὴ καὶ ἡ τιμὴ καὶ ἡ βασιλεία* (Theod.; so Chald.); *καὶ ἐδόθη αὐτῷ ἐξουσία καὶ τιμὴ βασιλική* (LXX.).

[3] It is worth notice that while the A.V. has *the kingdom and the power and the glory*, the rendering in the Prayer Book has *the kingdom, the power, and the glory*.

[4] I refer to Lagarde's text. The Editio princeps (see Lagarde's Preface p. iv.) in the latter place has simply *ἡ βασιλεία*.

supplies one more confirmation of the theory that the doxology is a liturgical accretion. At least when the period of purely oral transmission was over and the Gospel of St Matthew and that of St Luke were in general circulation and were seen to present two different forms of the Prayer, a longer and a shorter, the natural desire for fulness and completeness would ensure the longer form as given by St Matthew being employed in the public Prayers of the Church and being as time went on embodied in the Liturgies. Thus to this longer form the doxology would become regularly attached. This obvious conjecture as to the earliest devotional usage of the Church is confirmed by the evidence of the *Didaché*. Thus even from sub-Apostolic days liturgical custom would suggest the interpolation of a doxology in St Matthew's Gospel alone.

To sum up, the evidence which we have considered seems to shew that several different forms of doxology, ultimately to be traced to the Old Testament, were in common use in the earliest years of the Church's life; that the public prayers, especially those of the Eucharistic Service, generally concluded with one or other of these doxologies; that from the first the Lord's Prayer, like other prayers, had attached to it now one doxology, now another; that, as the *Didaché* in particular seems to suggest, the Lord's Prayer was in this way frequently adapted for use at the Service of Holy Communion; finally that one form of doxology, which appears to be a conflation of two distinct forms, was added to the Prayer in the 'Syrian' text of St Matthew's Gospel and so has remained the common conclusion of the Prayer since the fourth century.

INDEX.